LACAN AND THE GHOSTS OF MODERNITY

STUDIES IN LITERARY CRITICISM & THEORY

Hans H. Rudnick
General Editor

Vol. 20

PETER LANG
New York • Washington, D.C./Baltimore • Bern
Frankfurt am Main • Berlin • Brussels • Vienna • Oxford

Marshall Needleman Armintor

LACAN AND THE GHOSTS OF MODERNITY

MASCULINITY, TRADITION, AND THE ANXIETY OF INFLUENCE

PETER LANG
New York • Washington, D.C./Baltimore • Bern
Frankfurt am Main • Berlin • Brussels • Vienna • Oxford

Library of Congress Cataloging-in-Publication Data

Armintor, Marshall Needleman.
Lacan and the ghosts of modernity: masculinity, tradition, and the anxiety of influence / Marshall Needleman Armintor.
p. cm. — (Studies in literary criticism and theory; v. 20)
Includes bibliographical references and index.
1. Psychoanalysis and literature. 2. Lacan, Jacques, 1901- —Contributions in criticism. I. Title. II. Series.
PN56.P92A76 809'.93353—dc21 2003012907
ISBN 0-8204-6906-8
ISSN 1073-2004

Bibliographic information published by **Die Deutsche Bibliothek**.
Die Deutsche Bibliothek lists this publication in the "Deutsche Nationalbibliografie"; detailed bibliographic data is available on the Internet at http://dnb.ddb.de/.

The paper in this book meets the guidelines for permanence and durability of the Committee on Production Guidelines for Book Longevity of the Council of Library Resources.

275 Seventh Avenue, 28th Floor, New York, NY 10001
www.peterlangusa.com

Printed in Germany

For my mother
Lucille Miller Armintor
and to the memory of my father
Joseph Kirk Armintor (1943-2004)

Contents

Preface

This book is a substantially revised version of my doctoral dissertation, "Significant Returns: Lacan, Masculinity, and Modernist Traditions," which was completed at Rice University in 2002. An early version of the fourth chapter was presented at the inaugural Affiliated Psychoanalytic Workgroups conference, "On Feminine Sexuality," held at Boston College in May of 1999.

The project grew out of my desire to establish some historical context for Lacan's work, taking into account the ideas of his early colleagues and intellectual peers; hence this book's focus on the first few seminar years of Lacan, rather than on those texts that are by now more familiar to the Anglophone world, the selection of essays from *Écrits* and Seminars XI and XX. Given Lacan's proclivity for illustrating many of his concepts with reference to art, literature, and philosophy (among the more famous examples: Poe, Plato, Joyce, Holbein, Bernini, Aristotle, Hegel, and so on), I felt it was necessary to work out an approach that was appropriate in order to read Lacan along with literature, if only to justify my interest, as a literary scholar, in psychoanalysis. The result is more idiosyncratic than I perhaps would have liked, and indeed, this book is more of an exercise in a type of hermeneutics than historicity. Nevertheless, the strategy that emerges in this book is one that is, I hope, in the spirit of Lacanian hermeneutics, which derives its energy from a transferential hermeneutic relation to Freud's body of work.

This link to Freud is dramatized (literally) in the lecture "The Freudian Thing," in which Freud, long dead, is made to speak; Lacan thus raises the question of what it means to ventriloquize Freud. Undoubtedly, when explicit submission to the Law of the Father enters the picture, we find ourselves on fertile psychoanalytic ground. However, Lacan's idea of the "return" to Freud, and the assumption of the analyst's mantle from the spectre of Freud, involving a fundamentally ahistorical act of repetition, bring to my mind what MacQuarrie and Robinson's translation of *Being and Time* terms the "reciprocative rejoinder":

> The repeating of that which is possible does not bring again [Wiederbringen] something that is 'past', nor does it bind the 'Present' back to that which has already been 'outstripped.' Arising, as it does, from a resolute projection of oneself, repetition does not let itself be persuaded of something by what is 'past', just in order that this, as something which was formerly actual, may recur. Rather, the repetition makes a *reciprocative rejoinder* to the possibility of that existence which has-been-there. [Die wiederholung erwidert vielmehr die Möglichkeit der dagewesenen Existenz.] (BT 437–438)

The response of authentic Dasein to its past, considered in a temporal context, is not really a "return of the repressed," but rather a deliberate choice to investigate that which is normally hidden from view, and, in turn, respond to it in an authentic fashion. Heidegger further elaborates on the nature of this hermeneutic move: "But when such a rejoinder is made to this possibility in a resolution, it is made *in a moment of vision* [Augenblick]; *and as such* it is at the same time a *disavowal* of that which in the "today", is working itself out as the 'past'. Repetition does not abandon itself to that which is past, nor does it aim at progress" (BT 438). The nature of the "Augenblick" exempts Dasein from committing, Heidegger stresses, to either temporal alternative (BT 438–439).

It could be said of Lacan in general that his acts of Freudian exegesis, whether calculated as such or not, represent a gesture of authenticity in both the pedestrian and Heideggerian senses: as in Kierkegaard's "moment" of *Philosophical Fragments*, this resolute response lies outside of time, unbidden by the pressures of tradition. Indeed, the intellectual career of Lacan reveals that he did not simply begin his psychiatric training on an analyst's couch; his medical thesis *De la psychose paranoïaque dans ses rapports avec la personnalité* shows that Lacan was well versed in the vocabulary of phenomenology, a discipline which has roots in early experimental psychology. Lacan's interest in psychoanalysis cannot be construed as inevitable from the first, as his initial formally psychoanalytic work is not fleshed out until the late 1940s and early 1950s. The story of Lacan's sending of an early draft of *Le stade du miroir* to Freud, only to receive a dismissive postcard of thanks, is a legend that tidily crystallizes the phantasmic relation between the two men; as amplified by Derrida in *The Post Card,* one can see that the "legitimacy" of the enterprise of Lacanian analysis, given its emphasis on learning analytic truths through full speech, surely has a thin premise when one considers its origins.

But the question of the Lacanian return's legitimacy is not so easily dismissed. At issue throughout Lacan's work is the confrontation between the self-as-lack and its threatening Other, a distinctive feature of post-Sartrean phenomenology. In its questioning of the nature of the analytic relation, and implicit challenge to other psychoanalysts' legacies, Lacan's archeological gesture of the return to Freud is seen to be something more complicated, revealing, and old-fashioned. It is an expression of the desire for truth, framed by the atemporal dialectic of intimate conversation; it is an expression of the need to fashion an identity in the shadow of one's teacher; it is an expression of yearning for membership in a time-honored learned society with its own special discourse. However honorable one's intentions may be, the desire for this relation is never simple or easy, and even acknowledging a positive influence is an opportunity for great anxiety. The questions raised in this work are also intended to explore the crises of masculinity that arrive with the rehearsal of such anxieties, whether intellectual, familial, or sexual. The site of initiation into self-knowledge is always traumatic, and there is no elegant way of memorializing or explaining such trauma, either to oneself or to others.

For this reason, I have chosen as a main topic the development of Lacan's thought. His reinterpretations of Freud and others shed a unique light on the capacity for psychoanalytic reflection, in that such reflection depends on intersubjective relationships, whatever form they might take. As his work is grounded in the later "metapsychological" Freud, it speaks distinctively to various types of psychotic ailments, particularly paranoia, masochism, and narcissism. In the case of the aforementioned pathologies, the material I shall discuss relates to delusional masculine anxiety over the absence of a father figure, and the reactions (rationalization, self-absorption, fetishization, rampant paranoia) of the male subject when confronted with this situation, as depicted in the psychologically rich work of Henry James, Marcel Proust, and James Joyce.

The narrative of modernist intellectual and artistic movements features a series of decisive breaks with tradition, often between mentors and protégés, and almost always with manifestly traumatic results. A hidden history of conflict and repression has defined the psychoanalytic tradition from its very beginning, and marks it as a quintessentially modernist intellectual movement. In all of the texts that shall be treated in the following pages, relations among men are often greatly affected by the need to insulate oneself from trauma, potential trauma, or sexual anxiety by indulging in various forms of fantasy, which often involve the attempt to remedy feelings of alienation and rootlessness stemming from the father's absence. This motif plays out in various ways in both analytic writings and novels such as *Ulysses*, where Stephen Dedalus, upon spying his dissolute father Simon lurching around town, feels relief that no one ever need think that they are related; Stephen feels free to deny his father since paternity is a relationship that exists largely by virtue of family names, resemblances, responsibility, and trust, as opposed to the maternal relationship, which is built on blood, the breast, and the umbilical cord. The moment is symbolic of modernism itself, in that although Stephen makes (as did Joyce) a self-conscious break with the past, he shall always be confronted with its image in the mirror. At the same time, denial of the past is a dangerous invitation to repression, and as Joyce illustrates poignantly in *Ulysses*, the revenants of one's personal history never seem to disappear.

Acknowledgements

I would like to take this opportunity to thank the members of my dissertation committee, as they oversaw this work in its earliest stages and gave me help and encouragement along the way: Wesley A. Morris, Colleen R. Lamos, and Deborah A. Harter. Thanks also the English Department at Rice University for supporting my work. I would also like to thank the staff and administration of Fondren Library and the Office of Research and Graduate Studies at Rice University for their kind accommodation and unwavering support for my research.

Since completing my doctoral work, the additional revision of this book project has been conducted at the University of North Texas, and my deep appreciation goes out to all of my colleagues in the English Department for their dialogue and friendship.

Deepest thanks of all are due to my family, and especially to my wonderful wife Deborah, without whom none of this would have been possible.

Abbreviations

BT Martin Heidegger, *Being and Time*. Translated by John MacQuarrie and Edward Robinson. New York: Harper, 1962.

CL Sigmund Freud, *The Complete Letters of Sigmund Freud to Wilhelm Fliess 1887-1904*. Translated and edited by Jeffrey Moussaieff Masson. Cambridge, Mass.: Belknap, 1985.

E Jacques Lacan, *Écrits*. Paris: Éditions de Seuil, 1966.

E:S ———, *Écrits: A Selection*. Translated by Bruce Fink, in collaboration with Héloïse Fink and Russell Grigg. New York: W.W. Norton & Company, 2002.

FS *Feminine Sexuality: Jacques Lacan and the école freudienne*. Edited by Juliet Mitchell and Jacqueline Rose. Translated by Jacqueline Rose. New York: W.W. Norton & Company, 1985.

JJ Richard Ellmann, *James Joyce*. New and revised edition. New York: Oxford, 1982.

OP Gaëtan Gatian de Clérambault, *Oeuvres Psychiatriques*. 2 vols. Paris: Presses Universitaires de France, 1942.

M Gilles Deleuze and Leopold von Sacher-Masoch, *Masochism*. Translated by Jean McNeil. New York: W.W. Norton & Company, 1992.

MNI Daniel Paul Schreber, *Memoirs of my Nervous Illness*. Translated and edited by Ida Macalpine and Richard A. Hunter. Introduction by Rosemary Dinnage. New York: New York Review of Books, 2000.

PP Jacques Lacan, *De la psychose paranoïaque dans ses rapports avec la personnalité*. Paris: Éditions de Seuil, 1975.

RT Marcel Proust, *Remembrance of Things Past*, Vol. 1, *Swann's Way*, *Within a Budding Grove.* Translated by C.K. Scott-Moncrieff and Terence Kilmartin. New York: Vintage, 1982.

S Plato, *Symposium.* Translated by Alexander Nehamas and Paul Woodruff. Indianapolis: Hackett, 1989.

S.II Jacques Lacan, *The Seminar of Jacques Lacan: Book II, The Ego in Freud's Theory and in the Technique of Psychoanalysis (1954-1955).* Translated by Sylvana Tomaselli, with notes by John Forrester. New York: W.W. Norton & Company, 1991.

S.III ———, *The Seminar of Jacques Lacan, Book III: The Psychoses (1955-1956).* Edited by Jacques-Alain Miller. Translated by Russell Grigg. New York: W.W. Norton & Company, 1992.

S.VIII ———, *The Seminar of Jacques Lacan, Book VIII: Transference (1960-1961).* Unpublished translation by Cormac Gallagher, from an unedited transcript.

S.XX ———, *The Seminar of Jacques Lacan, Book XX: On Feminine Sexuality, The Limits of Love and Knowledge, Encore (1972–1973).* Edited by Jacques-Alain Miller. Translated with notes by Bruce Fink. New York: W.W. Norton & Company, 1998.

SE Sigmund Freud, *The Standard Edition of the Complete Psychological Works of Sigmund Freud.* Translated and edited by James Strachey, et al., 24 vols. London: The Hogarth Press, 1953.

SF Henry James, *The Sacred Fount.* Introduction by Leon Edel. Afterword by R.P. Blackmur. New York: New Directions, 1995.

U James Joyce, *Ulysses: The Corrected Text.* Edited by Hans Walter Gabler. New York: Vintage, 1984.

1

Transference, Pedagogy, and Psychoanalytic Traditions: Freud, Lacan, and Plato's *Symposium*

> *...after I had successfully analyzed myself it became an unrepeatable act, a unique act of history, that could be studied, but that could only be imitated.*
>
> *That was why it became important for me to train analysts. Patients needed guidance, or they would have come to the conclusions too quickly and failed to have understood what the process of self-discovery was all about. And, of course, the analysts, men and women whom I had trained, were themselves but shadows of myself.*[1]

In his 2001 novel *Freud's Megalomania*, Israel Rosenfeld depicts a wistful, disarmingly candid Freud at the end of his life, gamely engaging himself in the writing of one last monograph, entitled simply (and improbably) *Megalomania*. Rosenfeld puts this highly fictionalized, vulnerable Freud through some tortuous mental paces; his Freud frets about his role as the august father of psychoanalysis, muses on his disinheritance of those who broke with his teaching, and mercilessly critiques psychoanalysis itself as an intellectual sham stoked by his personal delusions of grandeur. Rosenfeld's conceit cleverly forces his confessional-minded Freud to commit to paper what should have been obvious: as it was Freud who shepherded psychoanalytic practice into being the institution and cultural phenomenon it eventually became, psychoanalysis could not lay claim to being the scientific discipline Freud wished it could have been as long as its most significant figure had the unchecked power to police it. In spite of this, the defections that resulted from Freud's personal disagreements (particularly those with Jung, Alder, and Fliess) did their part in spreading the practice of psychoanalysis rather than diminishing it. With the beginning of each new mode of psychoanalytic practice, differences with Freud hardened into new dogmas; personal estrangements were further codified by competing schools of analytic thought, and by the time of Freud's death, any chance psychoanalysis might have had at a more "scientific" integration of concepts, theories, and aims was effectively scuttled.

Considering the number of European modes of analytic practice that started with their chief progenitors' expulsion from Freud's graces, the career of Jacques Lacan is remarkable in that it was never defined by an explicit break with the master. Situated in prewar France at the edges of such varied intellectual movements as Freudian psychoanalysis, orthodox French clinical psychology, both German and French phenomenology, and Surrealism, Lacan established a strain of psychoanalysis that took all of these disparate influences into account. Like Freud, Lacan spent his career moving through different phases and trying various approaches to the problems of language, the subject, the Other, lack, desire, and so on. What distinguishes Lacan's work is its unique exegetical approach to Freudian texts, using the strategies of structuralism to extend the themes of Freud's later work into an analytic vocabulary founded on Freud's doctrine of the ego and its object relations. Yet, in everything that Lacan did, there is a remarkable openness to different avenues of thought both within the Freudian canon and outside of it. As if by virtue of the fact he did not explicitly rebel against any particular psychoanalytic doctrine, Lacan attempted to embrace and encompass as much intellectual territory as he possibly could.

However, in a November 1955 lecture entitled "The Freudian Thing, or the Meaning of the Return to Freud in Psychoanalysis," Lacan makes the uncompromising statement that psychoanalysis, having gotten too far away from its roots, must "return" to Freud in order to ensure its survival. At first glance, this topic would seem to be reactionary and uncontroversial, particularly considering that it was delivered to a Viennese audience. But underneath the surface, Lacan's fleshing out of this directive outlines what he feels is a full-blown crisis in psychoanalytic thought. During the course of this lecture, Lacan identifies a number of seemingly impossible hermeneutic hurdles in detailing the treacherous implications of a return to Freud, and therefore also the difficulties of taking on Freud as an intellectual forebear.

The importance of this lecture in Lacan's oeuvre cannot be overstated, both as a statement of purpose and an indication of Lacan's intentions in appropriating Freud's ideas. Much has been written about this theme of the return in Lacan's work, and Lacan's use of Freud, especially the works of Freud's later phase. Although Lacan's lecture is dramatic, vivid and at times fanciful in its language and scope, at the center of his manifesto is a deadly serious drama narrated by Lacan and enacted by Freud, once the living exponent of psychoanalytic truth, who must now be made to speak from beyond the grave.

"The Freudian Thing," above all, expresses the self-consciousness of the debt Lacan feels he owes to Freud in his psychoanalytic work. In turn, Freud had similar difficulties in trying to reconcile himself with the presence of his mentors; Freud's bizarre and confounding dreams, discussed in chapter six of *The Interpretation of Dreams*, reveal hidden anxieties over his relationships with his past teachers. Indeed, the Lacanian conception of transference with one's mentor receives an extended treatment in Seminar VIII, *Le Transfert*, as Lacan begins the seminar year with a discussion of the encounter between Socrates and Alcibiades in Plato's *Symposium*. Despite the all-encompassing, highly rationalized theories of both Freud and Lacan on the subject of transferential relationships, the initiation into psychoanalytic dialogue is nevertheless littered with the attendant obstacles of paternal and erotic attachment, and, in some instances, filial betrayal.

"The Freudian Thing" and the Spectre(s) of Freud

Lacan's 1955 lecture "The Freudian Thing, or the Meaning of the Return to Freud in Psychoanalysis," has the ring of a line-in-the-sand challenge to the psychoanalytic establishment. The nature of the claim that Lacan makes in the lecture is undoubtedly a strange one, given that Lacan has no especially privileged position with regard to the study of Freud's work, which was, by that time, already widely disseminated, accepted, and made an irreplaceable part of twentieth-century intellectual life. But Lacan's return to Freud demands a wholesale reevaluation of Freud's work, rather than suggesting a simple rejection or blind acceptance of Freud's ideas; Lacan's return to Freud is a prime example of the kind of creative interpretation commonly identified as deconstructive reading, in its embodiment of the Heideggerian impetus to discover the "unthoughts" of an intellectual tradition.

For Lacan, Freud's death poses both historical and clinical problems for psychoanalysis. The historical calamity of Freud's absence is seen by

Lacan as a paradoxical consequence of its great success, particularly in the United States, where all manner of analytic schools, treatments and therapies flourished after Freud's ideas passed into the mainstream of American culture. Lacan sees the assimilation of Freudian ideas into American analysis as a product of the "categorical will that gives enterprises their style, that of a cultural ahistoricism characteristic of the United States of America" (E:S 108). More to the point, Lacan deems the fragmentation of the psychoanalytic movement (or at least its wandering afield from the roots of Freud's work) to be a personal betrayal of Freud "...by the very field that he has left in our care and by those to whom custody of that field was entrusted—that is, the psychoanalytical movement itself, where things have come to such a pass that to call for a return to Freud is seen as a reversal" (E:S 108).

Freud's depiction here as a Jeremiah-like figure, forsaking the bonds of country only to have his followers consign him to the ash heap of historical obscurity, cannily sets up the second aspect of Lacan's "return" to Freud. That the rejection and subsequent forgetting of Freud would come from "those to whom custody of [the] field was entrusted" alludes to the range of relationships that necessarily presided over the founding of psychoanalysis and determined its development. From its origins, the field of psychoanalysis has been constituted by a network of collegial and pedagogical encounters, as analysts can only begin to practice after undergoing an extensive training period that concludes with being fully analyzed by a trained analyst, a process often taking years and possibly decades to complete. In this sense, all psychoanalysts are direct beneficiaries of Freud's insight, passed on through a chain of concrete relationships and associations.[2]

The forgetting of Freud, for Lacan, is tantamount to a forgetting of psychoanalysis's identity. Lacan attempts in this lecture to shock the psychoanalytic community at large, to confront it with the reality that the psychoanalytic discipline no longer has the living presence of Freud presiding over it. As this work was composed shortly after the 1953 lecture "The Function and Field of Speech and Language in Psychoanalysis" (also known as the "Rome Discourse"), Lacan's concept of "full speech," and the primacy of speech in the analytic encounter, come into play here. Only in the face-to-face (or mouth-to-ear) interaction between analyst and analysand, Lacan says, can psychoanalytic truth be produced. As Freud is no longer alive to train more analysts and to guide psychoanalysis, the source of the original psychoanalytic insight may only be found somewhere in his body of writings.[3] When Lacan talks about the question of the return to Freud as an attempt to recover Freud's presence in the texts, he is also conscious of addressing the historical moment in which he speaks. The language Lacan uses to outline what he sees as the task of Freudian recovery carries with it a sense of Hegelian gravity:[4]

> We are not seeking to emphasize a return of the repressed here, but want to use the antithesis of the phase that has passed in the psychoanalytic movement since Freud's death to show what psychoanalysis is not, and to find with you a way of putting back into force what has continued to sustain it, even in its very deviation, namely—the original meaning [le sens premier] that Freud preserved in it by his mere presence [par sa seule présence], which I should like to explicate here. (E:S 109/E 403)

Without Freud, Lacan understands himself and his work to represent the negative movement of a dialectical relation. In this sense, Lacan writes as one who was never analyzed and trained by Freud, or indeed even met him. Rather, he is speaking as one who is in the same position as all other analysts; he is an analyst practicing in a world without Freud's earthly presence. Lacan's feeling for the nature of the psychoanalytic insight precludes any imperative to begin again from first principles, the "scientific" impulse that derives from the French tradition of post-Cartesian philosophy.[5] At the same time, his rejection of the Cartesian *cogito* (where the solitary, skeptical, "objective" mind separates false beliefs from the true) implicitly signals that any uncovering of truth must occur in the encounter with the Other, specifically in the analytic situation. Lacan declares that analysts must therefore seek their truth in the Freudian embrace of the analytic couch, in spite of its unscientific appearance: "Its objectivity is, in fact, strictly tied to the analytic situation, which between the four walls that limit its field, can work perfectly well...Psychoanalysis is the science of the mirages that appear within this field" (E:S 112).

Lacan's reassertion of the primacy of the analytic experience in understanding Freud reveals a deep dissatisfaction with the way that Freud has been represented by so-called Freudians (perhaps paradoxically), and the way that Freud's work has become commonplace, his ideas merely boiled down to a set of popular intellectual buzzwords. Lacan wryly remarks that to distinguish these ideas from merely ordinary ones, they are often marked with "the sign of the spirit [du signe de l'esprit]," so that one can "[recognize] them as having come from another world," essentially, from the world of the Freudian text (E:S 113). The "truth" of psychoanalysis, as it must be rediscovered again and again in the psychoanalytic encounter, is revived with each act of psychoanalysis, as it participates in the practice inaugurated by Freud. The elements of analytic theatre—the couch, the analyst's taking of notes, the autobiographical interrogation, the discussion of one's familial relations with one's analyst, and so forth—not only call up the ghost of Freud, but constitute the laboratory of psychoanalytic discovery and rediscovery.

The philosophical stance of Lacan's new, exuberantly imaginative intellectual persona is self-consciously outside the French rationalist tradition. In a highly lyrical passage, Lacan animates the corpse and corpus of Freud, allowing it to speak for itself; Freud speaks not as a human being but as an "object," existing in the same manner as desk or a rug (E:S 113–116). This necessitates an irreverent and tongue-in-cheek leap in thought, and possibly puts Lacan in an intellectually suspect position. Elsewhere in Lacan's imagination, Freud appears as Actaeon, descending to the underworld to divine "the locus in which the symbol substitutes for death in order to take possession of the first budding of life" (E:S 117). The stock-in-trade of psychoanalysis is the play of symbols and their relation to the unconscious, but Lacan worries here about his inability to produce a way of talking about the ego that corresponds with the practice of analysis:

> They began merely to repeat after Freud the key of his discovery: it [ça] speaks, precisely where it was least expected—namely, where it suffers....Be that as it may, since then, there have been more meetings between the psychoanalyst and psychoanalysis in the hope that the Athenian would reach his apex with Athena having emerged fully armed from Freud's head. Shall I tell you of the jealous fate, ever the same, that thwarted these meetings? Behind the mask where each of us was to meet his betrothed—alas! thrice alas! and a cry of horror at the thought of it, another woman having taken her place, he who was there was not him either [celui qui était là, non plus n'était pas lui]. (E:S 117–118/E 413)

With this embellishment of Freud's legacy, Lacan serves notice that we are now no longer in the realm of merely speculative psychoanalytic theory regarding the hermeneutics of Freudian reading. The act of psychoanalysis engages with Freud himself, the figure who embodies the first emergence of the analytic insight. In the pursuit of analytic truth (a favorite word of Lacan's), one shall forever find Freud where one least expects him, however much one wishes to repress him. Rather than meeting the "betrothed," the distinctively female figure representing the truth ("where one surprises her naked"), Lacan sees Freud's glowering visage instead, its ubiquity not to be underestimated.

"The Freudian Thing" is a powerful broadside indicting the psychoanalytic community for its scientific pretensions to produce ultimately objective "truths" about the human mind. As Freud was the first to be burdened with the psychoanalytic insight, and therefore charged with the responsibility to forever seek out the truth in his work, his stamp on the field can never be erased. Lacan expresses here an ambiguous desire to follow Freud down the same path of inquiry. That path, however, also led Freud into equally ambiguous territory; his work took on broader and more difficult subjects, to the eventual ruin of the libidinal theory in favor of the id-ego-superego model and the death instinct.

Lacan's command to "return to Freud" stakes out a claim to the origin of psychoanalysis that transcends the proprietary presence of Anna Freud and the International Psychoanalytical Association, and side-steps the issue of the very real institutional legacy represented by the IPA. In the time-honored fashion that has marked the evolution of the psychoanalytic movement, Lacan would found his own school (in the form of the *École freudienne de Paris*) in order to disseminate his ideas and teachings, and would also eventually dissolve it when he no longer thought it served its purpose. What the return to Freud signifies for Lacan is the importance of understanding an intellectual tradition as a live entity, in much the same way as did Heidegger and other modernists. With his imperative of the return to Freud, Lacan sets the terms for a confrontation with the presence and burden of the past, the spectre of mortality, and the problems of personal identity in taking up someone else's intellectual legacy.

Freud and His Forbears: *The Interpretation of Dreams*

Freud himself was not free of conflicted feelings regarding his mentors, and his anxieties about them are on vivid display in his first major work, *The Interpretation of Dreams*, which is the Freudian text with the most pervasive impact on Lacan's work overall. Its treatment of the dream-work as an assemblage of symbols providing the keys to the unconscious is the cornerstone of Lacan's view of language, and its role in the analytic relation. Lacan's mid-1950s writings such as the Rome Discourse and "The Signification of the Phallus" present the reading of the symbolic order as the primary goal of psychoanalysis, not only in the analysis of dreams, but also in the events of one's everyday experience. If one follows Lacan's exhortation in the Rome Discourse to read the opening paragraphs of the chapter entitled "Die Traumarbeit," one will find Freud's confident declaration of the power in interpreting dreams as one would a language. Instead of dismissing dreams with nonsensical content as irrelevant, Freud declares that they may be interpreted and made meaningful in some fashion, as one might do with a rebus. Nonsense may be magically transformed into sense if one takes each element in the dream, juxtaposes it with the others, and attempts to link them together:

> The words which are put together in this way are no longer nonsensical but may form a poetical phrase of the greatest beauty and significance. A dream is a picture-puzzle of this sort and our predecessors in the field of dream-interpretation have made the mistake of treating the rebus as a pictorial composition: and as such, it has seemed to them nonsensical [unsinnig][6] and worthless. (SE 4: 278)

One striking aspect of this declaration is Freud's insistence that dream interpretation is foremost a logical (or linguistic) assessment of the manifest content of dreams, rather than a narrative, impressionistic, or affective one. Because the dream echoes the unconscious wishes of the dreamer, one must not confuse the manifest content with a proper reading of the dream, which should correspond in a meaningful way with the dreamer's life-experience.

There are inevitably some dreams where interpretation is a stretch at best, and Freud takes care over the course of the work to address those points where his faith in the intelligibility of dreams is sorely tested. Although some anchor of meaning in the dreamer's waking life can almost always be found, Freud concludes that the nonsensical or disturbing manifest content of some dreams expresses the inability of the dreamer to cope with a difficult situation.[7] Most of the examples Freud provides of these nonsensical dreams are drawn from a record of his own dreams; typical of Freud's early work, these accounts provide an unusual insight into the early years of psychoanalysis, in much the same way as his letters to Fliess and other early colleagues. In each of these dream readings, Freud suffers interpretive problems when trying to analyze dreams where he encounters his deceased father or a late former professor, and his inability or unwillingness to read these dreams thoroughly speaks volumes about his unconscious feelings concerning his erstwhile mentors. Such dreams account for most of the section "Absurd Dreams" in the sixth chapter, "Traumarbeit." Although it would be some time after *The Interpretation of Dreams* before Freud outlined the Oedipus complex in detail, it would seem that the "absurd dreams" are symptoms of Oedipal tension, a set of potent images that evade easy interpretation and impart to Freud a palpable sense of dread, signaling buried feelings of anxiety about his intellectual endeavors. Just as Lacan sees his intellectual inheritance from Freud as being fraught with pitfalls, so does the young Freud of the *Interpretation* experience trepidation when recalling his days as a student.

At the end of "Calculations in Dreams," Freud discusses some of these curious examples from his own dream-life, in order, he says, to illustrate a dreaming subject's ratiocination within the context of a dream. The brief dream that stimulates his investigation is this: after going to his professor's laboratory at night, a knock at the door prompts Freud to open it, revealing the dead Professor Fleischl, who has arrived with a number of strangers in tow (SE 4: 421). This dream caused Freud some puzzlement, until, he says, he recalled a dream that had occurred the night before the one featuring Fleischl. In the previous dream, Freud happens upon P., a deceased former professor of his, and Wilhelm Fliess having a conversation in the street. The three then sit down at a table where Fliess relates the sad news that at that very minute, as they converse, his sister is dying. P. fails to understand what Fliess says, whereupon Freud emphatically attempts to make P. understand the situation. This leads to Freud's epiphany concerning the appearance of the dead in dreams:

> *...overcome by strange emotions, I tried to explain to Fliess that P. (could not understand anything at all, of course, because he) was not alive. But what I actually said—and I myself noticed the mistake—was,* 'NON VIXIT.' *I then gave P. a piercing look. Under my gaze he turned pale; his form grew indistinct and his eyes a sickly blue—and finally he melted away. I was highly delighted at this and I now realized that Ernst Fleischl, too, had been no more than an apparition, a 'revenant'* ['ghost'—literally, 'one who returns'];[8] *and it seemed to me quite possible that people of that kind only existed as long as one liked and could be got rid of if someone wished it.* (SE 5: 421)

Freud notices a fault in his declaration to Fliess in the dream in that he says "Non vixit," the past perfect form of "Non vivit" (the correct form of the phrase), which is the present tense-form of the declarative statement "he does not live." Freud's perturbation arises from his guilt at having wished P. not only dead, but also in having wished to erase him from his memory for selfish reasons: "I am capable of doing so—of doing, that is to say, what I did in the dream, of sacrificing to my ambition people whom I greatly value" (SE 5: 422). Freud acknowledges, however, that the glance with which he destroys P. was a repetition of a similar gesture P. once made to him, as P. had once scowled at Freud when he was tardy to one of P.'s lab sessions. After some thought, it occurs to Freud that the occasion of these two dreams was the dedication of a memorial at the university to Fleischl. At the time, Freud remembers, he rued the fact that there was no memorial for P., because Freud felt that P. was an unjustly ignored scholar whose work was vastly underrated: "As he had deserved well of science I built him a memorial but as he was guilty of an evil wish (which was expressed at the end of the dream) I annihilated him" (SE 5: 423).[9]

What Freud expresses in this passage is not ambivalence, but a series of distinct, conflicted wishes and sentiments: I wish revenge on P. for having judged me when I was his pupil, but at the same time, P. should be memorialized for his service to science and the university; I harbor the feeling that P. should never have lived but regret that I killed his ghost in the dream; I wish that I were not too willing to forget those who have helped me, but it annoys me that Fleischl persists in disturbing me at my work, even in death. This logjam of separate and distinct feelings presented here indicates Freud's overpowering desire to bury his forebears once and for all, so that those who taught him are extinguished from his *living* memory, and leave him to work in peace without their interference. Freud's feelings about his old teacher P. seem to epitomize his attitude toward all his tutors. All in all, for Freud, P. is best memorialized: not forgotten, but ossified into a bureaucratic memory.

Freud continues this line of thought in the next section of "Die Traumarbeit," "Absurd Dreams," which finds him analyzing his own dream-thoughts with respect to his deceased father, Jacob. The second dream Freud looks at in this section is one of his own, and it would seem at first to place his father in a flattering light:

> *After his death my father played a political part among the Magyars and brought them together politically.* Here I saw a small and indistinct picture: *a crowd of men as though they were in the Reichstag: someone standing on one or two chairs, with other people round him. I remembered how like Garibaldi he had looked on his death-bed, and felt glad that that promise had come true.* (SE 5: 427–428)

"What could be more absurd than this?" Freud asks. His reading of the dream parses out the image of his father into two impressions: first, his memory of a small woodcut depicting an 18th century Austrian political crisis, and second, his linking of his father's death to feces. Freud remarks that a major symptom of his father's fatal illness (intestinal paralysis), and the autopsy of an old schoolmate's father (which revealed that the man soiled himself upon death), connected for him the spectre of death to excrement. Freud even allows himself a pun on the word "Stuhl," noting its meaning as both "chair" and "stool specimen," and he remarks that this homonym is of some significance in having produced this triumphal image of his father. This reading sets forth an explanation for the imagery of the dream, but falls short of explaining its meaning. The mental picture of his father in death, who appears to be as dignified as the famed Italian revolutionary, recasts his father as the progenitor of a nation, rather than as the progenitor of Freud himself. In addition, Freud's seeming paternal pride at this prospect further confuses any clear reading of this dream. The basic premise remains consistent, however, with the dream of P. and Fleischl. The dead paternal figure is once again disconnected from Freud's biographical narrative and transformed into a symbolic entity that Freud may admire and respect, but whose authority Freud evades, because his aggrandized character is entirely due to Freud's imagination. Once raised to the status of a monument or totem, such figures are abstracted from Freud's life, and Freud may choose to pay homage to them, or ignore them altogether.[10]

Another dream from the same section of the book succinctly describes another aspect of Freud's dilemma concerning his relationships with his father figures, whether biological or pedagogical. Upon seeing Count Thun driving a cab in Vienna one day, Freud dreamt that same night that he was sitting in the passenger seat of a coach, traveling alongside some railroad tracks (SE 5: 432). In the dream, Freud explains to the driver (who was not Count Thun), that he is afraid he is not able to continue driving with him, and that soon he will have to get off. Left with only this brief impression of a dream, Freud has very little to go on in constructing an interpretation. The answer is ultimately found in quite an obscure place. Freud's analysis of this dream leads him to theorize that this brace of riddles, popular at the time, may have been a key in sparking the dream's narrative. Although Freud does very little in the way of interpreting these riddles, they nevertheless fit in very well with his discussion of his other dreams:

Der Herr befleht's,
Der Kutcher tut's,
Ein jeder hat's
Im Grabe ruht's.

[With the master's request
The driver complies:
By all men possessed
In the graveyard it lies.]

Der Herr befleht's
Der Kutcher tut's
Nicht jeder hat's
In der Wiege ruht's.

[With the master's request
The driver complies:
Not by all men possessed
In the cradle it lies.] (SE 5: 433–434)

The answer to the first riddle is "Vorfahren," which in this context is a pun. As a verb, it means "drive up," as to a destination, but as a noun it means "ancestry," indicating those who have preceded one in life, and in the instance of the riddle, those who have preceded one in death. The second answer is "Nachkommen," which means both "follow after" and "progeny." Freud provides very little in the way of commentary on the dream except to say that the quatrain seems to have precipitated it, but there are several interesting narrative elements to this dream. The first is Freud's occupying of two different roles in the dream: initially, he acts the part of the master, ordering the driver along his route, but at the end, he plays the part of the apologetic underling, explaining to the driver that he is obligated to get off soon. Freud's power fantasy soon gives way to a plea to be released from servitude. Underlying this is the threat of death, clearly spelled out in the riddle; the path to immortality as an ancestor necessarily, but paradoxically, stops in the cemetery. In this dream, Freud betrays a desire to depart from the set path before him, as such a journey requires an acknowledgment of the past and its mastery over him.

Moreover, the overriding theme of this dream, the fear of death, touches on the element common to all the dreams in this section of the *Interpretation*. One may agree with Freud's initial assessment that in the dream of the dead friend or father, one confronts one's own death. But the death Freud fears is the abstract death that awaits him as a forerunner to a future generation of medical minds, and represents the only lasting success he can ever hope to have as a scientist and researcher. The legitimacy that death extends to one's deeds is not inconsiderable, as it provides an elusive, resounding validation of one's genius and works. In a sense, Freud's reputation depends on his eventual death.

After that event, he can be memorialized and accorded his proper place in the pantheon.

In Freud's attempts to explain the phenomenon of the revenant, he perhaps inadvertently sheds some light on the tendentiousness of his dreams concerning his own forbears. Not surprisingly, Freud stresses that such dreams are not necessarily harbingers of disturbance or fear, but are reflective of the dreamer's need to connect with the past and validate one's wishes or soothe one's anxieties: "It often happens that we find ourselves thinking: 'If my father were alive, what would he say to this?' Dreams are unable to express an 'if' of this kind except by representing the person concerned as present in some particular situation" (SE 5: 429). "Concerned as present" are the key words in this account: the dead are "present" in such a way that they are being made to *speak* on demand, in a situation engineered (however unconsciously) by the dreamer. Freud then remarks that "what we look upon as a criticism of the dream is in reality either a consoling thought that the dead person has not lived to witness the event, or a feeling of satisfaction that he can no longer interfere in it" (SE 5: 430). Freud tells the story of a patient who repressed his wish that, as his father was suffering terribly during a long illness, his father should die rather than linger on in pain; the patient then dreamed that his father, now dead, was speaking to him as if he were still alive, without realizing that he himself has, in fact, died (SE 5: 430). Freud attributes this repression to a sort of Oedipal guilt, as the dreamer felt ashamed to have had what was, in essence, a sympathetic wish. However, Freud also notes, "I willingly confess to a feeling that dream-interpretation is far from having revealed all the secrets of dreams of this character" (SE 5: 431).

Freud's ambivalence here is supposedly rooted in his inability to comprehend the nature of the dream. One should also question his steadfast belief that the manifest content of such a dream should be taken with the utmost literality. For Freud, there is no call from the grave, no willful projection of the dead into the land of the living; the dead appear as an unreachable apparition, unable to speak or make themselves understood. The figure of the dead father appears as a testament to death itself, grim, final, and unyielding as a tombstone. But reading these dreams also reveals that the dreamer's unstated wish (in this case, the wish of Freud himself) is to reanimate the father figure, only to take over his apparition and recast it as a presence from the distant past, remote from living memory.

Freud's dreams of the fatherly revenants and the hermeneutic concerns of Lacan about relating to one's predecessors are pertinent to any account of the history of psychoanalysis, if only for the simple reason that these issues of legitimacy and intellectual parentage are central to the life of intellectual inquiry. In light of the personal dreams that Freud recounts, Freud's principal insight in this section of "Die Traumdeutung" is inevitably anticlimactic, considering the evident richness of Freud's dream-life:

> Dreams, then, are most often profound when they seem most crazy. In every epoch of history those who have had something to say but could not say it without peril have eagerly assumed a fool's cap....the dream-work produces absurd dreams...if it is faced with the necessity of representing any criticism, ridicule or derision which may be present in the dream thoughts. (SE 5: 444)

When contemplating his dead colleagues, Freud understands them only in the second context outlined above, that the absurd dream forms as a response to the criticism that one may receive from a teacher or mentor. Freud's initial unconscious reaction is to take such criticism personally, but this manifests itself as a tendency to situate the father or mentor as an icon, a figure with no real history other than a mythical one. This comes full circle when, in the subsection titled "Feelings in Dreams," Freud recalls attending the funeral of his poor friend P., whose ghost he killed in the midst of his dream-conversation about Fliess's dying sister. At one point during the service, Freud's companion remarked to him that the eulogist had taken an obsequious tack by inflating P. into a larger-than-life personage (SE 5: 485). Freud notes that, at the time, he felt it was an inappropriate thing to say at a funeral, but he also relates his thoughts during the eulogy: "It's quite true that no one's irreplaceable. How many people I've followed to the grave already! But I'm still alive. I've survived them all; I'm left in possession of the field."

The element of play in his own dreams is not lost on Freud. The phantoms that drift in and out of his dreams are, to him, nothing more than symptoms of his feelings of being in complete command of himself and his fortune, and they cause him no anxiety. Still, the figure of the revenant is representative of the rebirth that remedies an irretrievable loss, and with that, they indicate Freud's apprehensions about reckoning with the past. This in itself may be, as Freud asserts in the above excerpt and elsewhere in *The Interpretation of Dreams*, a reflection of Freud's own anxiety about death. Yet Freud's conjecture that these figures compensate for the absence of childhood companions throws such a tidy reading into disarray. Regardless of his power to populate his life with replacements for these primal attendant personae, it may be well argued that Freud felt compelled to do so; his need for companionship spurred him to call forth the revenants, to make good his losses from childhood. Thus the revenant-dreams, for Freud, reflect his struggle to take responsibility for his place in the world and the profession, to defend his chosen solitariness, and at the same time assert a claim on the psychiatric field. Irreplaceable or not, Freud's acknowledgment of the presence (and absence) of those who have gone before him informs his inability to interpret these dreams in the same manner as those of his patients, or those dreams of his that have mundane content (losing teeth, climbing stairs, flying, and the like). These aberrant dreams, dealing with the figure of the father, put into question the authority of Freud himself as an analyst and also as an authoritative interpreter of his own dreams.

Seminar VIII: Lacan, Plato, and Psychoanalytic Pedagogy

The question of transference as it relates to the progress and training of analysts is, needless to say, crucial to psychoanalytic thought. Lacan's views on transference, couched in a reading of Plato's *Symposium*, engage in a set of metaphors that fit in neatly with his concerns about the function of speech in analysis and its connection with the classical tradition, and explore the concept of analysis as "the erotic science of the body," a notion assuredly rich with interpretive possibilities. I wish to develop a reading of Lacan with Freud that takes into account the full weight of Freud's classicism and the implications of the Socratic dialogic model for psychoanalysis; in so doing, I hope to distinguish Lacan's thought from the poststructuralist milieu in which it is commonly placed, and to ground it in the older tradition of dialogue and self-examination characteristic of Western philosophy.[11]

Lacan's intention in reading the *Symposium* is to set the tone for his investigation of transference. The significance that Lacan puts on transference in the psychoanalytic situation is often overlooked. Often, the popular, pejorative image of Lacanian therapy is that of the gnomic analyst handing opaque pronouncements to the hopelessly confused analysand. The Lacanian analyst transmits the meaning present in language, and does so specifically in the language of the analysand, but cannot remain completely inert in the analytic encounter. Lacan's discussion of transference attempts to draw a more complete picture of the analytic situation in accord with his linguistic and discursive concerns. Typical for Lacan, he sees that transference is a less than benign phenomenon; in a foreshadowing of Seminar XI, he posits the analysand as, roughly speaking, the *objet petit a* for the analyst.

Lacan's investment in the spiritual and blatantly sexual meanings of transference is displayed up front, at the very beginning of the seminar. The seminar year begins auspiciously with the phrase "In the beginning there was the word," and a stated intention to take on both Plato and Freud in the course of the seminar. Lacan foregrounds the question of transference as being about love:

> I intend to begin, I want to begin, I am going to try, by beginning with all the necessary awkwardness, to begin today around this, that the term "In the beginning" certainly has another meaning.
>
> At the beginning of analytic experience – let us remember– was love. (S.VIII I 2)

For Lacan, the spurious starting point of the psychoanalytic discipline occurs in a one-to-one relationship based on trust and a certain level of intimacy, in the broad sense of the word. Lacan then recalls the first analytic relationship, in which psychoanalysis received its appellation "the talking cure"; Breuer described his patient Anna O.'s hysterical symptoms in an attempt to cure them, and referred to the process as "*chimney sweeping*" (S.VIII I 2). In this case, it seems that Breuer's practice of inducing Anna to describe her hallucinations really did the trick. After speaking to him, she reported that her visions, once named and described in dialogue with him, seemed to melt away.[12] The term "chimney sweeping" (which appears in English in the text of Lacan's seminar) is fraught with sexual connotations, and indicates a habit that demands constant attention on the part of the analysand. It would seem that the beginnings of analysis, as a form of doctor-patient communication, provided the foundation for a cure that took into account the closely observed needs of the patient. The analyst imparts a certain sense of self-awareness to the analysand, in order to prevent such problems from reoccurring in the future. In this sense, every analysand becomes an amateur analyst.

However, Lacan's tone quickly changes in his consideration of how the practice coalesced into a set of dogmatic precepts that could be wielded to the detriment of both analysand and analyst. In hindsight, Lacan seems to imply that such dogmatism was unavoidable. An initiate newly confronted with the rigors and concepts of analysis may not only find them intimidating, but also may be apprehensive about the process of analysis itself, out of a realization that he or she is at the utter mercy of the analyst in the intimate analytic encounter. The set of practices that came to be known as psychoanalysis, Lacan says, fulfilled these expectations from a sociological point of view, and became part and parcel of the "manual of instructions" of analysis itself (S.VIII I 3). The problem is formulated here as if the analytic "operating manual" did indeed contain some kind of defensive rhetoric against the idea that such a relationship should be explained or sanctioned within the context of polite society. Yet Lacan's point makes clear that although there are plenty of examples in psychoanalytic literature that illustrate and dissect the nature of familial, sexual, and societal interaction, there is no guide to define the relation between the teaching analyst and the analyst-in-training, and, by extension, the links between Freud and his successors. Lacan asserts that the analytic relationship must conform to some guidelines for interaction, and that the typical characterization of intersubjectivity does not hold: "The Freudian experience becomes rigid once it appears, it only flourishes in [intersubjectivity's] absence" (S.VIII I 8). The Freudian experience, an intimate exchange, is therefore a special arrangement in which both analyst and analysand submit themselves to the situation, eschewing the roles of oracle, mind-reader, and guinea pig.

However, Lacan provides something of an opposing view in his discussion of the psychoanalytic tradition itself. The closest description of this phenomenon is found in the following passage, which attempts to treat psychoanalysis as a body of work which, like that of Plato, offers untold treasures and insights; in exchange, one must accept a foreign set of metaphors to explain one's inner life. Lacan suggests that the originary Freudian figures of psychoanalysis dictated the direction of the field in the same way that Plato's philosophy was meant as a corrective to the purgative drama of Sophocles, constituting an intellectual justification for ethical behavior:

> I will only recall that it was along the path of the properly ethical reference which is constituted by the wild reflections of Sade, and that it is along the

> offensive paths of Sadian *jouissance* that I showed to you one of the possible access points to this properly tragic frontier where the Freudian *Oberland* is situated, and that it is at the heart of what some of you have baptized the *between-two-deaths* ...I think I can say that we have introduced a reference point in the ethical tradition, in the reflection on the motives and motivations of the good. This reference point, in so far as I properly designated it as being that of beauty in so far as it ornaments, has the function of constituting the last barrier before this access to the last thing, to the mortal thing, to this point at which Freud's meditation came to make its final avowal under the term of death instinct. (S.VIII I 4)

Elsewhere in the seminar, Plato is referred to as "a sort of Sade but funnier" (S.VIII VI 6). Lacan speaks of the "repérage," the "marking" which is Freud's entry into the analysis of the death drive, latent in Freud's work until the composition of *Beyond the Pleasure Principle.* The whole of Freud's work can be understood as playing both sides of the Oedipus narrative, first from the point of view of sexual development (which analyzes the patient's early experiences), and secondly from the power of the images of death and fate presented in the tale. In the former, the content of the Oedipus story gives the unfolding of sexual development its shape; in the latter instance, it is the context surrounding the story, that of Oedipus' blindness to the meaning of his actions, which spurs the approach to the death drive, characterized as the opposite of the libidinal drive, namely, a desire to regress to a inert state. Numerous impulses come under the heading of the death drive, all exemplified by the desire to return to the nihilation of the womb. The fixation on the death drive reveals the impetus behind psychoanalysis to probe the initial wound reflecting the insight's emergence: "Narcissism explains everything....It must be said that at that time I was already reticent about the function of the narcissistic wound but it does not matter!" (S.VIII I 7). Although the broad parallel that Lacan draws between Freud and Plato is a rather mystifying one (the ascent to the Good and the trauma of the Oedipus complex could hardly be more dissimilar), Lacan's intent is to reflect on the construction of a dialogue with another person. The student speaks to the master, but the aim in the discourse is not communication—every utterance is another step in the search for truth.

Alcibiades presents a superficial challenge to Socrates in that, as an interlocutor, he refuses to agree with Socrates' explanation of the ascent to the Good, or indeed engage in any conversation with Socrates. The presence of Alcibiades disrupts the proceedings of the banquet, in

Lacan's words: "...this irruption of this personage who has all the same the closest relationship with what is in question: the question of love" (S.VIII II 7). Such opposition forces Socrates to consider the meaning of the amorous relationship between himself and Alcibiades.[13] Similarly, if the comparison between Socratic and Freudian dialogue is to be drawn, the physical features of the discursive object (in this case, the pupil-analysand) are specifically at issue; in Alcibiades, he encounters someone ready to spar over the inspirational conception of erotic love in the service of the Good. The unasked question that Alcibiades nevertheless embodies is: where is the value of the sexual relation, not to mention the palpable intersubjective proof of it? The problem here is brought up again in reference to the speech of Eryximachus:

> ...immediately we find a formula which I note, which I can only pin-point on the page. It is not that it gives us very much, but that it should all the same for us analysts be the object of a type of interest in passing, when there is some sort of surface noise that interests us. [Eryximachus] tells us that "medicine is knowledge of body's loves: ἐπισήτη τῶν τοῦ σώματος ἐρωτικῶν" (186c). One could not give a better definition of psychoanalysis, it seems to me. (S.VIII V 8)

Lacan casts the Socratic method as a form of diagnosis, which feels out the depth and seriousness of an illness. This erotic science of the body of which Lacan speaks fits the bill as a definition of analysis, which takes into account the vagaries of sexuality. Despite the implicit notion of exchange here, Lacan's earlier equation of Plato with Sade still holds: "...thus spoke Socrates. A force is transmitted in it 'which raises up those who approach it' the Platonic texts always say, in short, that the simple murmur of his word, some say 'at its contact'" (S.VIII VI 6).

Although Lacan initially characterizes truth as a function of Socrates' presence, the situation is not all that one-sided. As the seminar progresses, Lacan develops the notion that the idea of truth in the transferential relation is produced by both interlocutors. In Lacan's estimation, the imaginary golden idols Alcibiades sees within Socrates provide the touchstone for their master-slave dialectic. Lacan's evocation of the Greek tradition of religious idolatry here puts a spiritual spin on the decidedly strained relationship between Alcibiades and Socrates, and in essence trumps the Diotimean narrative of the loving, singular god of truth rather than might.[14] The *agalmata* is Alcibiades, whose presence raises the "enigma" of the gods, that of "scandal...hence the demonic incarnation of their scandalous exploits. And it is in this sense that I say that Alcibiades is the demon of Socrates" (S.VIII XI 13). Lacan develops this idea of the relationship between the two men by positing Alcibiades, once spurned by Socrates, as Socrates' "moi ideal," a necessary component to his having been enamored with him in the first place. Socrates himself is led on by the vision of the Good, inspired by (and moderated through) the person of Alcibiades. In rejecting the privileged place of the superego in Freud's model of the subject, Lacan asserts that the ideal "Other" originates in the narcissism of the subject's ego, and also in the projection of the ego through the image of the other, aggrandized (S.VIII XI 11). The specifics of Socrates' encounter with Alcibiades show that his interest in the young man is not an object that can simply be wished away:

> It is not beauty...nor the identification with God that Alcibiades desires, but this unique object, this something which he saw in Socrates, and from which Socrates diverts him because Socrates knows that he does not have it. But Alcibiades, for his part, always desires the same thing and, what Alcibiades is seeking in Agathon, you can be sure, is this same supreme point where the subject is abolished in the phantasy, his *agalmata.* (S.VIII X 10)

Earlier in the seminar, Lacan remarks that the great discovery of psychoanalysis has been the discovery of the "partial object," that which spurs desire in the subject: "partial" in that the subject is deluded into thinking that the object can be possessed completely, and therefore is something of an illusion (S.VIII XI 9). Socrates, also embodying the *agalmata,* makes himself available to Alcibiades, and in so doing, Alcibiades is fooled into believing that he can possess it, and therefore also Socrates' body itself: "...precisely because he knows that he is destined to deceive himself about it, namely to overlook the essential function of the object aimed at, constituted by the *agalma*" (S.VIII XI 10).

In Lacan's discussion of the *Symposium*, the transferential relation is seen to be crucial in the production of Platonic truth, and the truth of psychoanalysis. This is to be expected from an analyst who prizes the dialogic interaction between analyst and analysand so highly. For all that, Lacan's discussion of the *Symposium* is interesting in that the mutual desire between Socrates and Alcibiades is grounded in object relations. Each seeks out the other for a certain kind of fulfillment, a situation with implications and motivations that Socrates can fully comprehend, but which Alcibiades does not, leaving him unexpectedly wanting what he cannot have. The language Lacan uses to characterize the relationship between Alcibiades and Socrates touches on some of his favorite concerns: the death drive and its place in Freud, the effects of obsession and the illusions they produce, and the importance of full speech in the analytic relation. The overarching problem that Lacan seeks to address in this seminar is the status of analytic truth, and how it is adumbrated in the analytic relation. With both analyst and analysand as equally active participants in dialogue, what kind of truth is discovered, and what exactly is learned? Is analysis simply a cure, or can it be expected to produce something approaching moral truth? And how does it work between analytic teacher and analytic pupil?

"Gold in Exchange for Bronze": Pedagogical Illusions and Plato's *Symposium*

A closer look at the *Symposium* reveals that Plato himself provides no simple answers, and indeed the dialogue frustrates any simple interpretation in light of this theme. Socrates' philosophical teaching is variously characterized in the Platonic dialogues; indeed, the origin of the word "philosophy" is found in Plato, as he appears to have been the first to use the term. I shall not attempt here to give a Platonic account of philosophical knowledge, as every Platonic dialogue is, more or less, devoted to the rehearsal of valid arguments and the ethical value of such knowledge. However, one finds with Alcibiades' candid description of Socrates in the latter sections of the *Symposium* an extended exchange on the nature of amorous philosophical discussion between teacher and pupil; the earlier sections of the dialogue foreground the argument between Socrates and his former admirer by exploring the erotic elements of intellectual exchange, a feature common throughout the Platonic oeuvre. The context of the Socratic encounter, and the wisdom passing between both parties in dialogue (and, to a certain extent, in love) center on the question of *possession*; it is found, most notably, in Alcibiades' bitter complaints about Socrates' supposed indifference, but the dialogue as a whole deals in a set of metaphors depicting knowledge as a precious commodity to be swapped, bought, and coveted.

In the opening pages of the *Symposium*, Socrates greets Agathon, recent victor in a poetry contest and the reason for the feast, with the customary satirical fulsomeness he usually reserves for rhapsodes, rhetors, and other discursive con men:

> Socrates sat down next to him and said, "How wonderful it would be, dear Agathon, if the foolish were filled with the wisdom simply by touching the wise. If only wisdom were like water, which always flows from a full cup into an empty one when we connect them with a piece of yarn—well, then I would consider it the greatest prize to have the chance to lie down next to you. I would soon be overflowing with your wonderful wisdom. My own wisdom is of no account—a shadow in a dream—while yours is bright and radiant and has a splendid future. Why, as young as you are, you're so brilliant I could call more than thirty thousand Greeks as witnesses.
>
> "Now you've gone *too* far, Socrates," Agathon replied, "Well, eat your dinner. Dionysus will soon enough be the judge of our claims to wisdom!" (S 175d–176a)

Socrates' comment poses knowledge as a kind of zero-sum game: no doubt that as the level of Socrates' wisdom rose, Agathon's would be depleted just as quickly. The sexual imagery of this rhetorical figure fits into the primary topic of the evening's discussion, the probity of intertwining love with knowledge. In his praising of Agathon's beauty (in oratory, as well as that of his physical attributes) Socrates hits a note that will sound throughout the *Symposium*, as beauty is the first step on the path to love of wisdom, and the Good. Socrates' choice of a visual impression for the Good (namely, that which is "bright and radiant") asserts the link between knowledge and sight, another favorite theme of Plato's, and which is more often than not used to ironic effect. Before the night is over, it will be shown, unsurprisingly, that Agathon's closed-minded view of love as temporary infatuation with beauty shall prove to be morally bankrupt in light of the theory outlined by Socrates, with the aid of the Diotimean narrative. Despite Socrates' dismissal of Agathon's speech, the question of the limits of intergenerational pedagogy shall return to the fore, by way of Socrates' acknowledgment of the transactional nature of such relationships, in direct opposition to the strain of inquiry he explores with Diotima as his guide.

The theory of the ascent to the Good that Socrates puts forward in the *Symposium* is based on the dialogic progression of the inquiry into the nature of love, culminating in the emblematic image of the ladder ascending to the vision of the Good. Such an engenderment of knowledge in the individual occurs in a greatly different fashion than that of the homoerotic model Socrates purportedly excoriates. Diotima's explanation for the motivation to teach wisdom lies in the individual's desire to evade the inevitable mortification of the flesh:

> "And in that way [memory] everything mortal is preserved, not, like the divine, by always being the same in every way, but because what is departing and aging leaves behind something new, something such as it had been. By this device, Socrates," she said, "what is mortal shares in immortality whether it is a body or anything else, while the immortal has another way. So don't be surprised if everything naturally values its own offspring, because it is for the sake of immortality that everything shows this zeal, which is Love." (S 208a–b)

The figure Plato uses to describe the origin of this desire for knowledge is that of pregnancy, and indeed Diotima's explanation counters the suggestion that beauty, like knowledge, is a thing that can be possessed: "It is giving birth in beauty, whether in body or soul" (S 206b). Diotima remarks that once we get to a certain age, "we naturally desire to give birth" (S 206c). Love wants not beauty but "reproduction and birth in beauty" (S 206e). The Platonic imperative to orient oneself toward the eternal and incorruptible is manifest here, because that which longs for the beautiful must not in itself be beautiful or perfectly good; Eros is often portrayed, in antiquity, as being the ugliest of the gods, fomenting desire for that which he himself lacks. In turn, the passing on of such philosophical knowledge engenders the desire for the beautiful within the pupil. Diotima elaborates: "For among animals the principle is the same as with us, and mortal nature seeks so far as possible to live forever and be immortal. And this is possible in one way only: by reproduction, because it always leaves behind a new young one in place of the old" (S 207d).

Although this conversation may imply that Socrates is doing good by fostering relationships with younger men in the hopes that they will turn toward his brand of philosophical inquiry, the link between Socrates and his students, even if it is a bond of affection, is one fraught with complexity and danger. The emotion most often invoked with Socrates when his students talk about him in the dialogues is admiration; far from being a common lover, Socrates is the one above all others who provided his followers with a moral example and a model of how to conduct honest inquiry. However, Diotima assigns Socrates the role of Eros in this scenario, as one who desires love's beautiful effects, rather than casting him as a wise, abiding parent. Diotima's further exploration of this metaphor provides Socrates with an erotic role to play in his fostering philosophical interest within young men: "...others are pregnant in soul—because there surely *are* those who are even more pregnant in their souls than in their bodies, and these are pregnant with what is fitting for a soul to bear and bring to birth" (S 209a). Diotima's description of love's operation, process, and proper object allows Socrates a parallel role as one sowing the seeds of philosophy and procreating in spirit rather than body. Typical of the masculine role in procreation, Socrates imposes a *form* on the pupil, giving a context and method for the search for truth rather than doling out the content of such knowledge. Further textual parallels with this impression of Socrates arrive in Diotima's description of Love as being "homeless" and "a lover of wisdom," the same trappings as the pauperish Socrates (S 203c–d). The vision of the ascent to the Good Diotima presents is, most significantly, one of high moral purpose occasioned by the presence of another.

Nevertheless, Plato sees fit to give a voice to the status quo of pedagogical relationships. Pausanias' speech is the only one of the *Symposium* that takes the pedagogy between men and boys somewhat seriously, for much the same reason that Diotima seems to value the heterosexual one between men and women. The lover *develops* the beloved in an intellectual sense, so that after the affair is over, the older man leaves something permanent to the younger. Here, Pausanias outlines the lover's commitment to a potential love interest:

> I am convinced that a man who falls in love with a young man of his own age is generally prepared to share everything with the one he loves—he is eager, in fact, to spend the rest of his own life with him. He certainly does not aim to deceive him—to take advantage of him while he is still young and inexperienced and then, after exposing him to ridicule, to move quickly on to someone else. (S 181d–181e)

Pausanias' lines are echoed by the bitter Alcibiades later on, when he says he believed that Socrates genuinely cared about him and that he felt wronged when he realized he could not possess Socrates. Pausanias remarks that, ideally, the adult lover should obey two principal laws: one for the love of boys, the other for love of wisdom (S 184d). It is impossible to legislate rational behavior in a truly love-based relationship, as both parties are in such an excited state that neither one has any externalized view of their actions, which resolutely oppose each one's instincts for self-interest: "And, what is the most extraordinary thing of all, it is popularly supposed that the lover is the one man whom the gods will pardon for breaking his vows, for lovers' promises, they say, are made to be forsworn" (S 183b). In this sense, pedagogical love, regardless of the age difference, takes on a kind of phantom status in the network of relationships that comprises Greek society, as it cannot be measured by the number of children in a household, or other outward symbols of possession and domain. The lover of knowledge, whose object is heightened ethical discernment, shall instead retain qualities of mind and soul wholly independent of his former lover, and having been instructed in morality and truth, shall reap the benefits in perpetuity (S 183a). In sum, the moral education of a Greek youth, existing outside of a heterosexual economy, is a boon in his life; having been taken in hand by an older citizen, the younger benefits from the wisdom of old age, and takes these lessons, literally, in Pausanias' estimation, to heart. The question of whether such a relationship counts as "real love" is, in a very pointed way, taken up by Alcibiades when he seizes his turn to speak.

The presence of Alcibiades serves as the obverse of Diotima's ode to philosophical love; in keeping with this dialogue's character, Socrates engages neither Alcibiades nor Diotima in any substantial argument, and each is allowed to speak with little interruption. The principal conflict for Alcibiades in the *Symposium*, which he airs in the opening moments of his speech, follows on the questions raised by Pausanias: what are the boundaries of affection and knowledge in the pedagogical relationship, and what claims does the younger lover have on the older? The fundamental problem for Alcibiades, rejected and embittered, stems from his misapprehension of his role in his relationship with Socrates. Still smarting from the sage's rebuff of his amorous entreaties, Alcibiades enlarges on his enraged and spluttering initial response to the presence of Socrates, claiming that Socrates' seductive voice will surely overtake him in no time:

> He always traps me, you see, and he makes me admit that my political career is a waste of time, while all that matters is just what I most neglect: my personal shortcomings, which cry out for the closest attention. So I refuse to listen to him; I stop my ears and tear myself away from him, for, like the Sirens, he could make me stay by his side till I die. (S 216a–216b)

The difference between Alcibiades' view of his relationship to Socrates, and Socrates' own view of their tryst, is that of the aspiring teacher's pet versus that of the jaded teacher who realizes all too keenly the shallowness of the former's crush. Alcibiades' reflection that he has been unfaithful to Socratic tutelage causes him to feel embarrassed in the presence of the great man:

> Socrates is the only man in the world who has made me feel ashamed—ah, you didn't think I had it in me, did you? Yes, he makes me feel ashamed: I know

> perfectly well that I can't prove he's wrong when he tells me what I should do; yet, the moment I leave his side, I go back to my old ways: I cave in to my desire to please the crowd. (S 216b)

Alcibiades' adherence to moral rectitude is bound to his feelings of attachment to Socrates, despite his initial estimation of Socrates as a momentary fling. In a rare show of candor for Plato, Alcibiades goes on in his tale of failed seduction to describe his ardor for Socrates and the impossibility of letting him go:

> To begin with, he's crazy about beautiful boys; he constantly follows them around in a perpetual daze. Also, he likes to say he's ignorant and knows nothing. Isn't this just like Silenus? Of course it is! And all this is just on the surface, like the outsides of those statues of Silenus. I wonder, my fellow drinkers, if you have any idea what a sober and temperate man he proves to be once you have looked inside. Believe me, it couldn't matter less to him whether a boy is beautiful. You can't imagine how little he cares whether a person is beautiful, or rich, or famous in any other way that most people admire. He considers all these possessions beneath contempt, and that's exactly how he considers all of us as well. In public, I tell you, his whole life is one big game—a game of irony. I don't know if any of you have seen him when he's really serious. But once I caught him when he was open [ἀνοιχθέντος] like Silenus' statues, and I had a glimpse of the figures he keeps hidden within: they were so godlike [θεῖα]—so bright [χρυσᾶ] and beautiful [πάγκαλα], so utterly amazing—that I no longer had a choice—I just had to do whatever he told me.[15] (S 216d–217a)

Alcibiades makes the mistake of identifying the figure of Socrates exclusively with the truth he dispenses. The English word "idea" ultimately derives from forms of the root εἴδω, the Attic verb which means *to see* but is used for a broad range of meanings, most especially *to know*; the method of revelation Alcibiades describes is ἀνοιχθέντος, most precisely meaning in this context "laid open." Those things to which Alcibiades refers, here rendered as "images," are ἀγάλματα, a term that reaches back to Homer, indicating the honorific symbols of a god.[16] In this case, such idols would put the lie to Socrates' disavowal of his store of knowledge. Alcibiades himself, however, does not consider if the images themselves are real are not; they are a fantastical delusion that holds sway over him, and overwhelmed by Socrates' intellectual wealth, Alcibiades sees nothing for it but to put himself in Socrates' hands. The prophecy of Socrates' flip remark at the beginning of the dialogue has come true. Philosophy, here, is not something external to the self;

Alcibiades has deluded himself into believing that Socrates possesses a store of knowledge, which he hoards jealously. The images represent, one might say, the glittering truths offered by philosophy, which evaporate as soon as they are examined too closely.

Not only is the love Alcibiades feels for Socrates imaginary, but the possibility of any relationship with Socrates is precluded by his unwillingness to open himself up for an amorous exchange. Alcibiades reflects after spending the night sleeping next to Socrates: "Be sure of it, I swear to you by all the gods and goddesses together, my night with Socrates went no further than if I had spent it with my own father or brother" (S 219c–219d). The disappointment Alcibiades feels relates primarily to his inability to seduce Socrates successfully. After pursuing him for more than a day or so (Socrates simply cannot take the hint), Alcibiades finally confronts Socrates with the fact that he wishes to sleep with him, revealing, to Socrates' ambiguous chagrin, that his desires are quite basely sexual. Socrates' dismissive reply to his suit plays on Alcibiades' metaphor of the golden images:

> ...You seem to me to want more than your proper share: you offer me the merest appearance of beauty, and in return you want the thing itself, 'gold in exchange for bronze.'
>
> Still, my dear boy, you should think twice, because you could be wrong, and I may be of no use to you. The mind's sight becomes sharp only when the body's eyes go past their prime—and you are still a good long time away from that. (S 218e–219a)

Socrates' implication here is that Alcibiades (naturally) has given up too much of himself in his amorous pursuit: the pleasures of the flesh, his real aim, will be denied him as long as he continues chasing Socrates. The education that Alcibiades receives from Socrates may be morally instructive, but cannot fill the lack that Alcibiades feels; in psychoanalytic parlance, Alcibiades has projected the power of Socrates' images onto the man himself, such that he alone merely transmits the idea of the Good: it is authorized by his presence, real or imagined.

This sense of betrayal that Alcibiades feels certainly does not invalidate what he learned from Socrates; however, in the case of Alcibiades, it leaves a savage example to follow. Socratic pedagogy may ply the student with a set of metaphors to uncover what he has forgotten and in fact already possesses. But although it works for mathematical demonstrations and the like, ethical decisions cannot be thought processes locked up inside someone who constantly holds mental vigil in front of images of the Good. They are only available in the relationship with the teacher, the daimon, and disappear when he is absent. Platonic love, as depicted in the *Symposium*, is nothing less than intellectual seduction and abandonment, with the bereft student left to reassemble the lessons after the master's permanent physical departure, the master's voice ringing constantly in his ears. The rejection by Socrates of his putative pupil seems to have fired Alcibiades' philosophical imagination, however, as his declaration seems to betray:

> And, furthermore, you know what people say about snakebite—that you'll only talk about it with your fellow victims: only they will understand the pain and forgive you for all the things it made you do. Well, something much more painful than a snake has bitten me in my most sensitive part—I mean my heart, or my soul, or whatever you want to call it, which has been struck and bitten by philosophy, whose grip on young and eager souls is much more vicious than a viper's and makes them do the most amazing things. (S 217e–218a)

Here, Alcibiades inverts the imperative suggested by Pausanias: the education of a young man cannot be legislated, and that the older man should simply proceed as he sees fit. Alcibiades puts the responsibility on the teacher rather than the pupil, and suggests that such a relationship can be nothing but destructive, with the teacher assuming the role of the predator, and the pupil becoming the prey. The narrative of the *Symposium* establishes a philosophical justification of love as a noble feeling which induces one to act in accordance with a morality that is congruent in an aesthetic sense; that which is beautiful is but a physical reflection of the Good. Where Alcibiades and Plato go astray is in falling for the images themselves rather than being mindful of what they represent. The analogic relationships upon which so many of Plato's arguments depend melt into thin air if one does not adduce truth to them: in the words of Socrates, one must blindly take bronze for gold, in order to participate in the game of philosophical truth.

Lacan, Oedipus, and Revelation

An important question that Lacan seeks to answer in his earlier work is that of the origin of the psychoanalytic insight. Lacan attempts to determine what psychoanalysis is by investigating how one should proceed with psychoanalytic inquiry, as it depends on a theorization of analytic dialogue. It is only fitting that Lacan should turn his attention toward the historical and philosophical bases of dialogue, and interrogate them as to their relevance to analytic practice; from the foregoing, one can see that this is a mightily vexed issue. The very thing that gives psychoanalysis its value, namely dialogue between the analyst and analysand, is, in the end, impossible to rationalize. The conflation of love and philosophical dialectic is a significant one. The two-term Socratic dialectic removes all semblance of objectivity, and the manufacture of philosophical truth becomes a contest between the teacher and student, negotiated across the treacherous territory of expectation, miscommunication and desire. All the trappings of the analytic-pedagogical relation are subject to shift, including the roles of teacher and student, doctor and patient, seducer and seduced.

For Lacan, if one expects to uncover the "real" Freud, one will always uncover an individual mind at the center of his work, and ventriloquize it in the name of making it speak. The *meaning* of Freud's story must be discovered in the act of dialogue. This is the purpose of psychoanalysis, and the instrumental reason for Freud to have chosen Oedipus as the central figure of psychoanalysis. With his guilt so obvious, the motivations and import of his crimes remain hidden until they are revealed through some thorough detective work, placing his identity and birth within a larger narrative of destiny. Leaving questions of sexual development aside, Lacan's implied reinterpretation of the Oedipus story has mostly to do with the explicit concerns of analysis. Lacan regards Oedipus as the first analysand:

> But that [Oedipus' crime] is not why he [Freud] chose it. There are many other heroes besides Oedipus who are the locus of this fundamental conjuncture. The important thing, and the reason why Freud rediscovers his fundamental figure in the tragedy of Oedipus is because "he did not know...." that he had killed his father and had slept with his mother. (S.VIII VII 5)

The drama of Oedipus is one of revelation rather than action. The exposition of the layers of the Oedipus narrative, each more damning than the last, dooms Oedipus to his ultimate fate. As Lacan points out, the audience witnesses the revelation of the tragedy of Oedipus, which has already occurred; the outcome is already set, and Oedipus can do nothing during the play to change his fate, as he becomes aware of his crime. Most of all, the Oedipal tragedy is one of identity—it is the truth that wounds.

As described in this chapter, the full consequences of transference for analytic pedagogy are difficult to assess with regard to their meaning within the context of analysis itself. At best, training in analysis offers an education in analytic technique. As for the truth of psychoanalysis, it remains exclusively in the province of the subjective, not responsive to any possible "scientific" interpretation. The maladies that psychoanalysis aims to cure and the remedies it prescribes are products of the tendentious relationship between analyst and analysand; they do not derive from some philosophical ideal (a concept invalidated by the presence of Alcibiades in the *Symposium*), but are a result of friction in the subject-other relation, and in the reading of the unconscious. The reckoning with Freud that Lacan calls for is a charge to continually rediscover the orientation and identity of analysis in the works of Freud, whose corpus constitutes the substrate of analytic meaning. Any analytic hermeneutic must take into account the act of analytic reading as dialogue. One cannot pretend, with psychoanalysis as with philosophy, that there can be any abandonment of past masters, as the roles of master and pupil analyst are perpetually, and by definition necessarily, up for grabs. Lacan's ultimate suggestion in the Rome Discourse is that the overt professionalization and confident footing of contemporary psychoanalysis have finally buried the corpse of Freud, and the natural corrective to this lamentable state of affairs should be to dig it up again.

What Lacan's return to and obsession with Freud dramatizes is a romance of identity. The anguished lament of Alcibiades, rather than being the cry of someone lost or confused, is the outrage of someone who knows himself for the first time, but cannot reconcile it with his newly-discovered desires. The gift Alcibiades receives peels away the veneer of his self-regard to reveal a profound lack, and foolishly he continues to pursue Socrates, believing that Socrates alone harbors the secret that shall complete him. But beyond this, what Alcibiades regrets most is that he ever engaged himself in the illusions of philosophy, as Socrates appears to offer him access to a gleaming treasure that he could not possess. In the same way, Lacan recounts the story of Alcibiades as a counterbalance to the illusion that anyone who takes up psychoanalysis learns a discipline that leads to a kind of clairvoyance about human behavior, a golden key to some universal secret. The lure of psychoanalytic knowledge is not some marvelous realm of abstract truth, but the promise of self-discovery, with all its attendant anxieties.

2

Clérambault and Heidegger: Of Our Antecedents

> ...it should be noted that this experience [in analysis] sets us at odds with any philosophy directly stemming from the *Cogito*.
>
> —"The Mirror Stage" (E:S 3)

From its beginnings, psychoanalysis has always been a mongrel, un-"scientific" discipline of sorts, an eclectic amalgam of lab psychology, neurophysiology, philosophical reflection, and literary analysis. Any new idea will have its share of scoffers, of course, but this is precisely the kind of common-sense criticism still leveled against psychoanalysis by those who believe that the practice of medical diagnosis relies on a rigorously tested body of tried-and-true knowledge internalized by their physician, clad in a spotless white coat. Even the Greek origins of the term "diagnosis" invalidate the prejudice that healing is the province of an impartial observer examining a human being in the same way as one would a bacterium under a microscope; questions and answers reveal symptoms that the flesh will not or cannot yield to the scrutiny of a physician. In the same way, the practice of analysis depends on the co-creation of each analysand's analytic story in the interaction between analyst and analysand. By extension, the interpretation of any analyst's body of work cannot begin by taking his or her crucial ideas as inviolable dogma; as with any science, such knowledge is highly contingent on its context. The differences between psychoanalysis and what are typically thought of as the "scientific disciplines" are found primarily in psychoanalysis's raw materials (human experience), laboratory (the couch), and medium of discovery (analytic conversation). As for the theoretical side of analysis, Freud sets a precedent for others to follow by drawing heavily from classical literature, art and anthropology, in order to build the intellectual and metaphorical scaffolding for each phase of his work. In the same eclectic manner as Freud, Jacques Lacan drew ideas from a number of thinkers, artists and intellectual movements. To get at the origins of Lacan's thought, and the environment that made them possible, one must examine Lacan's training and early influences.

It is an often-obscured aspect of Lacan's work that he initially wished to found an alternate basis for psychoanalysis in then-current research being done in the arenas of experimental psychology and psychological phenomenology, particularly the work of Henri Ey, Eugene Minkowski, and the group Évolution Psychiatrique, whose eponymous journal still thrives to the present day. Lacan's clinical direction was also immeasurably influenced by the work of his mentor Gaëtan Gatian de Clérambault. Although not explicitly affiliated with the burgeoning field of French phenomenology, Clérambault established, according to Lacan, a structural model for examining the mental life of the subject, one that resembled the Freudian model in *The Ego and the Id*, although Clérambault professed no interest in psychoanalysis. Through his association with Clérambault, Lacan was able to formulate his primitive ideas of the split subject and *l'objet petit a*, and reconcile his theoretical approaches with clinical observation; Clérambault's discussion of erotomania prefigured Lacan's medical thesis on psychosis, which drew its case study, that of Aimée, from this time with Clérambault. The personal conflicts Lacan endured with Clérambault were neither unusual in any teacher-student relationship nor specific to Lacan, but they illuminate the quirkier pedagogical and clinical aspects of Lacan's personality.

Lacan's relationship to Heidegger has also been difficult to explain. In the 1950s, Lacan sought Heidegger's friendship out of an interest in his work, possibly influenced by his earlier association with the more formally phenomenological Évolution Psychiatrique. Heidegger's somewhat flattered and amused responses to Lacan's offers of collaboration, intellectual exchange, and friendship may have been more about Heidegger's postwar need to rehabilitate his reputation than any intellectual interest in translating his thought into psychoanalytic terms. Estimations of Heidegger's impact on Lacan's thought have, in the past, been focused on the later phases of Heidegger's work, primarily with regard to Lacan's approach to language as the medium and justification for psychoanalysis. Heidegger's earlier, more formal work has been overlooked as to its influence on Lacan, and it is this crucial aspect of the Heidegger-Lacan confrontation that I wish to elucidate here. In exposing the roots of Lacanian thought in the work of Clérambault and Heidegger, I offer an assessment of the aim of Lacan's work to bring a kind of scientific rigor to psychoanalysis, in order to articulate Lacan's ties to the modernist movements of transcendental phenomenology and "scientific" clinical psychology. The obsession of modernist intellectual movements with the ego is never truly abandoned in the postmodern era, with its emphasis on the "decentered" subject. Rather, this assuredly anti-Cartesian view of the subject is present everywhere in Freud, Heidegger, and particularly Clérambault, whose view of the split subject in large measure formed the basis for Lacan's mature work of the 1950s.

Clérambault: Maître de Lacan

In "De nos antécédents," a short piece near the beginning of *Écrits*, Lacan declares that he wishes to recall where psychiatry made its entry into his life. At the auspicious occasion of the publication of this book, a summary of his life's work, one might expect a statement reflecting on his life in thought, which Lacan delivers—although perhaps in an unexpected way. After making references to both Évolution Psychiatrique and those Surrealists who shared his point of view, Lacan remarks that the birth of the clinic ("naissance de la clinique," an unsubtle reference, perhaps, to the Foucault work of the same name) was, the analytic community believes, brought about by Freud, although the trappings of modern psychiatric practice, Lacan says, were established primarily through Kraepelin, master of the empirical, formally neurophysiological approach. However, writes Lacan, his career, and the character of French analysis, finds itself in "la trace" of Clérambault, "notre seul maître en psychiatrie" (E 65). Lacan goes on to say that it is because of Clérambault's structural rigor that Lacan and his colleagues, whether they were aware of Clérambault's influence or not, were able to advance the practice of French psychiatry. By 1966, Clérambault's work had been out of print since the mid-1940s, all but forgotten in the wake of the emergence of French psychoanalysis and criticism.

At the time of Lacan's publication of *Écrits*, Clérambault's fame rested principally (as it does now) on his theory of erotomania, a form of hysteria in which the female sufferer (invariably female, it might be said) believes that a noted man of wealth, importance or prominence is desperately in love with her. "Clérambault syndrome" is a near-universal term for this concept, and is uniformly used to describe sexual obsessions that transcend social class.[1] Although this idea has a great deal of currency in the psychological landscape (particularly from the Anglo-American perspective), Clérambault's clinical work has, for the most part, remained almost completely uninvestigated, save for a few brief biographical works and collections pertaining to his investigations of *l'automatisme mental* and fabric fetishism among women, which contain excerpts from his massive posthumous anthology *Oeuvres Psychiatriques*. Published in 1942 through the efforts of Clérambault's students several years after his death, it is a chronologically organized collection of case studies and clinical writings, divided into topical chapters; it ends with an account of Clérambault's suicide, the circumstances leading up to it, and the controversy surrounding it. As Garrabé notes in his preface to the collection titled *L'automatisme mental*, the size and whimsical, somewhat arbitrary presentation of the *Oeuvres Psychiatriques* certainly prefigures Lacan's *Écrits*.[2] Indeed, the appearance of *Écrits* at such a late point in Lacan's life might be construed as Lacan's succumbing to the demands of the intellectual marketplace, out of the realization that he had long since exhausted his best ideas and that they could finally be yielded to public examination, as a kind of monument to his intellectual legacy.

The intellectual debt Lacan owes to Clérambault is a concrete one. Lacan's concept of the split self, partitioned into the *je* and the *moi*, is grounded in the *scisson du moi* formulated by Clérambault, with the delusions of psychosis forming a large part of Clérambault's theory of personality. In a primitive sense, the delusion of desire is the reflected unconscious of the subject, superadded to the immutability of the symbolic order. As such, the dividend of the self effaces the ratiocinative side of subject. Clérambault's vivid descriptions of the deluded subject, found in his writings on "the delusional passions," provide the basis for the Lacan of *Les Psychoses* and also Seminar XI, with its presentation of the gaze, the blot, and anamorphism.

Clérambault, *L'Automatisme Mental*, and the Split Self

Up through the first half of the 1920s, Clérambault's clinical work took place in number of venues, and benefited from his long-running affiliation with the prefecture of the Parisian police. A significant number of Clérambault's subjects were, as a result, drawn from the criminal sphere of Paris; already subjected to humiliating treatment at the hands of the police, they received nothing less from Clérambault himself. His collected clinical writings are filled with rather primitive (by today's standards) neurological experiments concerning the effects of various toxins (alcohol, ether, narcotics) on the nervous system, assessments of criminal behavior, and the like. The writings of Clérambault were, with very few exceptions, produced for medical journals and a professional audience. As a result, Clérambault's style is terse, blunt, and often inconclusive, as he tends to leave questions open until more data can be found. Often, his more theoretical writings will pursue an idea over several installments, developing them with each iteration. Clérambault's persona was one of looming eminence, yet he was mercurial and unpredictable. He went at his tasks with the objectivity of a true clinician and inspired great loyalty, yet he jealously guarded his ideas and forbade his students to talk about them outside of seminars.[3] That Clérambault's thought emerges from a site of pathology is not really in question; one could say the same of Lacan's work during and just after this period, focusing as it does on frustrated desire.

The structural element of Clérambault's work, as Lacan himself points out, cannot be underestimated, particularly as it seems to have provided Lacan with some of his more recognizable concepts. Clérambault's most noteworthy abstract psychological construct is the phenomenon he termed *l'automatisme mental*. In Freudian terms, "mental automatism" is Clérambault's description of the relation of the ego to the unconscious. The "automated" portion of the subject's consciousness is that which organizes the data of perception and forms the substrate of conscious existence. In essence, this layer is that which most closely comprises the self, with distortions of this functionality making themselves manifest in one's subjectivity in the form of delusional passions. Clérambault differentiated these "passions" from hallucinatory psychoses, which were what he deemed to be the cause of real mental illness. At once, the Clérambaldian theory of personality is formed, more or less wholly; the personality of the subject, superimposed on the base of the *l'automatisme mental*, is dictated by the feelings that external stimuli and interest provoke in the subject. From this, one may see the eventual development of the Lacanian picture of the *moi/je* dyad, where the image of the self from the point of view of society, the *moi*, is the effect of the intersubjective relation of the subject with others in a societal context, and the subjective perception of experience, *je*, is the irreducible dividend of self and personality.

The formation of the concept of *l'automatisme mental* is itself worthy of examination. The central idea supporting A.M. (as Clérambault often refers to it in shorthand) is that of *anidéisme* or *anidéation*, which, for Clérambault, described the organic mental processes that operated outside the conscious life of the brain.[4] The initial idea of A.M. was established in Clérambault's pre-1926 clinical work. In a sense, the presence of the unconscious is the root cause of mental instability in that the subject's unnatural attention to its machinations disturbs the rational side of consciousness. The awareness of unconscious processes bubbling under the veneer of the conscious gives rise to their misinterpretation by the subject, possibly inducing paranoia. The symptoms of such a "disorder" are, according to Clérambault, the "echoing" of one's thoughts, internal narrations and arguments about one's acts, thoughts, and motives, such that the subject is whipped into a kind of hyper-aware state. The operations that are normally invisible to the subject's consciousness are *too* present, leading the subject to exaggerate their significance; Clérambault observes that the explication of mental disorders requires an understanding of the subject's perceptive mechanism as it relates to the phenomena disturbing them (OP 464). Clérambault remarks elsewhere that A.M. is a "primordial phenomenon," which falls under the same category, "secondary delusions," as do feelings of persecution, megalomania, erotism, and mysticism; Clérambault also refers to A.M. as a "primitive process," extant in a more or less "pure state" (OP 465). Again, the psychological maladies aggravated by the subject with reference to A.M. are important in that they are *delusions*, products of the misinterpretation of mental cues and processes with reference to the outside world. "Délire," Clérambault laconically asserts, "n'est qu'une Superstructure" (OP 466). Therefore, A.M., according to Clérambault, is a syndrome fundamental to all kinds of psychoses (OP 466).[5] However, Clérambault notes that delusionary hallucinations featuring persecutions are necessarily of mixed form; the experience of persecution and paranoia has a great many layers, the pathology of which takes into account many factors in the production of full-blown paranoia.

L'automatisme mental, in its original conception, is, simply put, a basic, universal structure for mental functioning. It provides for the processing of stimuli and the staging of thoughts. But when used as a sounding board in conscious life, it becomes a spur for delirium to emerge. As delirium is a composite state with many causes and factors, the problem of treating such an illness is to work out more than one course of treatment, given that psychosis and related maladies have histological causes, and mental functioning, belonging to a psychological domain, follows afterward (OP 523–524). The cause of psychosis is somatic, albeit in a metaphorical sense relating to the structure and theory of nervous organization, and is a key to the investigation of mental illness. Because it is a universal feature of consciousness, it does not solve individual questions of personality (OP 493). Although it is developed much later in the sequence of his work, at the heart of the theory of A.M. is Clérambault's doctrine of *anidéisme*, a concept similar to that of the Freudian unconscious, along with various descriptions of A.M. under the rubric of *l'Automatisme Ideo-Verbal*.

In later writings, Clérambault becomes even bolder in his theorizing of the subject, opting for an almost Cartesian method of talking about the unconscious. In the clinical writings of 1926, Clérambault discusses the various forms of psychosis previously covered in his work, and allows that all of the psychoses, from perceptual distortions (either chemically induced or organic) to recurring thought patterns, are "mechanical" in origin; the hallucinations are disorganized, not related to any train of thought or visual perception, and as such they are proof that the images are "automatically" generated (OP 63). Owing to the neutral aspect of this mode of mental functioning, Clérambault maintains that the categories of mental activity he describes as an effect of A.M. are not themselves necessarily positive or negative, but merely different effects of the same structure (OP 64–65).[6]

Where Freud theorizes that slips or parapraxes come from the unconscious and erupt into the conscious, Clérambault's picture of psychosis is such that each symptom of delusion violates the Cartesian picture of consciousness, disrupting the evenness of rational thought. But rather than subscribing to the Cartesian model of the "theatre" of consciousness, which entertains or rejects ideas, Clérambault constructs a view of the mind as a collection of systems automatically organizing and evaluating experience. Clérambault realizes that his insistence on the operation of "anidéisme" establishes the mind as an essentially permeable entity with little hard-wired internal structure, open to the whims and stimuli of everyday life. Thus, Clérambault's conception of the subject closely mirrors that of Freud; Clérambault, by 1926, observes that "anidéisme" opens one up to "inconscients directives," analogous to the Freudian vision of the conscious mind constantly holding the unconscious at bay. However, in this passage, Clérambault uncannily prefigures the postmodern vision of the subject as the nexus of a web of influence, drive, and attraction, incorporating everything under the heading of subjectivity; with the development of psychosis, all visual impressions, ideas, memories, and traumas are subsumed and overtaken by the disease (OP 76). The idea of the "subject" is merely an effect of the neurological system; it appears that the psychotic subject is at the center of a vortex of stimuli, and it desires to project itself outward into them. The trick of subjectivity is seen to be merely the effect of the aggregated neurological impulses in subjective experience. Here again, the neurological bias is shown to be alive and well concerning the matter of subjectivity and psychosis, although this move toward outlining the structure of consciousness happens to fall into step with the abstractions of Freudian analysis.

The distortion resulting in the psychotic personality, then, is aggravated through two tendencies. First, the exaggeration of the operations of the mind balloons into the irritation of psychosis; second, the intrusion of external stimuli is such that the personality expands to include them. Through these two causes working in concert, the psychotic personality develops. Speaking of the error in interpretation (which strongly resembles Lacanian *méconnaissance*), the impossibility of distortion-free perception appears here perhaps for the first time in the conversation of French psychiatry: not only does Lacan carry its implications to their logical extreme in his idea of *méconnaissance*, but the fact of *méconnaissance* is replicated in any relation between subject and other, or subject and analyst. The relationship between psychiatrist and patient, rather than being subject to legible transference and countertransference, is necessarily viewed through the warped lens of subjectivity.

Clérambault's influence on Lacan is reflected in a number of ways—specifically, in the ways that Lacan himself had advertised in "De nos antécédents"—most notably, in the fissure of the human subject into two separate portions, A.M. and the ego (or personality), both of which govern the actions of the subject. However, the abstraction of biological processes into objects of study for psychiatry, already a feature of Freud's work, emerges in Clérambault as the method for devising theories of psychological functioning. *L'automatisme mental* operates on such a level as to stand in for the involuntary processes of the brain. At the same time, the recognition of the personality as wholly secondary to the operation of these processes permits Lacan to establish the ego as being at the mercy of external forces, tossing the rationalist concept of free will aside.

Clérambault and Lacan's Early Assessment of Paranoia

In addition to utilizing a Clérambaldian view of the complexity of psychosis, Lacan's *thèse de médecine, De la psychose paranoïaque dans ses rapports avec la personnalité*, bears the unmistakable mark of his absorption of phenomenological thought. Lacan justifies his scientific interest in the question of the psychoses by remarking on the need for a taxonomy of the forms of madness and the structure of their integration into the conception of the subject. Because the concept of psychosis is so broad, Lacan says, it should instead be known by the individual names of folly, paranoia, delirium, discordance, schizophrenia, and the like (PP 14). The role of personality in relation to the psychoses is an important one, as "personality" is a name for an intentional phenomenological construction, referred to by Lacan as an intentional reality (PP 32). The vicissitudes of personality are only understood in the societal context in which they are lived: Lacan mentions as being significant the qualities of synthesis, intentionality, and responsibility, and they are the pillars of personality (PP 33). Lacan also includes a footnote at this point mentioning phenomenologist Max Scheler's work, itself deeply invested in exploring the phenomenological aspects of social life. Lacan's interest in developing a more structured account of personality stems from his distaste for overly theoretical ruminations resulting in dogmatic conclusions that inaccurately represent the subject, and Lacan further stipulates that any subject must not merely be considered as an empty container filled by stimuli, desires, and mental images (PP 37).

The ideal "image" of the "moi," despite its hardening later on into the monolithic construction of Lacan's later work, is, at this early stage, merely the rubric under which the experiences of the "I" are collected; the image of the *moi* is present in interior experience and is grounded in affective complexes (PP 39). Lacan then makes a gesture toward the abstractions of pure phenomenology, saying that the system of personality must be structured so that the elements of it are easily traceable and organically related (PP 49). This is Lacan's first hint at his later direction, which focuses on the self as being at the center of series of external forces, all of which impinge on the subject in one way or another. The problem of "knowing" the subject (which is essentially unknowable) is "solved" by examining the objects of desire for the subject, and pursuing the question of how that desire operates. Concerning the constitutional factors of paranoia, Lacan also notes that the "délires passionelles," the cornerstone for Clérambault's theory of the development of personality, can cause problems for the subject once they reach the level of erotomania, which Lacan defines as an excess of sexual pride (PP 73).

Lacan makes the case, however, that this type of delirium is not something that arises merely from an organic process. Referencing Clérambault's discussion of toxicity in relation to how it affects one's consciousness, Lacan makes it clear that psychosis is not merely a result of this form of abstract aggrandizement, but is rather a combination of ingredients, including organic ones (PP 107). Lacan also makes mention of the various factors in the subject's environment, seeing fit to include a mention of Minkowski's work on affective disorders (PP 139). Lacan follows with a consideration of the onset of paranoia as a process (PP 146), which can, above all, be unpacked and explained. Using an excerpt from Jaspers, Lacan remarks that the best description of paranoia is that of an erroneous judgment only understood within the context of subjective experience, and extrapolated rationally (PP 140). However, solving the problem of the psychoses is not simply a question of coming up with a thoroughgoing worldview of the operation of paranoia in the subject.

The series of approaches that Lacan considers in the first part of the book are merely preliminary to his presentation of the case of Aimée, to which Lacan devotes the second half of his thesis. For this, his analysis of a case of paranoia, Lacan examines the story of Aimée, an obsessed fan of an actress (known only as Mme Z.), whom she stabs in the hand outside the stage door of a theatre (PP 153). She is incarcerated for two months, then moved to a clinic at L'Aisle Sainte-Anne, where she is pronounced by the attendant physician as having a persecution complex with megalomaniacal tendencies and a "substratum érotomanique" (PP 154). The actress, notably, does not press charges. It is found that Aimée has a rich interior life, and in addition to her powerful fixation on theatrical performers, she features herself prominently as a character in romantic, highly literary fantasies (some of her prodigious works: two novels, which she sent to Buckingham Palace, a life of Joan of Arc, the letters of Ophelia and Hamlet), excerpts of which Lacan includes in his thesis (PP 181–199) with biting commentary. Lacan sums her up, cannily, as being "bovaryque," and no description could be more apt. Most important in Lacan's assessment is the character of her literary output; her fantasies, written down in overripe form, provide a guiding thread in any appreciation of the texture of her personality.

In the section following the discussion of Aimée's case, Lacan takes up the question as to whether or not Aimée's illness is necessarily organo-psychic. In doing so, Lacan indicates his eventual direction and investment in human sexuality as the key to understanding the psyche. Lacan acknowledges the toxico-neurological aspect of Aimee's predicament (PP 209) and entertains the idea that her madness was caused by certain glandular reactions in her body, but remarks that he wishes to focus on the state of mind that he terms "d'état oniroïde," where different impressions collide. Lacan also stresses that the interpretation of such phenomena is also extremely important, as it helps to assess each case in a more subtle way (PP 210). Beyond this, however, Lacan considers that sexual phenomena may have a part in it, and justifies his interest in this topic thus: "L'évolution de la *libido* dans la doctrine freudienne nous semble correspondre très précisément, dans nos formules, à cette part, considérable à l'expérience, des *phénomènes de la personnalité* dont le fondement *organique* est donné par le *désir sexuel*" (PP 255). In other words, the impressions that society puts on the subject have their own sort of organic impact; in Lacan's later work, this idea develops tremendous importance.

As a way of sharpening his argument, Lacan is quick to point out that despite his interest in Freud, he does not wish to engage in an analysis or valorization of the unconscious; indeed, he says that "la psychanalyse du moi" is more important than that of the unconscious (PP 280). In the same way that Freud assesses Schreber, he mentions that the perturbations of the *ideal-moi* lead to homosexual identification (PP 263). The constitution and origin of psychosis may remain somewhat obscure, but Lacan places highest priority on any systematization that identifies the problems (PP 270–271); always, it is in the analysis of the ego that one shall find the answers to the question of paranoia (PP 308). Far from being an anolmalous aberration of desire, the tendencies of the subject with regard to desire indicate the distinctive shape of the illness.

As for the phenomenological aspects of Lacan's analysis of the case of Aimée, he considers that desire should be seen as comportment (PP 311). But how does this differ from Clérambault's position? In Lacan's view, *l'automatisme mental* fails when all the symptoms do not line up in the way that the diagnostician expects (PP 312). The problem of interpretation does not surface when there are plenty of "concrete examples" of delusion to examined, each unique in their own way. In short, there can be no singular interpretation of a mental illness relating to the personality. As there are many different types of delusion, there cannot be one conclusive reading, and the pursuance of all the various factors leading to a mental illness cannot be resolved in one diagnosis (PP 313). Lacan proposes, rather, a construction of a positive science investigating the interaction of the subject in the context of "l'ordre social," where the network of meanings is found (PP 315). The construction of the self is only comprehensible within a societal context, and Lacan construes the dialectical progression of delirium as the further derangement of the subject by society (PP 317). The fiction of the subject hovers over a nest of desires and influences, such that devising an analysis of these phenomena and maladies is simply a problem of constructing "une analyse psychologique *concrète* [Lacan's italics]," which takes into account the reactions and history of the subject entirely within a social milieu (PP 346).

Even in this early phase, although Lacan's attachment to the idea of psychoanalysis had not quite yet been formalized, the familiar elements of Lacan's work are nevertheless seen to be taking shape. This selective overview of Clérambault's impact on Lacan's work reveals it to be one element (albeit a formative one) in the intellectual milieu of the period between the wars that contributed to Lacan's psychoanalytic approach. Although Lacan maintained silence on the topic of Clérambault for the better part of thirty-five years,[7] his remarks in "De nos antécédents" make clear his heavy debt to Clérambault, both in terms of intellectual content and style.

Heidegger: Society, Death, Desire

Lacan's engagement with Heidegger began in earnest after the end of World War II. Sartre and Lévinas had already imported Husserl's philosophy into France, but the intermediary presence of Jean Beaufret facilitated Heidegger's real entry into French intellectual life, delivering, as it were, Heidegger's "Letter on Humanism" to the French intelligentsia, according to Elisabeth Rudinesco's biography of Lacan.[8] Lacan was the respected figure Beaufret chose to aid him in this task. The concept of transference is Rudiensco's guiding principle in her highly analytic and opinionated investigation of Lacan, and she declares that the initial meeting between the two during Easter 1955 in Freiburg was a meditation on that very topic. Rudinesco's other theme concerning the relationship between Lacan and Heidegger is that their encounter was a missed opportunity for the both of them to connect with one another. Lacan's translation of a piece of Heidegger's, entitled "Logos," a commentary on Herakleitos' fragment 50, was based principally, she claims, on the growing Lacanian obsession with language and Levi-Strauss, not Heidegger's increasingly "mystical" and mystifying discourse.[9] Despite Lacan's solicitousness, Heidegger famously wrote to Swiss psychologist Medard Boss, on receiving a newly printed copy of Lacan's *Écrits*, "It seems to me the psychiatrist needs a psychiatrist" (230).

Rudinesco also believes that Lacan's intention in translating Heidegger was to sacrifice intelligibility in order to more closely imitate his expressiveness, so the words themselves would retain their "supreme significance"; this desire speaks to the self-conscious phatic aspect of Lacan's work. Yet Lacan benefited to a great degree from the influence of Heidegger's ideas, and it is clear from Lacan's early work that he did not simply cling to Heidegger's concepts as though they were mere totems. The Lacanian concept of intersubjectivity, as expressed in Seminar II, is crucial to an understanding of Lacan's position regarding the operation of the subject in an intersubjective world, and the relationship of the subject to the symbolic; namely, that the symbolic is the ontological understanding of being-in-the-world, and being-with others. Again, Lacan's contact with French- and German-language phenomenology, having been borne out in his early writing, comes into play in the first phase of his mature work, and these concepts throw a much-needed light on the central Lacanian figures and tropes. By the same token, the Heideggerian poles of authenticity and inauthenticity can aid in an understanding of the Lacanian ego, with view to its enmeshment in the intersubjective world.

Commentators on the Heidegger-Lacan connection who have made previous attempts to assess the relationship between the two thinkers quite rightly see Heidegger's impact on Lacan as being principally in the area of language as the medium and basis for intellectual inquiry; coupled with this, language is something that emerges, in a sense, unbidden, from the subject's environment. The operation of language, and the subject's interface with society and the natural world, is of prime concern for both Heidegger and Lacan. Heidegger's struggle to reformulate his philosophical vocabulary in his post-*Kehre* period reflects this desire to let language "speak for itself." In the same sense, all of Lacan's work reflects this same imperative. As it is a phenomenological, diagnostic discipline, psychoanalysis cannot prescribe meanings for words. The impetus for Lacan's early work is the uncovering the structures of the unconscious, such as they emerge from the symbolic order, which is Lacan's gloss for the norms of societal interaction. As we have seen from the Rome Discourse, this understanding of the social dimension of life is crucial to the understanding of the ego, as the ego of the analysand is that which receives healing in the process of analysis—and its condition is understood to be healthy or aberrant by the analyst in contrast to his or her symbolically prescribed role.

The primacy of Lacan's version of the ego as expressed in the essay on "the mirror stage" cannot be ignored when reviewing Lacan's ideas about language. However, this early essay gives a relatively untextured account of the Lacanian imaginary. Lacan's first two seminars offer a deeper reading of this process of ego-formation, as the impression one gets of the Lacanian world from *Écrits* is that there exists only the subject, with just the symbolic order and the Big Other to keep this benighted soul company. This is also part of the reason why it seems that the later Lacanian subject is adrift in a Cartesian universe: the mysterious Other, emerging from the ground of being (the unconscious) is seen as a malevolent figure.[10] The subject's interaction with the culture is something that can be gauged and analyzed. The horizon of analysis, after all, is the attainment of a cure that returns the analysand to normal functioning within a societal context, the main subject of Heidegger's early work.

Heidegger's immediate task in *Being and Time* is to isolate and distinguish Dasein by the means of eliminating everything that Dasein is not, and this strategy is also at work in the 1929–1930 seminar on worldhood, finitude, and solitude. Heidegger differentiates individualized, philosophical for-itself Dasein from its environment by first analyzing comportments that do not uniquely belong to the provenance of the individual self. The world of animals is discussed only in relation to the questions of world, as they are "captivated" by their environment in such a way that the existential questions of philosophy would not, as such, be interesting questions to answer for them. In *Being and Time*, Heidegger characterizes human beings as initially undifferentiated from each other, then moving toward a conception of identity through a somewhat traumatic process of becoming anxious, fearful, then resolute out of a realization of their own mortality. The description of this intersubjectivity is the subject of the fourth chapter of *Being and Time*, which covers "Being-With" (*Mitsein*). Although this chapter is quite brief compared to the rest of Heidegger's masterwork, it forms the basis of Heidegger's philosophy on the subject of the Other by initially outlining the modes and structures of intersubjectivity, through a unique strategy of disavowing any need to reclaim experience through some kind of intensive Cartesian examination. The primary fact of one's existence is that, from the beginnings of life, one first learns how to *be* in the world by adopting the behaviors of others. Being-with entails one's identification with what Heidegger calls the *they*. Heidegger's aim is to show that because one's everyday behavior is determined by habitually and necessarily conforming to society's mores and norms, this is how the subject must first be understood, philosophically.

Heidegger admits from the beginning that in philosophizing about the subject one must always begin with "I," as one cannot ignore its "givenness." In other words, the subject is always saddled with the self, and it cannot easily (if at all) be ignored (BT 151). But in philosophizing about the existence and behaviors of others (or "the Other"), it must be said that the Other, far from being alien, is necessarily present in the most ordinary of circumstances:

> Theoretically concocted 'explanations' of the Being-present-at-hand of Others urge themselves upon us all too easily; but over against such explanations we must hold fast to the phenomenal facts of the case which we have pointed out, namely, that Others are encountered *environmentally*. This elemental worldly kind of encountering, which belongs to Dasein and is closest to it, goes so far that even one's *own* Dasein becomes something that it can itself proximally 'come across' only when it *looks away* from 'Experiences' and the 'centre of its actions', or does not as yet 'see' them at all. Dasein finds 'itself' proximally in *what* it does, uses, expects, avoids—in those things environmentally ready-to-hand with which it is proximally *concerned*. (BT 155)

In other words, the Other is encountered in the everyday settings of social interaction. However, the import of this passage is that one finds oneself first and foremost in the actions and behaviors of others, determined as they are by social normativity. In this sense, the subject identifies itself first (however tacitly) as being just like everybody else. Heidegger thus deftly solves the problem of the existence of the Other; rather than being a mysterious doppelgänger to the self, the Other is one we know most intimately, as his or her behaviors are "ours" as well.

What concerns Heidegger the most is that the life of the subject should not be exclusively identified with the *they* (*das Man*), a condition that Heidegger indicates by the word *lostness*. As nothing in the life of the subject is certain, and there is no having of "self-knowledge" in any complete sense, the "authenticity" of the subject is something that remains obscured in everyday life (BT 152). Losing "oneself" in the mundanity of daily life is not a catastrophic occurrence; to the contrary, it is a necessary condition of daily existence. Leaving aside the ontological question for the moment, the question of the Cartesian subject's selfhood is complicated by the involvement of the "I" in the network of relations between other subjects. The question of the identity of the subject is, therefore, bound up with distinguishing the subject (which Heidegger refers to as "individual Dasein") from the *they*. Heidegger's observation that Dasein remains "ontically" concealed underscores the difficulty of the subject's disentanglement from the vagaries of learned behaviors, so that the question of self-identity remains perpetually complicated and compromised. Even when individualized Dasein physically separates itself from the world, it is still part of it, and the discussion of the absence of the Other is brought up within this context of individualized Dasein: "Yet Being-alone 'among' many does not mean that with regard to their Being they are merely present-at-hand there alongside us. Even in our Being 'among them' they are *there with* us; their Dasein-with is encountered in a mode in which they are indifferent and alien" (BT 157). The concept of Being-with is necessary for the contextualization of the subject within the world, and as an existential fact, it must be acknowledged that this is the primary fashion in which the subject lives his or her life. The Other is an ever-present entity that, like objects and Being-in-the-world, can only begin to be understood through personal contact. As in the structures devoted to Being-in-the-world, other people become known in terms of "use," in other words, through the world of work: "They thus become *authentically* bound together, and this makes possible the right kind of objectivity, which frees the Other in his freedom for himself" (BT 159). The foregoing sets the stage for Sartre's elaboration on the notion of freedom in *Being and Nothingness*, as ultimately the problem of the Other is bound up with the mystery of the Other.

At the same time, the question of the Other and judgment naturally enters the picture: what are the structures in place that produce this kind of relation with the subject, such that the subject is always under scrutiny? Recognizing that the presence of the Other constitutes a kind of ominous threat to the subject, Heidegger acknowledges the network of Others in this estimation and appreciation of the lostness of the *they*:

> This Being-with-one-another dissolves one's own Dasein completely into the kind of Being of 'the Others', in such a way, indeed, that the Others, as distinguishable and explicit, vanish more and more. In this inconspicuousness and unascertainability, the real dictatorship of the "they" is unfolded. We take pleasure and enjoy ourselves as *they* [*man*] take pleasure; we read, see, and judge about literature and art as *they* see and judge; likewise we shrink back from the 'great mass' as *they* shrink back; we find 'shocking' what *they* find shocking. This "they", which is nothing definite, and which all are, though not as the sum, prescribes the kind of Being of everydayness. (BT 164)

The network of Others, in a concrete sense, forces itself on the subject and not only offers judgment on various actions and opinions, but also threatens the authenticity of the subject, inasmuch as the authenticity of one's inner life can be said to be threatened: "The 'they' is there alongside everywhere [ist überall dabei], but in such a manner that it has always stolen away whenever Dasein presses for a decision" (BT 165). The illusion of the *they*, which offers judgment on individualized Dasein's desire and action, casts a shadow on the subject, regardless of its status as "merely" an illusion: "The Self of everyday Dasein is the *they-self*, which we distinguish from the *authentic Self*—that is, from the Self which has been taken hold of in its own way" (BT 167). Heidegger wishes to understand and distinguish the self from that which is necessarily authentic. However, Heidegger asserts that the way in which the subject can understand himself or herself is radically distinctive from the ontological self that the subject projects. The "I" is, necessarily, a reflection of how the subject understands itself, distinct from the place of lived experience.

It is here that the concept of authenticity provides a bridge to a discussion of the self in second division of Heidegger's work, where the subject is uniquely differentiated and validates its authenticity in death alone. Death outlines the finitude of life, and, most importantly, singles out the individual definitively (BT 277). The possibility of death, always "present-at-hand," cannot be predicted, ameliorated, or stayed by the expectation of its arrival, for its implicit preclusion of providing narrative closure is what prevents Dasein from shielding itself from trauma by anticipating it:

> As potentiality-for-Being, Dasein cannot outstrip the possibility of death. Death is the possibility of the absolute impossibility of Dasein. Thus death reveals itself as that *possibility which is one's ownmost, which is non-relational, and which is not to be outstripped [unüberholbare].* (BT 294)

The possibility-for-death is the distinguishing characteristic for individualized Dasein in that it is ownmost (BT 295), namely, that Dasein is removed from a cultural context ontically, and ontologically (BT 294n4). Being inured to the idea of death is only another form of fallenness, and ignorance of this possibility or indifference to it is yet another form of this (BT 299). This does not prevent death from being known and perhaps understood through the experience of events surrounding the deaths of others, however:

> Indisputably, the fact that one Dasein *can be represented* by another belongs to its possibilities of Being in Being-with-one another in the world. In everyday concern, constant and manifold use is made of such representability. Whenever we go anywhere or have anything to contribute, we can be represented by someone within the range of that 'environment' with which we are most closely concerned. The great multiplicity of ways of Being-in-the-world in which one person can be represented by another, not only extends to more refined modes of publicly being with one another, but is likewise germane to those possibilities of concern which are restricted within definite ranges, and which are cut to the measure of one's occupation, one's social status, or one's age. (BT 283)

The existential death analytic, a still rather controversial feature of Heidegger's thought, nevertheless provides an appropriate bookend to Heidegger's conception of the "I" as the "null basis of a nullity"; although one can judge, estimate, evaluate, measure, legislate and analyze the behaviors of the Other, what distinguishes the self is the constant grasping need to find something of one's own to claim, being that one is continually adrift in the business of daily life. The ownmost thing to Dasein—the cessation of one's existence—symbolizes this lack, turning absence into the supreme token of presence. Death assures one's place in the intersubjective landscape, as no one else can overtake or assume another's death.

From reading these issues in *Being and Time*, it is clear that there are two distinct ways of approaching the subject that correspond to authentic (having to do with the "ego," broadly) and inauthentic (having to do with social interaction) modes of being. The subject understands itself initially, and in an everyday fashion, within the context of inauthentic everyday interaction with other people; in itself, the self understands itself only as authentic in taking over and possessing those things that are closest to it, distinguished against the varied possibilities fulfilled by others in the intersubjective world. Although Lacan does not take up the early Heidegger's vocabulary to describe the subject's interaction with the world, Heidegger's influence on the Lacan of Seminar II is evident in the latter's discussion of the ego, the spectre of death, and the social nexus that defines certain identities taken up by the subject.

Heidegger and Lacan: Seminar II

> J. Lacan: And, to be candid, being purely phenomenological doesn't get us very far.
> M. Hyppolite: I agree.
>
> (S.II 38)

Early on in his seminar of 1929–1930, Heidegger defines the task of thinking as being a way of making oneself at home in the world. Taking his cue from Novalis, Heidegger begins the seminar discussion with a question about homesickness; it refers to "an urge to be everywhere at home. Philosophy can only be such an urge if we who philosophize are *not* at home everywhere....to be at home everywhere means to be at once and all times within the whole."[11] As Dasein, ensconced in societal ties, is naturally at home in the world, Heidegger observes that philosophy is the opposite of comfort and assurance in that it dispels the illusion that we are indeed at home in everything (Heidegger 19). Similarly, Lacan makes this statement at the beginning of Seminar II:

> Who is Socrates?...Here already there is a decentring – it is by starting off with this virtue that a domain is opened up to knowledge, but this very virtue, with respect to its transmission, its tradition, its formation, remains outside of the domain. (S.II 5)

The ostensible topic of the seminar is that of Freud's conception of the ego and psychoanalytic technique, but as in "The Freudian Thing," this type of inquiry entails, for Lacan, a full-blown consideration of what it means to do psychoanalysis. More specifically, Lacan sets the parameters of the analytic relation as that which can only occur outside of a typical intersubjective exchange; in other words, it must participate in a kind of Heideggerian authenticity, engaged in a search for, as Lacan puts it, the truth.

Lacan's second seminar took place during the years of 1954–55, roughly the period when Lacan was most involved with Martin Heidegger on a personal level. As such, the subject that Lacan tackles throughout the seminar is appropriate for a more traditional phenomenological approach: the question of the ego in Freud's analytic work. However, Lacan's Seminar II follows up on the topics pursued in Seminar I and yields the initial formulation of some principal Lacanian concepts, such as the *objet petit a*, revealed in the L-schema, which appears at the end of this seminar (S.II 243). Lacan's examination of the ego depends on the distinction of the ego from the world of social engagements; Lacan's discussion of the ego in Seminar II is, in the end, a study of the subject and its intersubjective relations, grounded in the negotiation of desire with the Other.

Lacan allows at the outset of the seminar year that the question of the nature of the ego could be bound up with narcissism, but Lacan claims that there are some "contradictions" in Freud that would complicate this issue (S.II 23). Lacan's discussion of the machine, introduced in the first seminar and continued in the second seminar, posits that all communication between subject and Other is mediated by the concrete societal interactions that comprise intersubjectivity:

> If the symbolic functions, we are inside it. And I would even say – we are so far into it that we can't get out of it. A large part of the problems which confront us when we try to scientificate, that is to say to bring order to a certain number of phenomena, first in line being those of life, in the end it is always the paths of the symbolic function which lead us, much more than any sort of direct apprehension.
>
> Thus, when it comes down to it, we always try to explain the living organism in terms of mechanism. The first question which we analysts must answer, and which can perhaps help us get away from the controversy which exists between vitalism and mechanism, is the following – why are we led to think of life in terms of mechanism? In what way actually are we, as men, parents of the machine? (S.II 31)

In "The Mirror Stage," Lacan declares that misrecognition is fundamentally a feature of the ego's relation to itself, but in a world where all subjects find a common ground of communication, desire nevertheless finds a conduit of expression, if not comprehension. Although there shall always be a *moi/je* split as a result of the intrusion of language into the life of the subject, desire nevertheless circulates among subjects as if it were electricity, pure and incorruptible:

> Recognition obviously presupposes a third thing. For the first machine which is jammed on the image of the second to be able to come to an agreement, for them not to be forced to destroy themselves on account of the convergence of their desire – which is in fact the same desire, since at this level they are one and the same being – it would be necessary for the little machine to *inform* the other, to say to it I – *I desire that.* That's impossible. Admitting that there is an *I* would immediately turn it into *you desire that.* I desire that means – *You, the other, who is my unity, you desire that.* (S.II 51)

However, even though desire is something that the subject experiences (and therefore it is an object of discourse), it is most directly understood by the subject alone. Lacan explains this kind of rough codification of desire in an attempt to make inroads into the mystery of consciousness. Following on this notion, Lacan notes that one cannot cling to a merely "existential" apprehension of the ego, lest one lose one's moorings in reality: "The ego only figures in it as a particular experience, tied to objectifiable conditions, within the limits of the inspection that is believed simply enough to be this reflection of consciousness on itself. And the phenomenon of consciousness has no privileged character in such an apprehension" (S.II 56). It is a relatively brief jump from this topic to that of the symbolic, and Lacan's appraisal of it corresponds to the Heideggerian conception of "lostness":

> Last time I told you that symbolism is essential to all the most basic manifestations of the analytic domain, namely to repetition, and that we must think of it as tied to a circular process of the exchange of speech. There is a symbolic circuit external to the subject, tied to a certain group of supports, of human agents, in which the subject, the small circle which is called his destiny, is indeterminately included. (S.II 98)

The imbrication of the subject in the external world, and the world of signification, is a guarantor of solid grounding for the investigation of the ego.

However, the appearance of the *moi* on the scene quickly removes any pretense of objectivity. Lacan here reproduces his famous diagram from Seminar I where a vase of flowers, reflected in a concave mirror, appears to be resting on top of a pedestal. This is meant to be an analogy of the mirages that are apparent in psychoanalysis, and Lacan uses this as a jumping-off point to talk about the presence of the ego as a mediator of experience: "In other words, all stimuli tend to produce hallucinations. The principle of operation of the ϕ apparatus is hallucination. That is what *primary process* means" (S.II 108). Lacan declares later on that the ego is the regulatory apparatus for the testing of the hallucinations that make up experience (S.II 145). The ψ to which Freud refers in the *Ego and the Id* system is the ego, which Freud calls the "nucleus." Referring to Freud's analysis of the dream of "Irma's injection," Lacan remarks that the dream reflects the existence of the ego within an intersubjective world:

> The subject enters and mixes in with things – that may be the first meaning. The other one is this – an unconscious phenomenon which takes place on the symbolic level, as such decentred in relation to the *ego*, always takes place between two subjects. As soon as true speech emerges, mediating, it turns them into two very different subjects from what they were prior to speech. This means that they only start being constituted as subjects of speech once speech exists, and there is no before. (S.II 160)

Here Lacan's reference is to the mythical prelapsarian period featured in the "The Mirror Stage." Moving on to the temporal horizon of naming, Lacan remarks that the name is the "time" of the object: the act of naming therefore is a "pact," and that signified objects are not simply a narcissistic reflection of the subject (S.II 169). In Lacan's words (also Heidegger's, in spirit): "The world of language is possible so far as we have our place in it anywhere" (S.II 278).

Because the Platonic form of knowledge is a dyad (S.II 87), where one side must be privileged over the other, Lacan remarks throughout the seminar that the model for societal and analytic relations should be a triangle, as the machinations of desire (for example, sin) pass through a third term between subjects. Then, Lacan notes that he needs a concept of repetition to outline the paths that information takes; in bowing to the "animal weakness" for visual diagrams, he hits upon the idea that the symbolic, rather than being hierarchical, is instead a circuit (S.II 88–89). From this, one can see Lacan's efforts to illustrate at one stroke the topography of both intersubjectivity and language, and the position of the ego with regard to both things. With reference to the diminishing status of the Freudian ego in the face of Freud's late moves toward metapsychology, Lacan says that: "...the further [we follow Freud's work], the more the ego is shown as a mirage, a sum of identifications" (S.II 209). In this case, the primary identification of the ego is found in death, the main link between the Freud of *Beyond the Pleasure Principle* and the Heidegger of *Being and Time*: "The relation of the ego to death is an extremely close one, for the ego is a point of intersection between the common discourse, in which the subject finds himself caught, alienated, and his psychological reality" (S.II 210). Here the familiar territory of *Being and Time* returns in Lacan's observation on desire, that the ego is itself lack personified: "Desire is a relation of being to lack. This lack is the lack of being properly speaking. It isn't the lack of this or that, but lack of being whereby the being exists" (S.II 223). The Freudian world is inescapably a world of desire, Lacan says, and this desire, a feature central to all human experience, "is the desire for nothing nameable" (S.II 223).

The nature of the ego, being a lack which defines the subject, cannot be, strictly speaking, that of an object, but rather that which makes objects possible. In introducing his well-known L-schema, Lacan makes a point of explaining the castrating effects of the symbolic:

> What analysis teaches us, on the other hand, is that the ego is an absolutely fundamental form for the constitution of objects. In particular, it perceives what we call, for structural reasons, its fellow being, in the form of the specular other. This form of the other has a very close relation to the ego, which can be super-imposed on it, and we write it as *a'*... (S.II 244)

Lacan further explains the nature of the intersubjective world as one being united in a vast network of death: "This life we're captive of, this essentially alienated life, ex-sisting, this life in the other, is as such joined to death, and is only drawn into increasingly large and more roundabout circuits by what Freud calls the elements of the external world." (S.II 233). The desire of the Other, that of mediating wants in the intersubjective world, is such that one cannot return to an "authentic" self. With the operation of *méconnaissance*, the ego can never apprehend objects of desire as they are, nor possess them. For Lacan, the question of death, a principal concern for Freud in *Beyond the Pleasure Principle*, winds up defining the subject in terms of desire; thrown into this existence, the subject's desires are stirred by the need to fill the lack that is the self, and in so doing, to acquire an identity.

Lacan's thought is, everywhere, concerned with origins, as is that of Freud. Lacan's interaction with Heidegger and the phenomenological situation of analysis in discourse is, for a start, an opportunity to rethink the process of analysis. Lacan's descriptions of what occurs in the analytic relation are meant to be abstractions of the process, not expressible of or in the healing process:

> In the beginnings of psychoanalysis, this beyond is the unconscious, in so far as we cannot reach it, it's the transference in so far as that is really what modulates feeling of love and of hatred, which aren't the transference – the transference is what makes it possible for us to interpret this language composed out of everything the subject can present us with, a language which, outside of psychoanalysis is, in principle, incomplete and misunderstood. That is what the beyond of the pleasure principle is. It is the beyond of signification. The two are indistinguishable. (S.II 188)

The symbolic order is beyond the limits of life: and, by the same token, the libidinal order is the ego, and "the death instinct is only the mask of the symbolic order" (S.II 326). The truth produced in the analytic relation must always, in a sense, be reflective of this fact: in essence, to analyze desire is to negate it, as language always castrates. When desire is analyzed in psychoanalysis, as is done in the Lacanian analytic relation, it is always as a prophylactic against the realization of specific desires; one could also extend this to the language of the return to Freud, invested in perpetually looking backwards to the past and tradition.

In these readings of both Clérambault and Heidegger, it is clear that Lacan's grounding in the intellectual milieu of the 1920s and 1930s provided him with a sound basis in an ego-centered model of consciousness, a notion that Lacan more or less stuck with for his entire career. Lacan's early effort to combine the phenomenological ego with a concept of the psychoses resulted in the mature Lacan of the L-schema, the *moi/je* split, and the notion of Freudian libidinal cathexes that would come to define the Lacanian theory of desire. That Lacan was able to make these influences his own is a testament to his genius and creativity; even though his ingenuity has, for a long time, effectively kicked dust over the tracks of his intellectual forbears, Lacan's roots in modernist intellectual traditions are long and deep.

Dénouement: The Death of Clérambault

Although Clérambault was known for his widely influential clinical practice, he was also known as one of the great characters of the Parisian intellectual scene. He lived a somewhat isolated life in a Mediterranean-style townhouse full of mannequins, which he clothed in the African and Arabian fabrics he would import from overseas; often, he would take pictures of them dressed in this fashion, as well as making portraits of himself dressed in Moroccan women's garb. It is telling that he made, in his own clinical work, a careful distinction between psychoses on the one hand and "delusional passions" on the other; as one who traveled in Surrealist circles, Clérambault firmly believed that cultivating one's passions was utterly necessary for living a fully realized life. It seems that when he could no longer pursue them, he committed suicide.[12]

It is also somewhat surprising that Clérambault, known for being so secretive, committed his ideas about his passion for fabric to paper. His works collected in a volume titled *Le passion des étoffes chez un neuro-psychiatre* look at the phenomenon of the highly aesthetic desire for beautiful fabrics as a transgressive sexual fetish; nearly all of the fabric fetishists he wrote about were women, and most of them were klepto-maniacs whom he encountered in the clinic of the Parisian Prefecture. In his view (and one can be sure that Clérambault regarded his own obsession in like terms), the presence of the fabric, being that of a fetish, replaced normal sexual functioning.[13] Clérambault goes on to give his own analysis about what this fetishism betokens for the sexual psychology of the kleptomaniacal subject. In describing the fetish itself, he uncannily anticipates the emergence of the *objet petit a* in Lacanian thought, saying that the *jouissance* experienced by the subject when rubbing the silk against the body is genital. For these women, the rubbing eliminates the need for sex and any other object or thing, as the feeling annihilates the world around them, thus rendering the women effectively asexual (Tisseron 38). Clérambault then adds that he believes that fetishism, because it is a replacement for genital sexuality, results in the (female) subject's frigidity. Obviously, Clérambault was unaware that he had a hand in demolishing the very concept of the biologically-driven libido with this discussion of his sustaining passion.

The story of Clérambault has an operatically tragic ending. Afflicted with cataracts, Clérambault sought relief in an experimental procedure developed by a Spanish surgeon. After traveling to Barcelona to have the procedure done, he discovered during his period of convalescence that his eyesight had been adversely affected by it. He could see, but could no longer perceive depth well, and, as such, could no longer appreciate the aesthetics of fabric-draping, as he had in the past.[14] Despondent over the loss of his vision, Clérambault drifted into a deep depression. One day in November 1934, having had enough torment, Clérambault went out into his garden, fired his pistol once to test it, then charged up the stairs to his bedroom, and shot himself in the mouth. He was discovered sprawled on the floor, having sat on a divan facing a chair with a full-length mirror perched on it, apparently so he could observe himself in the act of suicide. Clérambault's friends and colleagues quickly rushed to counteract the terrible publicity that followed: in the Joseph Kessel obituary that appeared in *Le Figaro*, the author (and friend of Clérambault) depicts a gathering at a salon on the Left Bank, where Clérambault's students and admirers had assembled to pay tribute to the man (Tisseron 113). Kessel paints Clérambault as a man of wisdom, science, and understanding whose passions simply got the better of him. Around the same time, Lacan is known to have remarked that he thought highly of suicide, in that it was one of the few arenas in which the subject was guaranteed to succeed;[15] as it entails the death of the subject, it provides firm closure for the subject's narrative, sealing a lasting image in the form of a tableau. In Clérambault's case, this tableau consisted of the determination to extinguish oneself, in the face of being cut off from one's passions and the defiant individuality of one's interior life.

3

Paranoia: Schreber, Lacan, and *The Sacred Fount*

The phenomenon of schizophrenia could have emerged only with the dawn of the twentieth century and the modern era. With its vivid perceptual distortions, hallucinations, and menacing fantasies, schizophrenia and related dementias are of a piece with the visual vocabulary of Modernism: the chiaroscuro phantasms of the cinema, the fractured distortions of Cubism, the bombast of Futurism. The visual culture of modernism expanded the expressive power of art into cultural communication, adding a new dimension to the experience of public life. The modern subject, confronted with a staggering range of symbols with which to interact, became an increasingly fragmented and scattered one. In *Anti-Oedipus*, the first volume of their magnum opus *Capitalism and Schizophrenia*, Gilles Deleuze and Félix Guattari settle on Daniel Paul Schreber, famous schizophrenic, as their classic model for twentieth-century subjectivity. The signal problem of modern subjectivity, as found in the French structuralists, is mastering the many discourses and signs at work in the culture at large. In essence, the subject must decide what stimuli to filter out in order to shape his or her own identity; the schizophrenic's ability to choose is absent, as every external sign is given equal weight, meaning, and menace.

The inner experience of the schizophrenic, as originally defined by Eugen Bleuler, has typically been characterized as an exaggerated interpretation of external events and language, taking on a life of its own within the subject through the operations of paranoia. As a result, the investigation of schizophrenia has been uniquely opened to psychoanalytic forms of inquiry. Contemporary work on schizophrenia prizes the psychologist's ability to interview the patient and to understand the illness by parsing out the schizophrenic's internal dialogue.[1] Although there is no possible analytic "cure" as such for schizophrenia, the impact of the figure of the schizophrenic on analysis has been unmistakably significant, beginning with Freud's treatise on Schreber's famous memoir. A major theme of psychoanalysis is, after all, the dissolution of self-created delusions.

The impact of Schreber was no less profound on Lacan's thought. After taking on the subject of the ego and psychoanalytic transference in Seminar II, Lacan turned his attention to the question of the psychoses in his seminar meetings of the following year. What followed was a continuation of the previous year's theoretical breakthroughs; Lacan turned to the topic of psychotic delusion, with constant reference to the case of Judge Schreber, as made famous by Freud's "case study." As a whole, the year's seminar meetings contain little of the structuralism that informs Lacan's miscellaneous writings of this period, later collected in *Écrits*. Lacan's major accomplishment in Seminar III is his justification for a psychoanalysis rooted wholly within the diagnosis of extrabiological drives, marked by rational processes gone awry. Just as Freud inaugurated a new analytic epoch with *Beyond The Pleasure Principle*, Lacan sought in this seminar to situate his analytic work outside of the biological models related to sexual development or trauma, and he had to choose a figure so that he could create a template for the ideal Lacanian analysand. In effect, Schreber is Lacan's Oedipus.

In this exploration of Schreber with Lacan, I wish to bring out the reasons for Lacan's selection of Schreber as the foundational persona of his work. Because Schreber's experience depends on a lively and, in its way, fruitful internal dialogue, I shall examine an echo of the Schreberian persona in Henry James's short novel, contemporaneous with Schreber's memoir, *The Sacred Fount*, itself a feast of repressed sexual content communicated through paranoid, highly visual thinking. Louis Sass observes in his study on Wittgenstein and Schreber that both men understood knowledge to be that which drained power away from the body;[2] with Schreber, Lacan, and James, the transposition of the body and its desires into the lofty realm of abstraction is a bellwether of modernity itself.

Schreber: *Memoirs of My Nervous Illness*

Schreber's *Memoirs of My Nervous Illness* was a bestseller when it was first published in 1903, but much of its reputation is largely due to Freud's famous "case study" of Schreber, "Psycho-analytic Notes Upon a Biographical Account of a Case of Paranoia," which first appeared in the *Jahrbuch für psychoanalytische und psychopathologische Forschungen* of 1911. Freud's analysis of Schreber is remarkable in that it is one of the few instances where Freud attempted an analysis on a psychotic, aside from the fact that he had never met the "patient," thereby compromising the very idea of analysis as a face-to-face endeavor. Freud acknowledges in the introduction to the essay that his analysis may be of limited intellectual value, given that he himself had no interaction with Schreber. He also notes, however, that the Schreber text affords him the rare opportunity to "work with" a psychotic (SE 12: 7). As a privately practicing physician, he adds, he could not avail himself of the psychotic patients most frequently found in public institutions. Freud owns up to the somewhat fanciful conceit of analyzing a patient by means of a diary, and justifies his interest in the Schreber case (and any possible psychoanalytic insight into his illness) with the following disclaimer:

> Since paranoiacs cannot be compelled to overcome their internal resistances, and since in any case they only say what they choose to say, it follows that this is precisely a disorder in which a written report or a printed case history can take the place of a personal acquaintance with the patient. For this reason I think it is legitimate to base analytic interpretations upon the case history of a patient suffering from paranoia (or, more precisely, from dementia paranoides) whom I have never seen, but who has written his own case history and brought it before the public in print. (SE 12: 9)

It doubtless helped Freud and all other potential armchair analysts that *Senatspräsident* Schreber was an articulate man of formidable intellect with a distinguished career as a jurist, which culminated in his assumption of the Chair of the Appellate Court of Saxony. Unfortunately, this prestigious appointment seems to have precipitated the first of his relapses; between the time of his being notified of his new position and the taking over of his duties, the added stress likely triggered a recurrence of his dementia. Even as he moved in and out of a delusional state near the end of his life, Schreber remained lucid, although aspects of his day-to-day life continually threatened him and encouraged his pantheistic (or, more accurately, pandiabolic) worldview in which God, all creation, and especially the various directors of the asylums in which he was incarcerated aligned to destroy him.

The psychoanalytic reading Freud draws out of Schreber's story is very familiar. As Freud was still focused in this phase of his career on treating the roots of neurosis, Freud determines that Schreber's problems are primarily about his persistent belief that God is slowly transforming him into a woman. This delusion was bolstered by Schreber's dressing up in feminine garb, tying ribbons in his hair, putting on make-up, and admiring himself for hours on end in the mirror. Freud's diagnosis of repressed homosexuality, therefore, is an open-and-shut case:

> But in the severe psychosis which broke out soon afterwards the feminine phantasy carried everything before it; and it only requires a slight correction of the characteristic paranoiac indefiniteness of Schreber's mode of expression to enable us to divine the fact that the patient was in fear of sexual abuse at the hands of his doctor himself. The exciting cause of his illness, then, was an outburst of homosexual libido; the object of this libido was probably from the very first his doctor, Flechsig; and his struggles against this libidinal impulse produced the conflict which gave rise to the symptoms. (SE 12: 42–43)

One can interpret Freud's attempt to analyze Schreber in libidinal terms as a reaction against the drier clinical assessments of Bleuler, whose work on the topic emerged just a few years before Freud's own essay.[3] There is no doubt that Schreber had rancorous feelings toward Flechsig, who is alleged by Schreber in several instances to have penetrated his body and committed other definite and indefinite forms of betrayal and mayhem against him. However, this rather literal reading of the *Memoirs* obscures the extraordinary perception on Schreber's part in his unique interpretation of his own condition, even to the point of absorbing the popular language of neurophysiology and incorporating it into his paranoid fantasy world; a portion of Schreber's paranoia is an intellectual riposte to his having lost his way in the world around him.[4] *Memoirs* is not only coolly logical in its rationalization for all sorts of miracles and menaces visited on Schreber. It is also a highly modern document presenting a scientific view of the world as Schreber finds it. Just as many writers after Schreber have found him to be an exemplar for (post)modern subjectivity, I shall take up the question of Schreber's madness with particular reference to the interplay between the degeneration of the body and its trauma at the hands of scientific discourse; with this aim in view, the purpose of Lacan's analysis of the Schreber case in Seminar III shall become clearer.

The content of Schreber's *Memoirs* is difficult to summarize in even a few sentences, although most readers of the book are familiar with Freud's opinions concerning it. Most accounts of the *Memoirs* take issue with Freud's characterization of Schreber as a repressed homosexual with a pronounced father complex, but this simplifies to a great degree the conflicts and opinions Schreber expresses in his book. The text of the *Memoirs* itself is comprised of Schreber's first-person account of his schizophrenia, and detailed explanations of his visions, complete with theological and cosmological discussions supporting and rationalizing Schreber's visionary particulars. Far from being the rant of a madman, the *Memoirs* presents an extremely vivid picture of the inner experience of a mental illness, written by a momentarily sane person who had experienced the delusions firsthand. The descriptions of Schreber's body and the world it inhabits are direct reflections of his efforts to assimilate and reconcile conflicting scientific and religious discourses surrounding his situation in life. On the one hand, Schreber is told that his nervous illness is a matter of the body; on the other, he struggles with his own conception of his condition as being occasioned by what he perceives to be the source of his torment, namely the evil god Ormuzd, who appears in various guises to bully Schreber by distorting reality. For Schreber, the world is revealed to be, after Plato's metaphor of the cave, a roiling manifold of shadows and apparitions, all manipulated by a host of minor deities under God's merciless thumb.

Since Schreber, the literature on psychosis has attempted, in one way or another, to describe and diagnose the purpose of the delusions experienced by the psychotic. In the main, psychosis is perceived as being a non-narratable state, where language refers to nothing but itself and narrative is, therefore, out of the question.[5] At the other extreme, Schreber's madness and the story it has to tell can be said to be an enlightening symptom of the modern condition.[6] But when viewed in primarily clinical terms, the Schreber case takes on more immediate dimensions. The root cause of psychotic delusion usually manifests itself such that one controlling figure in the psychotic's world is attempting to *consume* him or her, and psychotic symptoms arise as a defense against this.[7] The presence of the analyst in such a situation is understood to be separate from the father figure. To reference Shengold's slogan, "to see the parent is not to be the parent," and the analytic dialogue is conducted with the tacit understanding that this is the way of mediating conflict with this figure (Shengold 315). Extrapolating from the physical bases of Kraepelinean psychiatry, Schreber's narrative describes a kind of disease to which only analysis could respond. Schreber's obsession with the biological explanation of his illness as a condition of nerves reduces physical explanations for his illness to absurdity, and as such, this thread of his story runs parallel to his theological explorations, exposing any notions of inviolable selfhood as being merely fiction. *Memoirs* reveals Schreber as a desiring subject struggling with the strife of the mind, not the body; he attempts to take his place as a figure of authority in his world, and to take over the role of analyst, after a fashion, in a therapeutic dialogue with his own madness.

Metaphors of the visual infiltrate Schreber's language at all points in his narrative, particularly with regard to his veracity as a witness to his own predicament. In the beginning of the memoir, Schreber feels the need to define what he means by soul-murder (*Seelenmord*), and explains that the human soul is "contained in the nerves of the body.... the total mental life of a human being rests on their excitability by external impressions...they are able to retain the memory of impressions received" (MNI 19). Schreber goes even further, claiming that sentient life can be reduced to individual nerves, which vibrate with these impressions:

> Circumstances seem to be such that *every single nerve of intellect represents the total mental individuality of a human being*, that the sum total of recollections is as it were inscribed on each single nerve of intellect, the greater or lesser *number* of nerves of intellect only influences the length of time for which recollections can be retained. While man is alive he is body and soul together; the nerves (the soul of man) are nourished and kept alive in living motion by the body whose function is essentially similar to that of the higher animals. (MNI 20)

Throughout the book, Schreber demonstrates that he does not discriminate between the living and non-living; the material world, directly reflecting the mind and deeds of its Creator, subsumes all life in a carnival of sensation, expression, and imprinting of "thought" onto matter. Schreber claims that the registers of human sense (sight, taste, and so forth) are secondary to the mind with which the human subject perceives the world. Those things experienced in this world, at least by him, are a result of God having projected them onto nerves:

> I use here the expression "seeing with the mind's eye," which I used before (Chapter 8, p.109), because I cannot find a more suitable one in our human

> language. We are used to thinking all impressions we receive from the outer world are mediated through the five senses, particularly that all light and sound sensations are mediated through eye and ear....in the case of a human being who like myself has entered into contact with rays and whose head is in consequence so to speak illuminated by rays, this is not all. I receive light and sound sensations which are projected directly onto my *inner* nervous system by the rays; for their reception the external organs of seeing and hearing are not necessary. (MNI 120–121, n61)

Schreber's deployment of scientific concepts in order to express his feelings of dehumanization is a persistent feature of his *Memoirs*. This interpretive strategy opens up Schreber to a form of religious experience that sets God in opposition to Schreber with no person or thing remaining neutral. In the profoundest sense, Schreber's metaphysical perspective is a curse of the highest order. The distinguishing feature of psychosis is the constant and interminable reference to the self, which cannot be escaped, subverted or thwarted. Schreber's memoir itself contains alarming examples of reflexivity, which in themselves appear to clinch the question of Schreber's madness: "Since God entered into nerve-contact with me exclusively, I became in a way for God the only human being, or simply the human being around whom everything turns...[and] must also relate all things to himself" (MNI 233). A significant part of Schreber's torture is the experience of the "writing-down-material," the anticipatory echo of his thoughts as they are recorded by God, and set down, as it were, in the "book of life." The difficulty then faced by Schreber is to say something that is not anticipated by the rays, in order to convey his own thoughts and feelings from his limited perspective; Schreber's feeling is that the voices are advising him that everything he thinks and speaks has been "taken down" and need not be expressed (MNI 128). Unable to contribute anything new, he is not able to speak for himself: "For instance, when read a book or a newspaper, one thinks that the ideas in them are my own; when I play a song or an opera arrangement for the piano, one thinks that the text of the song or opera expresses my own feelings" (MNI 234). This part of Schreber's memoir eerily resembles the process of psychoanalysis, in that thoughts are illuminated in the act of speech, just as they are in the conversation of the analyst and the analysand.

Schreber finds himself charged with a mission to redeem humanity in the face of a cruel and predatory God, and this directive causes him to leap to some terrible post-religious reckonings. That Schreber sees himself as the only significant figure in the world is not unusual (given that he is suffering from paranoid schizophrenia), but the surprising thing is that his explanation of some of his more exotic tortures superficially assumes the language and concepts of Catholicism. Daunted as he ventures into uncharted apocalyptic territory, he is filled with disgust and self-loathing at his perfidious condition, as in this passage where he describes himself as the "eternal Jew":

> The Eternal Jew (in the sense described) had to be *unmanned* (transformed into a woman) to be able to bear children. This process of unmanning consisted in the (external) male genitals (scrotum and penis) being retracted into the body and the internal sexual organs being at the same time transformed into the corresponding female sexual organs, a process which might have been completed in a sleep lasting hundreds of years, because the skeleton (pelvis, etc.) had also to be changed.... (MNI 60)

Schreber's description of this situation does not merely imply the changing of Schreber's sex (although this is true as well). This originary myth, in its inclusion of Judaism, implies a sudden reversal of Christianity's beginnings in the Judaic tradition. In this sense, Schreber's story upends the Christian narrative in favor of avoiding the dominant discourse of the father, dictated throughout history. That Schreber no longer sees himself here as belonging to an earthly father (noted by his invocation of the Mars myth) indicates the strength of his delusion and the repression of some father figure.

In Schreber's case, the father figure most in need of repression was his father, Daniel Moritz Schreber, author of *Illustrated Medical In-door Gymnastics or a System of Medico Hygienic Exercises*, and director of the Leipzig Orthopedic and Medico-Gymnastic Institute. This book, which was published in 1853 and went into regular reprintings in multiple languages even into the next century, prescribed exercises for the health and maintenance of the body, complete with diagrams to aid the reader in their performance. The book also offers various rules governing the conduct of the exercises: not to wear constrictive clothing, to perform them at least a quarter hour before eating in order to "afford the muscles of the stomach a period of repose," and so forth.[8] In his introduction to the work, the elder Schreber explains the purpose of the book and the necessity of exercise to maintain health. Schreber's claim that the modern era has ignored the physical aspect of human life by focusing instead on the mental has led him to the development of medical exercises in order to correct this imbalance:

> ...it is our intention to treat here of gymnastics only in as far as they present a welcome means of carrying out medical ends—as a remedy, *curative gymnastics*; as prevention, *hygienic* or *sanitary gymnastics*—for certain cases of disease or infirmity. Both of the above definitions are comprehended in the term *medical gymnastics.* (Schreber 6–7)

The first of his remarks declares that "man is a double being," with mental and physical sides. With the above explanation, Schreber decisively qualifies his ideas about the profound effect of physical activity on the human body. In all senses, the elder Schreber maintains an inescapably dynamic view of the human organism:

> We see then that a continual renewal and revivifying of [the body's] parts is necessary. All interruption of this process, if not soon remedied, causes sickness, disease, and death. Thus it happens that an insufficient assimilation of matter, and an insufficient throwing off of used-up and therefore useless matter (the remaining of the same in the body)—in short the want of balance between the amount of matter taken into the body and the amount of it which is consumed, is one of the most general causes of irregularity in the development and working of the mechanism of our nature. (Schreber 9)

As a whole, the book's exercises are designed merely to stretch the muscles of the upper body, as Schreber believes that they are too often neglected in one's daily routine (Schreber 15). The success of the book was such that Schreber was catapulted into the stratosphere of the medical profession, and his two sons (the other of which committed suicide) struggled to deal with his imposing legacy. At one point in the *Memoirs*, *Senatspräsident* Schreber makes this surprising allusion to his father's work when describing his transformation into a woman, which has been mandated by the rays of God:

> Souls knew very well that a man lies on his side in bed, a woman on her back (as the "succumbing part," considered from the point of view of sexual intercourse). I myself, who in earlier life never gave it a thought, have only learned this from the souls. From what I read in for instance my father's MEDICAL INDOOR GYMNASTICS (23rd Edition, p.102), physicians themselves do not seem to be informed about it. Further, the souls knew that male voluptuousness is stimulated by the sight of female nudes, but on the contrary female voluptuousness to a very much lesser extent if at all by the sight of male nudes, while female nudes stimulate *both* sexes equally....I do not know whether these phenomena are generally known and considered correct. (MNI 155)

The part of the book to which the younger Schreber refers has to do with the position of the body in performing various exercises. Although the elder Schreber designed the exercises to be performed by both sexes, he expressly forbids certain ones that in his view stimulate blood flow to the abdomen, so that women should not have undue trouble with menstruating (Schreber 37).

From the strongly biographical content of Schreber's delusions, it is nevertheless apparent that the rational apparatus justifying Schreber's fear enables to him explain away his current wretched state. Because Schreber understands that the basis of reality is simply ideas in the mind of God, the notion of *representation*—the impressions of Schreber concerning the world, and his own body—takes center stage in his private delusional mythology. Nevertheless, Schreber feels that the idea of his becoming a woman is slowly being impressed upon him from the inside out. As Schreber notes at the bottom of the page, this is how God runs the universe, by managing the appearances and even fraudulently manipulating the appearances of human behavior and judgment: "The notion of 'representing,' that is to say of giving to a thing or a person a semblance different from its real nature (expressed in human terms 'of falsifying') played and still plays a great role generally in the ideas of souls. In this vein it was said innumerable times on later occasions: You are to be represented as a scoffer of God, or as somebody who has committed soul murder" (MNI 124n62). Here is a vivid description of Schreber's body being invaded by the souls, which collectively supervise the process of his transformation:

> Small parts of Flechsig's soul which were distant, and therefore not in contact with my nerves for quite some time, used repeatedly to exclaim as if astonished: "Is he not unmanned yet?" God's rays frequently mocked me about a supposedly imminent unmanning as "Miss Schreber" [English in the original]; an expression used frequently and repeated *ad nauseam* was: "You are to be *represented* as being given to voluptuous excesses," etc. I myself felt the danger of unmanning for a long time as a threatening ignominy, especially while there was the possibility of my body being sexually abused by other people. (MNI 124)

Strangely enough, Schreber never explains this last comment. At the very least, he felt ill at ease about being incarcerated in an asylum with other men, seeing as he was about to be "unmanned," as it were. This paranoid point of view is more fully articulated in this passage where all objects in Schreber's experience take on a gendered valence: "...A very prominent part was played in the 'soul-conception' by ideas about the relation between the two sexes and their respective mode of occupation, their tastes, etc. For instance, beds, handmirrors, and rakes were considered feminine, basket-chairs and spades masculine; of games, chess as masculine, checkers as feminine, etc." (MNI 155). In this passage and others like it, there is a strong correspondence to Freud's symbology in *Interpretation of Dreams*, where objects themselves have definite genders. Marooned in this sexualized world, Schreber is simply another object to be transformed at God's will.

The picture that Schreber provides of his confinement is one of one-sided confrontations, innuendos, and unimaginable torture, while to all outward appearances he was the model of docile inmatehood. Schreber's rapid shift in sexual identification is his way of coping with the idea that he shall become a woman, and as he is the only flesh-and-blood human left in the universe, the significance of this change assumes tremendous importance. In an excerpt from the legal notes attending Schreber's memoir, the court observes that Schreber's behavior, while clearly pathological, seems to have a significant voluntary component:

> For some time the physical behavior of the patient showed only little change, the peculiar very loud forced laughter and the monotonous uttering in endless repetition of incomprehensible abusive language (for instance "the sun is a whore," and suchlike), which served apparently to a certain extent as counteraction against the hallucinations and disturbances of feeling (pain in the back, etc.), continued as before...the patient was frequently found in his room half undressed, declared that he already had feminine breasts, liked to occupy himself by looking at pictures of naked women, even drew them and had his mustache removed. (MNI 331)

This doffing of the mustache seems to be, in hindsight, irrefutable proof of Schreber's unmanning: he yields the hirsute phallus as the last vestige of his abandoned sexual identity.[9] From the foregoing, it is obvious that Schreber's delusions were not all-encompassing, and that despite his protests to the contrary, he had some hand in dealing with his own madness. Other legal documents from the period suggest that although he was not considered sane by any measure, Schreber was still allowed to partake in social life with asylum staff, who considered him to be a distinguished, well-behaved guest.[10]

What does it mean to have Schreber as one's model analytic subject, as does Lacan? Why is Schreber so popular in psychiatric literature? For one thing, Schreber's canniness is what separates him from the rest of the Freudian case studies: witness the level of interpretation Schreber brings to his own case. Schreber's status as one of the more well-traveled mascots of psychoanalysis rests on his unique distinction of having discovered the place of fantasy in psychic life. He hits upon the function of personal narrative as a therapeutic working-out of and coping mechanism for the psychoses. In all phases, Schreber's use of narrative in explaining external stimuli (for example, his "paralysis," which initiates his self-assigned gender reassignment) insulates his ego within the context of an intersubjective world, re-imagined from the ego outward. In this, Schreber's story buffers the confrontation with the predatory father figure by making himself the simultaneous victim and hero of the remade world. The dramatic arc of the Schreber story provides an alternate Freudian context for the narrative of sexual development, one in which the father is displaced and subverted via the "degenerate" fantasy of Schreber. It is in this sense that Schreber embodies the core Lacanian ideal of *méconnaissance*: Schreber's expectations and dreams are superadded to the phenomena observable in the world. Schreber takes the burden of trying to cure himself into his own hands.

With Freud's original case study of Schreber as a clue toward his turn to the "metapsychological" phase of the post-World War I period, particularly in *Beyond the Pleasure Principle*, a line can be drawn directly from the later Freud (including the religious and anthropological writings) to the beginnings of the Lacanian "structuralization" of the Freudian corpus. Turning the tropes of psychoanalysis back on analysis itself in order to analyze it yields something more than a simple critique or invalidation: it clears the decks of the possibility of the survival of the Oedipus myth, or the abuse of power in the analytic relation.[11] In the same way, Schreber might have understood his own delusions as being part of a fictive overlay superimposed on a world of inner experience, itself proven to be an endlessly rewritable palimpsest. As Freud puts it:

> And the paranoiac builds it [the world] up again, not more splendid, it is true, but at least so that he can once more live in it. He builds it up by the work of his delusions. *The delusion-formation, which we take to be a pathological product, is in reality an attempt at recovery, a process of reconstruction.* (SE 12: 70–71)

That it is a recuperative gesture is something that one can take for granted. At the same time, this gesture is something that puts the fantasist at a disadvantage. The paranoiac wishes to put himself to the side of the narrative of sexual development; he wishes to experience the world as a god, a king, as the eunuch father—and, most significantly, to take the act of interpretation a step further by rewriting his own sexualized narrative.

Lacan: *Les Psychoses*

> Since this level leaves you somewhat confused, I will put things to you dogmatically, which I detest doing – you know my style is dialectical.
>
> (S.III 149)

Lacan's most fertile period in his intellectual career was between the years 1953 and 1956, which saw the composition of "The Function and Field of Speech and Language in Psychoanalysis," "Seminar on the Purloined Letter," "The Instance of the Letter in the Unconscious," "The Signification of the Phallus," and, of course, "The Freudian Thing." After his explorations of Freud's later work in Seminar II, Lacan turns his attention, as promised at the end of the previous seminar, to the topic of the psychoses, as most pointedly exemplified in Schreber's *Memoirs.* Although the text of Schreber's memoir appears on the surface to be quite exotic, Lacan's point here near the close of Seminar II casts the emergence of psychosis in the subject as being a common problem. As everyday experience is constantly distorted by one's subjective outlook, the emergence of psychoses is simply a matter of degree, rather than indicating a severe abnormality of perception:

> ...everything the obsessional says has got nothing to do with his experience. It is through verbal conformity, social language, that he maintains his precarious equilibrium – which is nonetheless very stable, for what could be harder to catch out than an obsessional?...Post-analytical paranoia is a long way from being a mythical problem. You don't have to have pushed the treatment very far for it to give rise to a perfectly consistent paranoia....You don't need a very good psychoanalyst to get this to come about, it's sufficient to believe very fervently in psychoanalysis. (S.II 242)

Lacan then remarks that a fixation on "psychological facts" is enough to bring paranoia about. Given a "ready-made" language with which to obsess, the subject is all the more vulnerable to psychosis. The reason that Schreber is a prime candidate for discussion here is that, having a privileged perspective on his illness, his own reaction to his disease constitutes his attempt to contain it. Schreber's interpretive identification with his illness becomes its fabric, as his lamentations inveighed against the asylum staff indicate.

In Schreber, Lacan finds an archetypal figure, one that crystallizes the modern condition of the subject, its relation to the Other, and the very foundation of psychological pathology—namely, that all disorders that can be unraveled by psychoanalysis are found in the psychoses. The Lacanian analytic situation, with its stated emphasis on those "mirages" that appear within the field of the analytic relation, recalls the torments of Schreber. Throughout Lacan's work, and particularly in this seminar, the question of the psychoses is tacitly considered against the concept of the neuroses, the definition of which is often variable, but may be characterized as the bodily after-effects of sexual or developmental trauma.[12]

Schreber is the central figure of Lacan's investigation into the character of the psychoses because his delusions neatly exemplify a *complete* paranoiac fantasy, one which provides an unstinting example of fully developed paranoia. With psychosis, the subject abandons all objective references concerning his dealings with the world; instead, everything that occurs is an expression of an undifferentiated desire present in all objects external to the subject. This topsy-turvy dialectical relation with the world is illustrated in Schreber's preface to the book, in which he accuses the asylum director of having ordered his torture at the hands of various lackeys and henchmen. In the subject's everyday dealing with others, the interaction with the other adduces sense to the utterance (S.III 51). But in the case of the psychotic patient, this desire is represented in an exaggerated fashion. In Schreber's case, the legions of "small others" who haunt his consciousness are introjections of Flechsig and other personages from his life (S.III 53). Rather than each being a discrete entity, these are all shadows of the god Ormuzd, whose intention is to destroy Schreber.

It is the all-encompassing nature of the psychotic delusion that makes it unusually difficult to treat, as everything can be explained by the predatory intentions of the omnipotent, imagined persecutor. However, the effects of such a persecutory delusion can often appear to be entirely narcissistic, as Schreber himself points out above. Lacan references this quote from the early Freud-Fliess correspondence to describe the difficulty of reasoning with a psychotic subject: "Psychotics love their delusion like they love themselves" (S.III 157). Freud would write in a more focused way on the topic of narcissism much later, but here he demonstrates his understanding that the primary issue in dealing with the fallout of psychosis is that the necessary evil of subjectivity becomes the venue of, and underlying reason for, the illness. Moreover, the subject's self-understanding, only accessible through psychoanalysis, determined as it is to a large extent through traumas and the like, is guided by the signifying chain of the symbolic order, underwritten by the Oedipus complex, primal scenes, and so forth. Lacan asserts here that the primal scene, which dictates the character of the subject, is of great importance in the evaluation of narcissism:

> In *The Wolf Man* the primitive impression of the famous primordial scene has remained over the years, serving no purpose, though already signifying, before having its word to say in the subject's history. The signifier is thus primitively given, but it remains nothing as long as the subject doesn't cause it to enter into his history, which becomes important between the ages of one and a half and four and a half. Sexual desire is effectively what man uses to historicize himself, insofar as it's at this level that the law is introduced for the first time. (S.III 156)

Lacan puts the focus on the intervention of the symbolic in the human; the importance of this issue is unpacked later in the discussion of the insertion of the subject into the symbolic order, and elsewhere in Lacan with the emphasis on the interdiction of the symbolic as the primary procedure for analysis.[13] Certainly, in the case of this primal scene, the symbolic is Lacan's guide, as well as Freud's:

> The symbolic provides a form into which the subject is inserted at the level of his being. It's on the basis of the signifier that the subject recognizes himself as being this or that. The chain of signifiers has a fundamental explanatory value, and the very notion of causality is nothing else.
>
> There is nevertheless one thing that evades the symbolic tapestry, it's procreation in its essential root – that one being is born from another. (S.III 179)

The masculine valence of the symbolic is rarely expressed more clearly elsewhere in Lacan's work: the intersection of the synchronic, metaphorical symbolic with the life of the diachronic, metonymic subject produces what is known as reflexivity, and also opens the door to the possibility of solipsism. In "The Signification of the Phallus," Lacan states that the power of the symbolic is found in the supreme effect of the operations of the phallus, and its ability to create significance seemingly at will. Only in the process of conversation will the analyst and the analysand be able to reach a viable reading of the subject's complexes, through the selective reading of the symbolic life of the subject: "The continuity in everything a subject has lived through since birth tends never to emerge and doesn't interest us in the slightest. What interests us are the decisive moments of symbolic articulation, of history, but in the sense in which we say the History of France" (S.III 111). The history of the subject is never easy to outline, for attention must be paid to the sense in which the subject has self-understanding through the symbolic.

It is this doubleness in the life of the analysand that Lacan addresses in his discussion of psychosis. In the same sense that Lacan is careful to distinguish between the life of the subject and the history of the subject, so too there is a distinction to be made between the history-less subject and the subject able to balance desire and subjectivity in worldly interaction. As Lacan sees it, the *Verwerfung* of the paranoid subject occurs when the "primordial signifier," that of the father, perhaps, is rejected, and in doing so, the symbolic order is obscured from view (S.III 149), Lacan considers this to be the fundamental mechanism of paranoia:

> It's inside this primordial body that Freud posits the constitution of a world of reality, which is already punctuated, already structured, in terms of signifiers.... The subject's initial apprehension of reality is the judgment of existence, which consists in saying – *This is not my dream or my hallucination or my representation but an object.* (S.III 150)

The effect of this *Verwerfung* results in a confusion of signification with the object itself; thanks to the stamp of the primordial signifier, the subject can distinguish between objects and their interpretation via the symbolic. The subject wishes to know nothing about castration because the subject wishes to know nothing about the disjunction between language and the real. The psychotic subject deludes himself about possessing the power of the phallus to signify; not being subject to the symbolic order, the subject is free to attach meaning to objects at will. Lacan describes the psychotic state as lacking an intersubjective context, such that the psychotic's experience is guided by orienting phrases and words (in Schreber's case, "unmanning," "fleetingly-improvised-men," and the like) that take on greater significance than they do for others. Lacan sardonically remarks that although everyone engages in belief-making, "Obviously, we don't put them to the same use as the psychotic does" (S.III 110). The failure of the symbolic exacerbates the delusional persona of the psychotic; the dialectical relation between subject and world, as expressed within the subject's daily routine, is thrown off-balance by the lack of context for the proper operation of the symbolic:

> For want of being able in any way to re-establish his pact with the other, for want of being able to make any symbolic mediation whatsoever between what is new and himself, the subject moves into another mode of mediation, completely different from the former, and substitutes for symbolic mediation a profusion, an imaginary proliferation, into which the central signal of a possible mediation is introduced in a deformed and profoundly asymbolic fashion. (S.III 87)

The lack of identity is the root of delusion. As such, the interaction with the Other causes the obliteration of the *objet petit a.* Paranoid delusions lead the subject to a necessary confrontation with God, necessarily a narcissistic projection of the worst of persecution fantasies. God is the ultimate excuse for the paranoiac's misfortune, and as this conception of the Almighty is a reflection of Schreber's, God takes on the characteristics Schreber imagines (S.III 101).

One of the greatest abiding confusions in the poststructuralist milieu has to do with the question of surveillance, which Foucault cunningly explores in *Discipline and Punish.* The Lacanian concepts of the gaze and the "big Other" are often analyzed in the light of Foucault's work, and this results in a highly inaccurate characterization of Lacan's ideas. In this seminar, Lacan speaks lightly of having to identify with the big "O," the projection of the subject through the object of one's desire:

> For my part, within the generalized notion of communication, I state what speech as speaking to the other is. It's making the other speak as such.
>
> We shall, if you like, write that other with a big O.
>
> And why with a big O? No doubt for a delusional reason, as is the case whenever one is obliged to provide signs that are supplementary to what language offers. (S.III 37)

It is, asserts Lacan, the *unknown* in the equation that causes uncertainty about the fabric of reality, and perhaps projection on the part of the Other. God is the sticking point in Schreber's delusion (S.III 314–315), as the signifier that can be continually filled with more and more impressive characters. This "quilting point" is the moment at which the subject is gripped by the symbolic, and forced to interpret all of experience with regard to it. Yet, the primordial signifier of which Lacan speaks is not the organizing principle of the symbolic, personified; it is initiation of the subject into the symbolic order, and therefore socialization. This "big Other" subsists, then, as a necessary delusion, in order to express this illusion symbolically; namely, after Sartre, that the gaze of the Other stands in for the corrosive glance of infinite judgment.

Michel Arrivé singles out Jacques Lacan's remark in *Les Psychoses* that the Lacanian style, like that of God, has nothing of the Other in it.[14] The ultimate reason for this is that Lacan wished to have nothing to do with the influence of the Other on speech, as the analyst must tap as directly as possible into the matter of the unconscious to translate the symbolic into discourse. Lacan's lordly and enigmatic style *pretends* to speak the language of the symbolic in order to produce the illusion of its authoritativeness. In the relation between analyst and analysand, the analyst necessarily is the stand-in and embodiment for the symbolic. Rather than being a delusion of grandeur (although in Lacan's case, it probably would have been fitting), psychoanalysis demands the necessary delusion that an analysis be comprehensive and reflect the analysand's place in the symbolic. The subject's inner experience, experiencing oneself as both authentic and not, is taken to represent one's experience of the world, and the interpretation of this experience designates one's place in the world. The "Other" of psychoanalysis, the analysand, is in danger of being obliterated by the analyst, and the end result is that the analysand's ego is always aberrant. In the analytic relation, the analyst abnegates the ego in order to play his role. In a sense, the analyst's role is entirely illusory and inauthentic, *and so is the assumption of the role from other analysts, the authority of the analyst to interpret symptoms, and the bonds between analytic teachers and students.* The role of analyst must be assumed by fiat, and the illusion must be maintained by the analysand's faith.

It has been said that Lacan's style is to "ignore transference." This is patently wrong. Lacan simply views transference as being an inescapable condition of speech, and therefore it cannot be analyzed separately from any form of interaction with the analysand. On the other hand, Lacan strove to keep his personal and professional commitments to the analysand utterly separate, although he was often accused of blurring the line between the two.[15] Yet, within the smaller-scale framework of analysis, Lacan saw the whole of the social relation implied, and it is there that Lacan stages the presence of analytic truth. The shared mirages of therapy are made altogether valid by putting two heads together, as it is only in the analytic relation that they appear.

Henry James: *The Sacred Fount*

The Sacred Fount is a relatively obscure work in the Henry James canon; at the time of its publication, it was seen as little more than a puzzling and slight shaggy-dog story foisted on an unsuspecting reading public.[16] It may be said, however, that *The Sacred Fount* defines the stylistic agenda that James was to follow for the rest of his career, as the substance, characterization and plot of the novel yield completely to the ruminations of its implied narrator.[17] This style reaches its logical endpoint in *The Golden Bowl*, where the action takes place almost entirely by means of the narrator's discussion and dissection of the characters' thoughts and feelings. *The Sacred Fount* is also James's only long work narrated by a first-person narrator, who remains nameless throughout the action of the story. With this conceit, atypical in James's oeuvre, the narrator proceeds to tell the story of an odd weekend at the country estate of Newmarch, where the narrator himself interprets the weekend's gossip as proving a larger point about human nature: that love in couples mismatched with regard to age fosters a vampiric effect. As the younger, more vital partner ages faster, the elder grows more youthful. Naturally, the intellectual momentum that carries James's narrator through this book is predicated on his proving the theory, which brings the novel to its climactic set piece, a confrontation with the party's dominant doyenne, Mrs. Brissenden. This section alone takes up the final quarter of the book, in which the narrator discovers the "secret" that is known to all of the other guests, and that all of his conceits are for nothing.

The nature of this "narrative" tags it as a likely candidate for psychoanalytic reading; indeed, *The Sacred Fount* would seem to be a rich source of insights about the psyche in obsessional torment. Once the narrator reaches the house, his declaration appears to anticipate the chain of Lacanian signification: "The links, in fact, should I count them all, would make too long a chain. They formed, nevertheless, the happiest little chapter of accidents, though a series of which I can scarce give more than the general effect" (SF 24). However, the set of concerns that James brings to the table in many of his novels, especially those of obsessive observation, paranoia, and sexual isolation, receive their most bracing and reductive formulation in *The Sacred Fount*, such that the narrative can be said to be a meditation on James's narrative art itself. The narrator shoulders the classically Jamesian persona of the detached gadfly, engrossed in the fine analysis of social interaction and drama in high society, only to find that he is ultimately the butt of the joke, and that all his calculation has come to naught. As the story plays out, his sanity and judgment are openly called into question by the characters he so closely observes. Rather than wielding power over his hapless quarry, the narrator is blinkered by his near-fetishistic attachment to his own observations and theories. As the novel ends, the *story* is all the narrator has, as the delicious effects of his theory become the prize itself:

> A part of the amusement they yielded came, I daresay, from my exaggerating them—grouping them into a larger mystery (and thereby a larger "law") than the facts, as observed, yet warranted; but that is the common fault of minds for which the vision of life is an obsession. The obsession pays, if one will; but to pay it has to borrow. (SF 30)

James explores this question of balance throughout the novel, between vitality and decrepitude, between darkness and light, thus setting the dramatic agenda. In the narrator's obsession over the events of the country weekend, he exhibits some of the same qualities as Schreber in his predatory view of the world as a whole. The narrator's supposed aloofness presupposes a godlike access to the truth, and in loosing himself from the moorings of his predefined social role he is removed from the sexual economy of the novel. Yet, he plays a sort of vampire as well, as he is perfectly content to theorize and gossip.[18] As such, *The Sacred Fount*, in addition to providing a picture of paranoiac delusion, does so in a self-aware fashion, complete with metaphorical language, the knowing abstraction of sexual intrigue, and references to physiological ailments. The "primitive" Lacanian reading offered here accommodates both the aesthetic James of the finer grain and James the acute chronicler of social foibles; both are met in the persona of the narrator, who is at once formidable and embarrassingly naïve. Also, the superficially homoerotic exchanges between the narrator and Ford Obert produce a kind of shared insight reminiscent of psychoanalysis, all while going through the motions of seduction.

The primal scene of the novel would appear to be early in the narrative, after the initial greetings and scene-settings of the opening chapters. Some members of the Newmarch party, including the narrator and Mrs. Server, happen upon a striking painting in the library. The question of the meaning of the portrait is put at first to Gilbert Long by the narrator, and then to Mrs. Server; not coincidentally, these are two people assumed by the narrator to be possibly one of his matched love sets:

> "Do, my dear man, let us have it again. It's the picture, of all pictures, that most needs an interpreter. *Don't* we want," I asked of Mrs. Server, "to know what it means?" The figure represented is a young man in black—a quaint, tight black dress, fashioned in years long past; with a pale, lean, livid face and a stare, from eyes without eyebrows, like that of some whitened old-world clown. In his hand he holds an object that strikes the spectator at first simply as some obscure, some ambiguous work of art, but that on a second view becomes a representation of a human face, modelled and coloured, in wax, in enamelled metal, in some substance not human. The object thus appears a complete mask, such as might have been fantastically fitted and worn. (SF 50–51)

The oddest phrase in this passage is easily "in some substance, not human," as if in the vampiric world of Newmarch, the narrator wishes to pre-empt the question as to whether the mask is fashioned out of some fleshly substance. The reader is presented with a set of stark ambiguities: the face of the figure itself seems not quite human, as the pale skin and lack of eyebrows give the appearance of a clown persona. The mask, on the other hand, which one would assume would at once conceal identity and project a persona chosen by the wearer, instead appears here a mysterious blot, nebulous in its appearance, purpose and intention. The language James chooses to describe the mask instead appears to be a noncommittal gesture to suggest what the object is, a "complete" mask that "might have been fantastically fitted and worn." Most readings of the novel interpret the painting as representing the layers of social deception portrayed in the novel's narrative.[19] Rather, the painting foregrounds the enigma of the *meaning* of the Newmarch party: it stands as a symbol that offers a gesture of interpretation, namely, the exposition of human nature and behavior. The mysterious figure in the painting stands for, as in much of James, the misdirection of interpretational attention. The narrator's remark to Obert on finding the opposite numbers to the loving couple is yet another example of misdirection: "The real man must be the one she doesn't markedly collar" (SF 56). In a sense, it is a case of the narrator looking too hard in the wrong place and expecting the truth to be there, when it is in plain sight.

James's choice to place what may be described as his own narrative voice in the action of *The Sacred Fount* leads to some interesting contortions that undermine his, and the narrator's, authority. The tensions between "seeing to the exclusion of almost everything else" and the narrator's own preoccupation with acting as a bon vivant weigh on him such that his own position is endlessly compromised. Part of the narrator's anxiety must stem from the impossibility of seeing into the consciousness of the characters, as occurs in the best of James's work. However, the narrator feels that he is somehow endangered by all of his calculation and second-guessing:

> Reflection was the real intensity; reflection, as to poor Mrs. Server in particular, was an indiscreet opening of doors. She became vivid in the light of the so limited vision of her that I already possessed—try positively as I would not further to extend it. It was something not to ask another question...it was something to talk as hard as possible with other persons and on other subjects, to mingle in groups much more superficial than they supposed themselves, to give ear to broader jokes, to discuss more tangible mysteries. (SF 72)

In this passage, the simple act of analysis is shown to be the substance of Newmarch life, as opposed to the content of the relationships under scrutiny; it is an assertion about the power of observation and the narrator's estimation of it as the primary social gift, a ticket punched for entry into the ranks of the cognoscenti:

> Newmarch had always, in our time, carried itself as the great asylum of the finer wit, more or less expressly giving out that, as invoking hospitality or other countenance, none of the stupid, none even of the votaries of the grossly obvious, need apply; but I could luckily at present reflect that its measurements in this direction had not always been my own, and that, moreover, whatever precision they possessed, human blandness, even in such happy halls, had not been quite abolished.
>
> There was a sound law in virtue of which one could always—alike in privileged and unprivileged circles—rest more on people's density than their penetrability. (SF 77–78)

Because this "density" is at a premium to foster intrigue in social circles, the narrator immediately shows himself to be aware of the lures of gossip and innuendo. Over the course of the narrative, the narrator's perception of what constitutes density and penetrability changes. He must decide whether or not the riddle is worth pursuing, and at what cost to his prey. He harbors this "haunting principle," which occurs to him on meeting May Server, curiously demanding of himself that he determine the emotion he felt on upon greeting her: "Yet what *was* this feeling, really?—of which, at the point we had thus reached, I seemed to myself to have gathered from all things an invitation to render some account" (SF 97). This invitation is as yet unclear, and the act of the invitation itself is strange. The phrase "I seemed to myself" implies that the invitation issues from the "I," and that to have "seemed" to oneself implies that another persona has done all the collecting for him, and is only now going through the process of surveying his treasures. James saves this "render[ing of] some account" until the end the novel, in the argument with Mrs. Brissenden, where the narrator is then forced to give up every last bit of his gossip.

The encounter with Mrs. Server is the most pointed example in the book where James's figural violence rears its head, a motif common in the later works, as in *The Wings of the Dove*, where James envisions characters being violated, devoured, consumed, and so forth.[20] Here, we see the narrator preying on an unsuspecting May Server, an insect-like creature assuredly to be pitied rather than helped:

> She gave herself, in that minute, more than she doubtless knew—gave herself, I mean, to my intenser apprehension. She went through the form of expression, but what told me everything was the way the form of expression broke down. Her lovely grimace, the light of the previous hours, was as blurred as a bit of brushwork in water-colour spoiled by the upsetting of the artist's glass. She fixed me with it as she had fixed during the day forty persons, but it fluttered like a bird with a broken wing. (SF 99)

If May Server had been once a feared and treasured component of polite society, she no longer has any potency whatsoever. The ability to see, to express, and to exist in the visual language of pleasantry and exchange of greeting deserts her here. In the course of conversation with May Server, the nameless narrator injects this observation: "She was on my hands—it was she herself, poor creature, who was: this was the thing that just now loomed large, and the secret was a comparative detail" (SF 100). The "secret" of the vampiric affair is on the back burner for the time being, and for the moment, May Server's lifeless carcass is a burden he must bear: "She reminded me of a sponge wrung dry and with fine pores agape. Voided and scraped of everything, her shell was merely crushable....That was Mrs. Server's tragedy, that her consciousness survived—survived with a force that made it struggle and dissemble. This consciousness was all her secret—it was at any rate all mine" (SF 101). Not only has May Server's vibrancy supposedly been sucked out of her by her paramour, her bloodless dissection at the hands of the narrator seals her fate.

The organizing principle of *The Sacred Fount* is made more compelling for the narrator in that his scheme could be "found out." Waiting for the theatrical gesture of discovery that would bring the weekend to a close, the narrator reflects on the worth of his obsession: "Would the definite dramatic signal for ringing the curtain down be then only—as a grand climax and *coup de théâtre*— the due attestation that poor Briss had succumbed to inexorable time and Mrs. Server given way under a cerebral lesion?" (SF 121). The allusion to the "cerebral lesion" suggests that May Server's debilitating condition is the result of something hidden; her disabled self-possession, related to sight, must be part of her malady, but his clinical reference to the structure of the brain covers his scientific bases, and is at the same time an artistic conceit. The narrator comes through with the admission that his interest here in figuring out the situation is largely aesthetic:

> Things in the real had a way of not balancing: it was all an affair, this fine symmetry, of artificial proportion. Yet even while I kept my eyes away from Mrs. Briss and Long it was vivid to me that, "composing" there beautifully, they could scarce help playing a part in my exhibition. The mind of man, furthermore—and my generalization pressed hard, with a quick twist, on the supersubtlety as to which I had been privately complacent—the mind of man doubtless didn't know from one minute to the other, under the appeal of phantasmagoric life, what it would profitably be at. (SF 130)

The dichotomy of *The Sacred Fount* is all about the distinction between the "affair of symmetry" and seeing things as they are. The appeal of the so-called "phantasmagoric life," whatever James means by the phrase, is bound up in the pleasure of the voyeur. Without image and metaphor, there would be no delicious irony at which to poke. The "profit," again, is the affair itself, but the problem of objectivity, if it exists, is the possibility that he could be wrong. Here is the same declaration, where "returns" takes a double meaning: "It was on my way to the place, in fine, that my obsession had met me, and it was by retracing those steps that I should be able to get rid of it. Only I must break off sharp, must escape all reminders by foreswearing all returns" (SF 142). This foreswearing signifies the narrator's break with reality.

Perhaps it is no coincidence that the homoerotic prospects of this particular James novel arrive in the guise of the narrator's interactions with the artist Ford Obert.[21] Here, the only satisfying sexual relation that the narrator can forge is between himself and the artist, mediated by their exchanging of notes on the Newmarch scene. The scene is loaded with comical sexual innuendo, and it can be said, perhaps, that it is about everything but the plot:

> "You mean he contents himself with winking at *her*? My dear fellow, that wasn't enough for you yesterday, and it wouldn't have been enough for you this morning, among the impressions that led to our last talk. It was just the fact that you did wink, that you *had* winked, at me that wound me up."
>
> "And what about the fact that you had winked at *me*? *Your* winks—come"—Obert laughed—"are portentous!"
>
> "Oh, if we recriminate," I cheerfully said after a moment, "we agree." (SF 149)

This exchange speaks well enough for itself, and it is followed by this somewhat risqué description: "I turned, on it, a little more to him, and looked at him so long that he had at last to look at me; with which, after holding his eyes another moment, I made my point. 'Our hands are not clean.' 'Ah, speak for your own!'—and as he moved back I might really have thought him uneasy" (SF 149). The sexual intrigue gets thicker as the narrator says: "You excite me too much. You don't know what you do to me" (SF 151). The seduction the narrator has propagated throughout his weekend at Newmarch has overcome both men to the point that neither is sure what exactly has occurred during their discussion.

If there is sexual frustration, it is certainly felt by the ever-scheming narrator, who is attempting to place Obert in the continuum of things: "'Oh, the torch of my analogy!' I had so groaned it—as if for very ecstasy—that it pulled him up, and I could see his curiosity as indeed reaffected" (SF 152). Despite this phallic symbology, the overall effect is that the narrator continues the seduction of Obert by drawing him back in at various moments, such as this one. The climax of the meeting arrives, appropriately enough, with the appearance of Brissenden himself:

> "Oh," said Obert, looking, luminous and straight, up at me from his seat, "the man now, the actual man—!" But he stopped short, with his eyes suddenly quitting me and his words becoming a formless ejaculation. It was Brissenden himself who, to my supreme surprise, stood there, with rapid inquiry in his attitude and face. (SF 157)

The look of "rapid inquiry" on Brissenden's face is the subject of concern to the narrator: he may be suspicious about what they were doing, but the narrator's real concern is that Brissenden is also a reading subject, steadily constructing his own interpretation of the weekend's events. For the narrator, the initial shock comes from the mere presence of one of the objects of his obsession, as the man has intruded on the psychotic fantasy the narrator has so carefully constructed.

The dénouement of the story telescopes the abrupt entrance of Brissenden into the traumatic irruption ending the paranoid fantasy. The conversation with Mrs. Brissenden, which takes up the rest of the book, is itself a helix of confusion and miscommunication. For nearly forty pages, the nameless narrator and the revitalized doyenne talk over the events at Newmarch. The narrator tells her about the conclusion that he has reached: he accuses her of sucking the life out of Brissenden, to her ultimate benefit. However, the communication of this conceit is difficult; her puzzled denials are taken as mere dissembling by him, when in fact she cannot possibly understand his line of reasoning at all:

> She had taken at last again the time she required. "Do you know what I think?"
>
> "It's exactly what I'm pressing you to make intelligible."
>
> "Well," said Mrs. Briss, "I think you're crazy."
>
> It naturally struck me. "Crazy."
>
> "Crazy."
>
> I turned it over. "But do you call that intelligible?"
>
> She did it justice. "No: I don't suppose it *can* be so for you if you *are* insane." (SF 192)

The repetition here in this passage is a device that reverberates throughout the rest of the later James, where characters repeat the last words of their interlocutors, especially if there is nothing left to say. Of course, he really is crazy, and in that, his paramount concern is the intelligibility of his conceits, and he resorts to figural violence to explain their severity: "'No,' I quickly went on, 'I daresay, to do you justice, the interpretation of my tropes and figures *isn't* "ever" perfectly simple. You doubtless have driven me into a corner with my dangerous explosive, and my only fair course must be therefore to sit on it till you get out of the room'" (SF 196). Once again, the narrator participates in rhetorical violence, taking the figural for the literal.

The narrator allows himself, even as he loses the argument, that he shall be revenged upon everyone who had a hand in pushing him into this untenable position, however much pleasure he derives from it:

> I know not what heavy admonition of my responsibility had thus suddenly descended on me; but nothing, under it, was indeed more sensible than that it practically paralysed me. And I could only say to myself that this was the price—the price of the secret success, the lonely liberty and the intellectual joy. There were things that for so private and splendid a revel—that of the exclusive king

> with his Wagner opera—I could only let go, and the special torment of my case was that the condition of light, of the satisfaction of curiosity and of the attestation of triumph, was in this direct way the sacrifice of feeling. (SF 203)

As a private obsession, the enterprise of gossipy detective work is conducted as a private perversion of the very public activity of social life. Even though some scandal is to be expected under the circumstances, what the narrator has proposed, with the fetishism of the scene, is seen as a private pleasure, improper because it is solitary. When the narrator says "'My system, where so much made for protection...wasn't intended to have the effect of exposure'" (SF 209), he means the object of his obsession, not himself. Yet he has been exposed, and it is he who has committed the sabotage. When given the "wrong" answer to the complex sexual intrigue at Newmarch, he himself must be forced to understand his error: Mrs. Brissenden informs him that "Lady John *is* the woman," and the phrase is repeated three times (SF 208–209). His complaint that Mrs. Brissenden has no taste for the theory (because she has a reliable, spying husband) induces him to complain, lamely: "But she had no ear for irony, and she made out still more of her story: 'He's simple—but he sees.'" (SF 211). For the narrator, the inexcusable lack of irony is where the truth breaks upon the shore of consciousness, and the undeniable facts undo all of his beautiful abstraction, which is where the real value lies:

> I had taken her immediately up, and I held her by it and by something better still. "You, from your fortress of granite, can chuck them about as you will! All the more reason, however," I quickly added, "that, before my frail, but as I maintain, quite sublime structure, you honour me, for a few seconds, with an intelligent look at it. I seem myself to see it again, perfect in every part," I pursued, "even while I thus speak to you and feel afresh that, weren't the wretched accident of its weak foundation, it wouldn't have the shadow of a flaw. I've spoken of it in my conceivable regret," I conceded, "as already a mere heap of disfigured fragments; but that was the extravagance of my vexation, my despair. It's in point of fact so beautifully fitted that it comes apart piece by piece—which, so far as that goes, you've seen it do in the last quarter of an hour at your own touch, quite handing me the pieces, one by one, yourself and watching me stack them along the ground. They're not even in this state—see!" I wound up—"a pile of ruins!"..."I should almost like, piece by piece, to hand them back to you." And this time I completed my figure. (SF 214)

His despair at the prospect of unmaking this edifice—which would be in fact as pleasurable as its assembly—descends on him, because the crucial thing is *completeness* of the experience, not its permanence. The final answer to the puzzle is that it is indeed Gilbert Long and Lady John, and May Server and Mr. Brissenden who are conducting affairs (SF 218), and this throws the prospect of the narrator's proportion off balance, as two vital people and two depleted ones carry on with each other in full view. Matching like with like, taking appearance for the thing that it is, violates the spirit of symptom-reading that any good member of the social register prizes. The narrator cannot deal with the evidence, after all is said and done. The complicated business of undoing the theory would have to be recollected in private, aided, perhaps, by the writing of a memoir, such as *The Sacred Fount*: "I *should* certainly never again, on the spot, quite hang together, even though it wasn't really that I hadn't three times her method. What I too fatally lacked was her tone" (SF 219). These words end the book, and the tone that Mrs. Brissenden has mimics reality crashing in on the subject, and for all that she might as well be the voice of Jehovah speaking through the clouds. For the paranoiac, everything must fit together, and the impingement of anomalous, absurdly factical truth ruins everything.

Schizophrenia and Its Place in Psychoanalysis

Schizophrenia, particularly in the postmodern era, has taken on a near-shamanistic cast in popular culture; madmen (almost always men) are portrayed as enlightened visionaries, political radicals (as in *Madness and Civilization*), or romantic victims in a heroic struggle with fate. For someone like R.D. Laing, whose ideas have often been compared with Lacan's, the schizophrenic is the ultimate nonconformist, whose rebellion against a lack of freedom manifests itself in a liberation from reality.[22] That such outward impressions of madness have gained a currency in the culture at large is a testament to both the linguistic character of psychotic disorder (which manifests itself primarily through the effects of language on the subject), and the perception that such a disease limits its impact to a singular victim: schizophrenia (unlike hysteria) does not manifest itself in a class, group, or family. In essence, the madman is alone, like the prophet or oracle, and in many cases where the subject's external behavior is mostly benign (the mawkishness of the 1990s films *A Beautiful Mind* and *Shine* comes to mind), schizophrenia can be perceived as a superficial disorder of an outsize personality. As we have seen with Schreber and Freud, schizophrenia itself is diagnosed only through the lens of personality—there are no other symptoms to treat.[23]

In the foregoing analysis, I have attempted to outline the psychoanalytic characterization of paranoid thinking as it informs Schreber, Lacan, and James, in order to provide a context for a reading of all three from the metapsychological standpoint of Freud's later work. Most importantly, this reading takes as its theme the propensity for paranoid thought to propagate and contest illusions of authority, whether they are present in the subject's experience in the world, or on the analyst's couch. Following Freud, it can be seen that the paranoid fantasy is best "understood" as an attempt at "self-reparation."[24] The guiding principle that may be taken in each case is that the psychoanalytic assessment of paranoia is an *ex post facto* evaluation of some form of exclusionary trauma. In Schreber's case, it is the struggle with his father's legacy; in Lacan's case, the inability to sit in Freud's seat; with James's narrator, the foreclosure of his participation in the sexual intrigue of Newmarch.

The most celebrated symptom of schizophrenia, that of delusions of grandeur, reflect the desperate desire on behalf of the subject not to be dominated by the menacing world around him.[25] Thus, the tension in psychoanalysis is between the necessity of a controlling authority (the analyst) and exertion of this authority over the wounded analysand, already traumatized by the situation of being on the "outside" of discourse. To some degree, this is reflected in the history of the discipline. The final break the field of psychoanalysis made with the rigors of anatomical development and early experimental neurology constituted a potentially liberating and vertiginous separation from the implacable judgments of science in favor of a method that responded to the need for the psychiatrist to interact with the patient on a more "human" level. Yet, as Lacan's work on the psychoses indicates, such an arrangement courts a possibly steep personal cost in submitting to the illusion of the controlling Other.

4

Masochism: Reading Fantasy with Lacan, Sacher-Masoch, and Proust

The term "masochism" has, since being first diagnosed by Krafft-Ebing in the early twentieth century, achieved a circulation well beyond its original clinical description. The popular conception of masochism typically denotes a simple, perverse desire for suffering in any form, rather than describing a discrete set of circumstances initiated by the sexual fantasies of a particular subject. That the widespread definition of masochism has no component in it whatsoever of sexual fantasy may point to an incapability of the average person to adopt a masochistic frame of mind, or to put particular forms of sexual desire into a masochistic vocabulary of images.

This is not to say that some of the most eminent figures in psychoanalysis have not had difficulty defining masochism in an exclusively sexual context. In looking at psychoanalytic evaluations of masochism, one can see that it presents serious problems for the pleasure-oriented libido theory of sexuality, first advanced by Freud and later modified by Lacan; rather than being something explicable by libidinal operation, masochism inhabits the same abstract realm occupied by paranoia. In the literary work of Sacher-Masoch and Proust, the masochistic fantasy is primarily a function of nostalgia and is indicative of a longed-for mythical past, as a result of the absence of paternal authority. For Deleuze, the masochistic fantasy is a distinctively post-"pleasure principle" form of sexuality that represents, at best, a sort of liberation of the subject into a realm of potentially rehabilitative fantasy, demanding a wholesale rearrangement of the symbolic order in the masochistic imaginary.

The Lacanian exploration of masochism requires an examination of his views on feminine sexuality. At every turn, Lacan's psychoanalytic structures, centered on the idea of a masculine libido, frustrate his attempts to account for the sexuality of women, which is not surprising given his adherence to Freud. In Freud's "A Child is Being Beaten" and "The Economic Problem of Masochism," Freud's inability to deal with the female beating fantasy stems ultimately from his attachment to the Oedipus complex. Like all of Freud's theories concerning feminine sexuality, the masochistic fantasy, as imagined by Freud's test subjects, is thought to be an ineffectual shadow of the "real" masculine beating fantasy, modeled on the Oedipus complex. Where Freud hedges on the issue of female sexuality, Lacan's discourse has little recourse other than to follow Freud's refusal to investigate the "dark continent." In discussing psychoanalytic assessments of masochism, I shall first look at Freud's attempts to solve the question of female masochism, which reveal the limitations of his theory of the libido. In following Freud, Lacan comes to somewhat vague conclusions regarding female sexuality, and these also prevent him from resolving masochistic questions. The masochistic encounter, which gains its energy from hazy, indulgent nostalgia, strives to create sexual tension, released by each individual act of violence; it is, in every important respect, the classic masculine sexual fantasy *qua* narrative.

Freud, Masochism, and the Beating Fantasy

In his essays "A Child is Being Beaten" and "The Economic Problem of Masochism," Freud tries to account for what he sees as a disturbing phenomenon in the early genital phase of sexual development. The "beating fantasy," a somewhat elaborate narrative cultivated by children of both sexes, follows different scenarios according to the child's gender, but Freud in each case postulates that guilt is the primary motivating force behind the masochism. Freud asserts that the beating fantasy almost always involves masturbation; upon completing the act, the subject invariably feels guilt and shame, and these feelings are compounded by the fantasy's aberrant nature (SE 17: 179). The source of this guilt, as in most of Freud's work, is found in the Oedipus complex. The Oedipal triangle neatly accounts for the movements of the male fantasy: the first phase, in which the boy feels he is loved by his father, gives way to the second, in which he is beaten by his mother. Freud's substitution of "loving" for "beating" reveals the true structure of the fantasy and allows Freud to construct an intermediate stage where the father beats the son. The last stage of the fantasy, in which the mother beats the son, foreshadows the masochistic "perversion" later in life; at the same time, the action of "beating" also represents sexual contact. Therefore, the proper reading of the fantasy is that the male subject has been turned away from an incestuous love of the father to a "proper" lust for the mother (SE 17: 199). Freud warns, however, that an attachment to this fantasy leads to a destructive obsessional neurosis (SE 17: 182).

The analysis of the male beating fantasy is fairly simple. However, the larger part of Freud's group of subjects is comprised by young girls, and their version of the beating fantasy presents a serious challenge to Freud's tidy explanation. The stages for the female fantasy are quite different in structure and content, and may be summarized thus:

1. My father is beating the child (whom I hate).
2. I am being beaten by my father.
3. An authority figure (a representative of the father's authority) is beating a number of anonymous children, typically boys (and I am probably watching).

(SE 17: 185–186)

The initial problem in assessing this fantasy is, as Freud points out, that it violates the masochistic paradigm by the end of the narrative and turns sadistic in form. Moreover, it goes outside the familial boundaries of the Oedipal relation by featuring a crowd of other children and, most notably, it also excludes the mother. Freud considers these omissions to be anomalies, but decides in the end that the fantasy is a kind of assurance against losing the affections of the father (SE 17: 186). The female beating fantasy, so far, represses this forbidden love of the father, just as it does in the male version. In addition, this fantasy masks the fantasist's illicit sexual desire for the father by putting a group of boys in her place. According to Freud, this gender substitution is an expression of her wish to retreat to the sadistic-anal phase and to become a sexually neutral, non-threatening boy, whom the father can easily dominate (SE 17: 187). Although the ending phase of the beating fantasy seems decidedly sadistic, Freud still classes the fantasy as a masochistic one. In Freud's reading, the girl's voyeuristic role, removed from the "action" of the fantasy, negates any desire on her part to enter into a sexual relation (SE 17: 200). But if this is true, then why does the masochistic female fantasist appear to feel guilt? Freud's apparent response, that the girl's fantasy is her wish for the denial of the father's carnal attentions, makes some sense when compared with his reading of the male beating fantasy; yet, the appearance of the symptoms and his reading of the fantasy cannot be easily reconciled. The mere existence of the fantasy and its regularity of expression in young girls seem perverse to Freud, but he cannot provide an explanation as to what the fantasy represses, if the sexual tension in the fantasy is resolved by the girl's "de-sexualization."

Freud works out a more definitive answer to these questions in "The Economic Problem of Masochism." In this 1924 essay, Freud puts aside the question of childhood imaginings and offers a reading of masochistic behavior grounded in his structural theory of the ego, superego, and id. Of the three kinds of masochism Freud treats, the moral, the feminine, and the "erotogenic," he declares the erotogenic imperative to be present in all masochistic urges, because the pleasure of the body in pain supersedes all other libidinal goals (SE 19: 161). Guilt, the necessary end result of beating fantasies for Freud, transforms sadism into masochism by turning the dynamics of punishment inward (SE 19: 165). Thus "erotogenic" masochism gives the subject's superego a sadistic kind of control over the ego, but Freud observes that the sadistic goal of domination remains secondary to the pleasure gained by inflicting pain on the body. Freud extends his consideration of masochism as the outcome of infantile regression to the anal phase by likening the pains of the subject, beaten and dominated like a child, to the agony of childbirth (SE 19: 165). This can be seen analogically as an amplification of the stereotypically "passive" female role in copulation, and also a reflection of the final satisfaction of penis envy, the gift-child.

Despite the foregoing, Freud doubts that such female masochistic fantasies are common, although they well exemplify the classic female traits of passivity and infantile organization of sexual structures. The existence of the beating fantasy represses little or nothing, because Freud suggests that masochism recalls a part of the subject's life in which the relationship between the libido and death instinct had not separated fully (SE 19: 164). This inchoate mixture of urges results only in an indecisive libidinal direction: there is no trauma for the subject's psyche to repress. It is no accident that the effects of masochism are a faint imitation of sadism, an observation Freud whispers in parentheses:

> Being castrated—or being blinded, which stands for it—often leaves a negative trace of itself in phantasies, in the condition that no injury is to occur precisely

> to the genitals or the eyes. (Masochistic tortures, incidentally, rarely make such a serious impression as do the cruelties of sadism, whether imagined or performed.) (SE 19: 162)

Masochism, then, would appear to repress little, because it arises, of course, only from an improperly developed libido. Later in the essay, Freud remarks that because masochistic guilt is so deeply hidden in the unconscious, subjects do not immediately connect their symptoms with remorse (SE 19: 166). But in general, Freud cannot see a solution to what he sees as masochism's ultimate cause, the inadequate mastering of the death drive by the libido (SE 19: 164). Freud's need to construct a context for masochism as a fulfilling sexual activity finds its best expression in the superego's moral imperative to punish the naughty, selfish ego (SE 19: 167). In this way, Freud sees the sadistic superego and the masochistic ego as "complementary." As in "A Child is Being Beaten," the guilt induced by the masochistic fantasy reflects the subject's transgression against the Oedipus complex by not fixing on a proper sexual aim. Unfortunately, the masochistic subject is in danger of falling back into the Oedipus complex (SE 19: 167). Still, the erotogenic aspect of masochism avoids easy categorization, and Freud must simply abandon any analysis of this bodily pleasure that has no discernible libidinal goal.

If we follow Freud's judgment in "The Economic Problem of Masochism," that the masochistic disposition is rarely harmful and leaves indeterminate psychological scars, his effortless aligning of the fantasy with passive, shadowy "feminine" sexuality makes sense. The anatomical problems of making both genders responsive to the same developmental model impel Freud to construct ghostly psychoanalytic paradigms for which he can provide no concrete evidence, save readings of various symptoms. The cardinal characteristic of feminine sexuality, in Freud's eyes, is ambiguity. It is present everywhere for the Freudian woman in libidinal aims, genital organization, and relationships with other women. At least for men, psychoanalysis may provide a kind of cure that irons out these problems. For women, whose sex drives are motivated by penis envy, psychoanalysis provides a structure to explain their negation and lack, no matter how abstract it may seem. This *Penisneid* may help explain the attraction of some women to psychotherapy, as Freud writes in his 1932 lecture "Femininity":

> The wish to get the longed-for penis eventually in spite of everything may contribute to the motive that drives a mature woman to analysis, and what she

> reasonably expects from analysis—a capacity, for instance, to carry on an intellectual profession—may often be recognized as a sublimated modification of this repressed wish. (SE 22: 125)

Feminine sexuality, "unfinished" and regressive, must learn to express itself in masculine psychoanalytic terms in order to be analyzed.

The pathology of masochism as a form of masculine behavior is obvious and even plausibly explained in terms of the Oedipus complex. Yet masochism's manifestation in female subjects presents an even more worrisome problem for Freud's theories. How can one account for the operation of a fantasy that shifts in its libidinal aims (from sadism to masochism), is repressed even though it embodies a "proper" sexual attitude for women, and leaves, by Freud's account, no psychological scars or even interesting symptoms? It would seem that part of Freud's difficulty in bringing women into the psychoanalytic fold is grounded in the application of his already strong theories to a subject whose symptoms can only be misread according to a principally masculine paradigm. Masochism, in fantasy or in practice, resists elementary analysis here, because Freud puts such behavior outside of the parameters of the Oedipus complex. By treating the female beating fantasy as a narrative, the voyeuristic ending, that of the girl standing serenely next to the father figure and observing the beating, implies a kind of conscious independence from masculine sexual paradigms, an independence that Freud cannot openly acknowledge.

The same problem often occurs with Lacan's writings on female sexuality, as the reason for the difficulties Lacan encounters is found in his constant and necessary deferral to Freud. Lacan's brief commentary on masochism in "Guiding Remarks for a Congress on Feminine Sexuality" speaks volumes about the difficulty of assessing female sexuality with traditional psychoanalytic tropes. Lacan suggests that although female masochism may simply be a male "fantasy" (every man, after all, *should* desire a submissive woman), he questions the purpose of such a masochistic desire (FS 92). He then remarks in seeming exasperation, "not everything sexual may be made accessible to analysis," and his final puzzling statement on the matter appears as both a warning and cryptic dismissal of the question: "Have we remembered Freud's often repeated warning not to reduce the supplement of feminine over masculine to the complement of passive to active?" (FS 93). In coming to terms with Lacan's views, there is the inevitable problem of the masculine analyst adumbrating masculine-gendered concepts in the analytic relation with a female analysand. Through them, the female body, the focus of the masochistic relation, is elided in psychoanalytic discourse for the sake of an elegant model, and often the desire of the interpreter.

The Lacanian Perplex

Lacan's view of language as the principal issue of psychoanalysis allows him to translate Freud's mythic view of sexual and familial relations into well-defined structural terms. From the outset, Lacan models his psychoanalytic concepts on a distinctively masculine sexual organization, with his establishment of the phallus as a symbol for the object of desire and also the medium of linguistic expression. In "The Signification of the Phallus," Lacan comments briefly on the difficulties in determining woman's relationship to the phallus because women cannot, as such, participate in the castration complex as men do (E:S 272). However, because the castration complex exists as a "knot" in the libido, the subject, whatever its gender, cannot ignore the phallus's presence (E:S 271–272). As the progenitor of all the subject's desires, the phallus is "discovered" in and "speaks" through the Other (E:S 274). In turn, the "Demand" the subject puts on the Other is based on his expectations that the Other shall satisfy him with infinite love and possibly nourishment, the kinds of things a mother typically provides (E:S 275–276). But once the immediate need has been met and these hopes for the infinite satisfaction of need have assuredly been dashed, the feeling left over after the subtraction of the object from Demand is felt by the subject as *love.* Lacan terms this love "the relic of an obliteration"; the force of desire blinds the subject to the inadequacies of what he has (E:S 276). This sentimental feeling helps the subject to connect this Demand to the object of his desire; love is, in a sense, the consolation prize for having been castrated by language, because *jouissance,* true possession of the desired object, is always impossible.

The creation of meaning itself, of course, occurs according to the movements of the phallus, which embodies a kind of sadistic imperative in its complete "possession" of those things it signifies. Lacan prudently takes up the Kleinian challenge as to whether the phallic stage signals a repression of some kind, and if so, whether or not the phallus is a symptom (E:S 273). By positing the phallus as the source of all intelligibility and as the goal of the subject's desire, Lacan's answer is enthusiastically in the affirmative. In a way, Lacan's dogmatic valorization of the phallus puts the question out of the Kleinians' reach. The phallus is the supreme signifier, able to create meaning at will, and directs the subject in all its diverse lusts. The *traces* of signification, the presence of the phallus, and the "Law of the Father" are everywhere in language, selecting what can be included or disavowed in "meaningful discourse." The phallus creates meaning by attaching signifiers to signifieds; on reflection, one finds that the phallus has "always" been hidden in the object it touches:

> All of these remarks still merely veil the fact that it can play its role only when veiled, that is, as itself a sign of the latency with which any signifiable is struck [*frappé*], once it is raised to the function (*aufgehoben*) of signifier. (E:S 277/E 692)

"Frappé" implies a whole range of more or less violent meanings, from *knock* to *stamp* to *stun*. Brought out into the light of intelligibility, the phallus, having always been there, "reveals" the truth of the signified. Once the phallus raises the object to signification, the phallus "[marks] it as the bastard offspring of its signifying concatenation" (E:S 277), needing, apparently, no feminine counterpart to reproduce meaning.

Thus the proliferation of signifiers proceeds by a kind of violation of the signified. One cannot extend signification to an object without altering one's perception of it, and this necessary difference results in the prohibition of *jouissance*. Language deludes one into thinking that the object of desire is identical to its corresponding representation in language. However, by positing that women are objects of sexual desire that embody the veiled phallus, Lacan encounters the expected problem of linking the phallus to an Other that typifies extreme lack. Again, Lacan reveals the inability of his linguistic metaphors to represent women accurately because of sexual difference:

> Paradoxical as this formulation may seem, I am saying that it is in order to be the phallus—that is, the signifier of the Other's desire—that a woman rejects an essential part of femininity, namely, all its attributes, in the masquerade. It is for what she is not that she expects to be desired as well as loved. (E:S 279)

The tension in Lacan's work between the poetics and the technique of his psychoanalytic discourse comes to a head here; the definition of femininity as deception and pretension precludes any analytic investigation of the female subject itself. The last line of this excerpt can be read in at least two different ways. Either a woman is naturally deceptive and cannot fulfill masculine desire, or a woman expects to be desired because she is not a man, that she expects to be valued because she has an attractive façade. In other words, men participate in an imagined possession of women by assuming that they are shallow and easily read, and we are again back in the territory of "undeveloped" genital organization. If the phallus is discovered in woman, psychoanalysis dispels the vision men have of women as the earthly representatives of the mystic Other, capable of infinite mother-love. Imagining them as entry points to the Other, the male subject cannot accept a woman as a creature with a physical body, or worse yet, a similar subjectivity, if this overpowering "love" is the end result.

Lacan's discourse on female sexuality can never get past the female body. This is also Freud's principal complication. In "Guiding Remarks for a Congress on Female Sexuality," Lacan explores his frustration with the inability of psychoanalysis to apply its theories to women. The masculine libido, its imperative and purpose so clear-cut in its relation to the penis, becomes irrelevant when trying to talk about the vagina (FS 87). Lacan's remark that the symbols used to represent woman and the symbols of woman remain inseparable reveals a psychoanalytic model in which women, by responding to the mark of the phallus, are made into non-"feminine" creatures (FS 90). Lacan even creates a kind of homogeneous feminine desire out of the Freudian conception of penis envy; the desires of all women are bound together in their sexuality by their uniform *envy of the desire for the penis* (FS 94). The problem of connecting women to a phallic economy of desire has, for the moment, been solved by making her a sexual object, lacking libidinal motivation.

The lecture "Intervention on Transference" provides a glimpse into the only method Lacan finds to investigate female sexuality in any detail, although Lacan himself does not acknowledge it. Through the failure of Freud's analysis of Dora, Lacan's reading of psychoanalytic transference makes it possible to see the narrative of Dora as one that outlines Freud's possession of Dora's body through the seduction of psychoanalysis. The levels of symptomatic interpretation, deepened by the addition of Freud's insight into Dora's condition, dramatize the analytic "encoding" of Dora's body into Freudian discourse. At the source of Dora's hysteria is her anxiety about being used as a pawn in the game being played by her father, his mistress Frau K., and her husband Herr K., to whom Dora fears she has been promised as payment for his wife's favors. As Lacan tracks the transference between Dora and Freud, he notices that the master uncovers, but fails to discuss, a possible homosexual attraction of Dora's to Frau K., first detected in Dora's refusal to speak about her rival for the affections of her father (FS 65–66). In attempting to uncover the motive behind Dora's refusal to speak, Freud suggests that her fascination with Frau K. stems from repetition compulsion (FS 67). In this case, the "compulsion" is turned away from Dora herself and onto Frau K., suggesting to Lacan that the real subject at hand in the "mystery" of Dora's "bodily femininity" is a subject closed to Freud too (FS 67–68). Because Dora cannot fathom woman, Lacan observes, she undergoes a process of bodily fragmentation and fulfillment of infantilistic desires, such as thumb sucking, to deal with her confusion (FS 67).

This last observation alone can support a reading of "Dora" as a masochistic text. All Dora wants to do is to avoid the destructive, family-rending implications of sexuality itself, and this leads her to Frau K., a mother figure who torments and fascinates her at the same time. Unfortunately, Dora cannot express this desire of hers to get closer to Frau K., but, as Lacan cannily observes, she could not get a proper vision of *herself* as an object of desire in order to assume a normal sexual development in the first place (FS 68). And because Freud was also guided by the phallus (his own, in this case, perhaps), he never saw this possibility either, because he was too bound up in playing the transferential "role" of Herr K. (FS 69–70). In the end, transference is a poor substitute for *jouissance,* but remains, nevertheless, a worthy consolation prize for the analyst: "In other words, transference is nothing real in the subject other than the appearance, in a moment of stagnation of the analytic dialectic, of the permanent modes according to which it constitutes its objects" (FS 71). Lacan calls transference the "ruse" because it fills the emptiness of the deadlocks reached in the dialectic and provides a record of the movements of the symbolic order (FS 71–72). Most importantly, it compensates for the incompleteness of the cure, after Dora's termination of therapy.

Transference resembles Lacan's view of love in "The Signification of the Phallus," as it bridges the chasm between subject and Other, crushing the subject's conception of the latter. The narrative of "Dora" is the record of Dora's symptoms, and an account of her place in the symbolic order. Through its subtle observations and its transferential narrative, Freud's work draws a picture of female sexuality entirely through suggestion, and cannot produce the body itself. Even if Freud had succeeded in a "cure," the body of Dora, like the Queen's purloined letter, could have still been read and possessed by numerous analysts, each knowing more than the last. This is precisely what Lacan does in critiquing Freud's inability to see Dora's homosexual tendencies. As a countertransferential statement about Freud's desire for Dora in the personage of Herr K., "Dora" tells the story of Dora's ravishing on the page, just as Lacan possesses and defies Freud by pointing out his transferential mistakes.

The story of Dora, which is, after all, titled "Fragment of an Analysis of a Case of Hysteria," assuredly cannot produce even a merely satisfactory map of female sexuality. Freud's analysis fragments Dora by parsing out her meaning bit by bit in the uncovering of the diagnosis, symptom by symptom. But the work is indicative of a superior reader of the analysand, and therefore Freud must position himself as Dora's seducer. He cannot remain disinterested; woman cannot be "produced" or possessed without the mark of the foreign phallus. In "Seminar of 21 January 1975," Lacan attempts to explain the structure of female sexuality by returning to the "disturbances" produced by the castration complex, but he cannot come to a definite conclusion about it. Lacan reiterates his insistence on the symbolic order as that which expresses the continuity of the real:

> Nothing supposes it [demonstration in the real] other than the consistency for which the cord is acting here as the support. The cord is the foundation of accord. And, if I make a leap, I could say that the cord thus becomes the symptom of what the symbolic consists of. (FS 163)

The relation of the body to the symbolic order, however, is more difficult for him to discern. Lacan admits that one assumes the body follows on the same lines as the symbolic, but this is an inadequate explanation for the feminine phenomenon he tries to explain (FS 164). Speaking about the body and the representation of the body in analysis cannot solve the problem. The object is the cause for the subject, and as a result of writing, the subject informs everything it reaches with its own discourse (FS 165). Therefore, the existence of writing itself validates the repetition of the symptom, and one can write the symptom endlessly (FS 166). Lacan implies that because the "woman" cannot stand for all "women," this "symptom" known as woman can never be written conclusively. The only way to account for the persistence of the woman, therefore, is through *belief* (FS 168–169). Lacan claims that the existence of woman relies upon belief in "love," which is the supplement left over from a failed attempt to contextualize feminine sexuality in psychoanalytic terms (FS 170).

The inadequacy of either Freud or Lacan to deal properly with female sexuality could be reduced to the fact that because they are male analysts, they cannot fathom living in the female body. But the implications of Lacan's concept of role-playing in the transferential relation suggest the capabilities of psychoanalysis in the interpretation of the symbolic. The intrusion of the psychoanalyst's masculine ego into the interpretation of the symbolic order may play a part in male schematization. If the ego plays the imaginary to the superego's symbolic order, then the ego of the analyst, in this case Lacan and Freud, can never be neutral. As Lacan observes in the Rome Discourse, Freud's countertransference fails him because he cannot adopt the objective stance the analyst should exhibit. If one's own ego could be suppressed, then it could conceivably be possible to think oneself into another interpretation.

The female subject's shifting role in the beating fantasy suggests that her imaginary need not be structured like that of the superego-oriented male, whose role remains consistent throughout the fantasy itself.[1] The most important part of the female beating fantasy is that there is no counterpart in her version to repress her "true" desire, to be loved by the father. Instead of the mother beating the son, an action which masks the incestuous attachment to the father, the female subject's fantasy can represent a sexual development "successfully" negotiated. The female subject can be said to play *all* of the "subordinate" Oedipal roles in the beating fantasy. Once she has finished playing the role of the child being beaten, she appears as a mother looking on with the father as he beats his son or sons. Freud's conclusion that masochism represents a "regression" seems to be too hasty, especially when one considers that the female subject's fantasy complements that of the male subject. Clearly, she participates in the sadistic gratification of the father.

The problem of determining the meaning of this fantasy revolves around the lack of evidence and phallic analytic paradigms. In *Male Subjectivity at the Margins,* Kaja Silverman agrees with Freud that the true impetus behind the beating fantasy is not incestuous desire, but is more specifically that of entering into a homosexual relation with the father.[2] Silverman follows out the female fantasy according to the male fantasy, and finds, not surprisingly, that masochism is an untenable position for women because it manifests "imaginary relations outside the psychoanalytic paradigm" (Silverman 203). The masochistic fantasy of the girl implies an identification with the pleasure of the boys being whipped in the final stage. The fantasy allows the subject to identify with a form of feminized masculinity (Silverman 204), and Silverman sees this as a possible entry into a sexual relation, as the "I" of the female subject becomes "heteroidentified" (Silverman 205). Like Freud and Lacan, Silverman concludes that the female beating fantasy must again ultimately be connected with the convenient sexual difference provided by a heterosexual paradigm. The role of fantasy in the life of the child, whether to indicate a hidden fear or unconscious desire, has, for both Freud and Silverman, a specific purpose, namely to initiate the child in a sexual relation and to force it to occupy a sharply defined role.

However, for all gendered subjects, masochism throws the typical reading of fantasy, as a symptom of repressed material, into doubt. In addition, it completely overturns all expected forms of the sexual relation under the symbolic order. As behavior, masochism seems obviously pathological, if simply for the reason that pain is the opposite of pleasure. With Deleuze, one can read masochism as an act of self-expression and liberation, in its mocking subversion of sexual roles. Unlike the libidinal sexual aim, the masochistic fantasy illustrates the facility of the psyche to occupy a multiplicity of perspectives. This is a facility denied by Freud, and hinted at though unexplored by Lacan. The figure of the woman in Freud's and Lacan's texts avoids the violence of the phallus, and turns every beating into a satisfying sexual relation, even if they are vicarious and fantastic ones. The location of the fantasy is so deeply buried that neither Lacan nor Freud can reach the "true meaning" of the fantasy by simply using the Oedipus complex as a guide.

Fantastic Narratives: Deleuze and Sacher-Masoch

The discrepancy between the two subjects of sadism and masochism can be described by the distinction between the superego and ego. Freud's declaration of only one valid masculine libido in "Femininity" fails at explaining the thoroughgoing masochist, and the incommensurability of the two impulses of sadism and masochism in relation to each other (SE 22: 131). The rift between sadism and masochism is easy to grasp, as it embodies the distinction between the body's needs and what the psyche demands of it. The former represents the proliferation of sexual discourse itself, and the latter calls attention to the body so ignored in the first place by psychoanalysis. As Foucault remarks in *The Order of Things*, the Sadeian narrative annihilates desire by manifesting every whim on the spot, "endowed with life in the living body of desire."[3] Sade's works can be read as a parody of sexual desire in action, over-emphasizing the power of symbol and discourse in sexual behavior:

> In Justine, desire and representation communicate only through the presence of Another who represents the heroine to himself as an object of desire, while she herself knows nothing of desire other than its diaphanous, distant, exterior, and icy form as representation. Such is her misfortune: her innocence acts as a perpetual chaperone between desire and its representation. (Foucault 210)

The dispassionate demeanor with which Sade's darkly humorous grotesques pursue their various and complex pleasures in *Philosophy in the Bedroom* heightens the impact of Dolmance's vituperative philosophical musings on morality. By contrast, the world of Sacher-Masoch presents sexual play marked by an ironic inversion of the Law of the Father, and the rules of sexual economy, roles, and representation. As such, it presents a sexuality based on a broadly organic model, focused on the wants of the body rather than the warrants of the libido, or its Freudian laws. More importantly, its couching of sexuality *as primarily a fantastic narrative* frees it up for looser interplay than when beholden to the superego. The emphasis on the ego stresses the imaginary's reconfiguration of the symbolic order for its own amusement and momentary suspension of the masculine libido's authority.

The struggle to define masochism in terms of biological drives is indicative of the wholly fantastic nature of sexual masochism. The operation of masochism, divorced such as it is from "normal" sexual behavior, presupposes a radical division between the body and any appraisal of its teleology: masochism disproves the theory of the drive and is, in the words of Deleuze, a "defusion" of the instincts (M 116). In opposition to the symbolic representation that characterizes sadism, masochism hands control of the self over to the wants of the body in an attempt to avoid psychoanalytic interpretation. In "Coldness and Cruelty," an extended study of *Venus in Furs*, Gilles Deleuze tackles the question of masochism in its original literary form. Deleuze assesses Sade as an author who exploits the demonstrative possibilities of language and fills up the page with rather voluble characters who attempt to indoctrinate the reader into Sade's particular way of viewing the world (M 116). By contrast, Sacher-Masoch's text seems remarkably accepting and seductive, as its first-person narrative allows readers to project themselves into the story more easily. The distinguishing characteristic of the masochistic fantasy is its vagueness of details, including the subject's awareness of his own body (M 26). The masochistic body, Deleuze asserts, does not come into being until the masochistic torturer hurts it. Wherever the whip strikes, the expression of pain focuses the reader's attention onto that part receiving the blow. Thus one can say that the body arrives already fragmented rather than as a whole entity torn apart by violence, as in Sade. The masochistic narrative proceeds in an atmosphere of suggestion, as opposed to action and desire; masochism postpones the brief episodes of sexual pleasure, and they only come after exaggerated periods of waiting (M 32–33, 70). The subject willingly puts himself into the hands of the torturer in a manner that would be inimical to a sadist, as, for Sade, the focus must remain on the pleasure felt by the subject directing the fantasy. The violence of masochism throws the ambiguity of the subject's desires into sharp relief.[4] The authority figure in the fantasy, always a woman, is a "nurturing" stand-in for the mother, with whom the male subject has an imaginary relationship (M 46). In the "masochistic situation," there are no traces of the father's authority "borrowed" by the mother. Deleuze calls the masochistic fantasy an "ironic" inversion of the sexual relation. The male subject represents the superego's humiliation at the service of the ego (M 125–126), enacted by the figure of the "beating woman," a maternal torturer bound to the subject not by blood, but by pain (M 127).

Throughout the essay, Deleuze cultivates a therapeutic reading of masochistic fantasy that allows for the subject's capability to rehabilitate himself to the pleasures of the body. It is worth noting that Sacher-Masoch's fantasies start with a sexual relationship that is impermanent and fleeting. In *Venus in Furs*, Wanda's domination of Severin proves to be the cure for his romantic, "supersensual" feelings, which invited this abusive treatment. In the atmosphere of the masochistic imaginary, the male subject inserts himself into the feminine position and woman brings about his rebirth, without the mark of the father. This rebirth reasserts the real blood links of the mother to her offspring; its violation creates a body ready for all forms of pleasure rather than binding it for possession, as does the phallus. The ephemeral constitution of this sexuality positions it as a "complement" to typical forms of psychoanalytically validated behavior, which insist on oppressing bodily pleasure of all kinds by legislating its perversity, as such.

As a narrative, Sacher-Masoch's tale is essentially a *Künstlerroman* detailing Severin's sexual education, initiated by Wanda's intervention. The arc of the story moves through his first encounter with Wanda, his subsequent discovery of his appetite for humiliation, and "cure"; once Wanda leaves him for good, he discovers that he no longer desires humiliation, and then graduates to a healthy sexual outlook in which his rightfully dominant masculine role is assumed. In its original literary formulation, "masochism" reflects a classically fetishistic phase that must be abandoned on the path to sexual maturity, and indeed the story is itself told in flashback by a well-adjusted, more mature Severin. In an odd re-staging of the Sadeian corpus, the text of *Venus in Furs*, framed by the device of Severin's telling of his story to a friend, is also shot through with intense, abstract discussions about philosophy, political ideology, primitive concepts of ethnography, and so on, sandwiched between the flamboyant set pieces featuring Severin's domination at the hands of Wanda. The destructive presence in this brief novel, in essence its villain, is Severin himself, the stand-in for Sacher-Masoch, and he astutely realizes the profound depth of his aberration too late. The ultimate point of the torture in *Venus in Furs* is the sacrificing of Christian love in the name of pleasure, and with that, it signals the triumph of perversion. One of the initial encounters with Wanda yields this high-minded, essentially comic, exchange:

> "I am beginning to believe the incredible and understand the incomprehensible, namely the philosophy of the German people and the qualities of their womenfolk. It no longer surprises me in the least that you northerners are unable to love, for you have not an inkling what love is about."...
>
> "Yes, madam, as far as love is concerned our feelings are honorable and virtuous and our relations are durable."
>
> "And yet," interrupted the lady, "you nurse a secret craving for a life of sheer paganism. You modern men, you children of reason, cannot begin to appreciate love as pure bliss and divine serenity; indeed this kind of love is disastrous for men like you, for as soon as you try to be natural you become vulgar." (M 144–145)

Severin's vision of the Venus in Furs, warmed with pelts so that she can survive in a northern climate (M 149), reflects his dream of the transplantation of the Hellenic ideal into a new pagan era: the survival of an enlightened goddess-ideal in the age of reason. The tension between Severin's paganism and his desire to be noble drives the action of the story. His compulsion to abase himself influences Wanda in turn to humiliate him through various beatings and other more dramatic scenarios. The problem with the arrangement, as Wanda points out time and again, is that it will lead her into infidelity with another man, as this should be the ultimate humiliation (and therefore, delight) for Severin. The boundless love that Severin wishes to experience demands the unraveling of the relationship, and this sets the novel's plot in motion. The secret of masochism is that Severin himself is an artist, rather than a philosopher, as are Sade's protagonists. The tableau of the Venus in Furs is exciting to him, but it is wholly alienated from human behavior, and therefore exists as his abstract ideal.

The basis of the masochistic situation is the personality of Severin himself. The alienation that he feels no doubt stems from his lack of ambition and status as a lazy student trapped in his studies, a mood not helped by his leisurely surroundings: "The days drift aimlessly by in the little Carpathian health resort. I see nobody and nobody sees me" (M 152). Severin's feelings of inadequacy are, in some ways, expressions of class difference that give his fetish some traction. The roots of Severin's perversion are, in this case, Sacher-Masoch's. The classic masochistic fantasy is founded in the traumatic episode of Sacher-Masoch's being beaten as a child by his fur-wearing aunt for his rudeness to the chambermaid and the cook. In the novel, Severin lets on that such an episode occurred in his youth, and that it predated his initial encounters with Wanda. He mentions his "Cato-like austerity," yet claims that his "room looked like that of Doctor Faustus," and that "I studied indiscriminately" (M 174–175); Severin is the very picture of the modernist flâneur, an idle dilettante waiting for a muse.

Wanda protests all of this (Sacher-Masoch employs her throughout as a sensible counterweight to Severin's derangement) by bridling at the idea of her assuming the dominant and destructive position in her relations with Severin: "If all you say is true, then you are giving vice a halo; your ideal is a brazen and inspired courtesan. Ah, you are the sort of man who will utterly corrupt a woman" (M 177). Severin's entreaties to her to beat him represent, in a certain sense, the unprecedented reversal of the symbolic order, as Deleuze points out. But the paradox of masochism gives shape to the fantasy: the breaks in between his encounters with Wanda give a texture to Severin's fixation. It is worth noting that the first domination scene in *Venus in Furs* is told entirely in the present tense, lending a special immediacy to the action (M 184–185). Despite Severin's being whipped and beaten, it is Wanda who cries out in seeming agony:

> "Severin!"
> "Tread on me!" I cry, throwing myself before her.
> "I dislike playacting," says Wanda impatiently.
> "Then hurt me in earnest."
> A disturbing silence.
> "Severin, I am warning you one last time."
> "If you love me, be cruel to me," I implore. (M 186)

Wanda's principal critique of Severin is directed at his insistence on the artifice involved in fulfilling his desires, and this indeed is the soul of masochism. Severin's command to "hurt me in earnest" constitutes a strange invitation to break the frame of their interaction *as* artifice. She does not desire to beat Severin as such, but only does it for the intriguing nature of the enterprise:

> She stops. "I am beginning to enjoy it," she says. "That is enough for today. But a diabolical curiosity has taken hold of me; I want to see how far your strength will go; I have a dreadful desire to see you tremble under my whip, to see you suffer, to hear at last your moans and screams, your cries for mercy, while I go on whipping you without pity, until you lose consciousness. Yes, you have awakened dangerous tendencies in me....Now get up." (M 186–187)

Severin, true to his current hazy state of being, is unsure that his fantasy has come true: "I wake after a feverish night troubled by nightmares.... Which of my confused memories are real? What have I experienced, what have I merely dreamed? I have been whipped, that much is certain....And it was she who whipped me. Yes, now I know it all" (M 187). Wanda's reaction is typical for her role as the voice of reason: "'Try to forget yesterday's horrible scene,' she says, in a trembling voice. 'For your sake I satisfied those mad wishes, now let us be reasonable'" (M 187). Severin counters with the assertion that his aberrant wishes are merely an acting out of his desire to be rid of them: "'I really believe,' said Wanda thoughtfully, 'that your madness is nothing but an unsatisfied, diabolical sensuality. Such afflictions are a product of our monstrous side – if you were less virtuous you would be perfectly sane'" (M 188). Severin promises that one day he shall relent in his desire to be beaten. Yet, Severin romanticizes the relationship to Wanda to such an extent that the desire to be beaten, the inconstant struggle of the flesh with its desire to be loved, mimics the novelties of a new love relationship, with its unexpected twists and turns, minor tiffs, and revelations.

The distinguishing feature of masochism, the willful ignorance as to whether one's love is received or appreciated by the other party, is agreed upon, more or less, in the theatrical interaction of the masochistic situation. At one point Severin is prompted to write this effusive paean to his own mental torture: "How exquisite is this agonizing doubt! It is not our judgment that leads us...We are driven by a gentle and mysterious power that deprives us of all will and reason, and we are swept along with no thought for the morrow" (M 198). Wanda surprises Severin with a contract which outlines their relationship, stipulating that he is completely in her power as a slave (M 196–197); even at that, the details of this agreement fall by the wayside in the eventual outcome of their relationship. The real question is whether or not such devices can guarantee a "genuine" masochistic relationship, as even the presentation of the contract (along with a ghostwritten suicide note, tailor-made for Severin) participates in the theatricality of the masochistic situation.

Wanda's fulsome panegyric to Severin's resolve captures the implacable asceticism of Severin's character. She marvels that he is so willing to relinquish his role as the "father," and that he takes on a steely determination to rid himself of all temptation:

> I must admit that I am impressed by your behavior; it takes a certain strength, and one can only admire strength. I actually believe that in unusual circumstances and in a more exalted age than this, what appears to be your weakness would reveal itself as impressive power. Under the first emperors, you would have been a martyr, at the time of the Reformation an anabaptist; during the French Revolution you would have been one of those inspired Girondins who walked to the guillotine with the *Marseillaise* on their lips. But today, you are my slave, my... (M 212)

It is Severin's single-minded pursuit of dissolution that causes him to remove all strictures from his stage-managed relationship with Wanda. Severin's stubbornness has landed him in this untenable situation, and although his womanly ideal of the Venus in Furs appears to him on an ice floe, symbolic of the survival of the pagan ideal in the trappings of Christian culture, the same impression finds him paralyzed, unable to control the effects of what he has brought about: "I awoke during the night with a cry of terror; I had been dreaming that I was stranded on a field of ice. An Eskimo appeared on a sled drawn by reindeer; he had the face of the servant who had shown me to my unheated room" (M 214). Severin spots Wanda skating nearby, and upon her approach to him, she suddenly transforms into a polar bear and starts to devour his flesh, a clear harbinger of the calamity that Severin brings upon himself. Despite her warm feelings for him, she acquiesces to his demands, becomes empowered by playing the dominant role, and their budding courtship is utterly destroyed. The novel arrives at its climax when Severin is ordered by Wanda to be whipped by her new lover, a Greek prince; supposedly, this fits in with the plan of Severin's humiliation (M 266). Severin cannot help but play along, and although he enjoys it he also feels intense shame, probably because he is being whipped by a man, which violates the masochistic paradigm (M 266–268). As Wanda and her lover leave him for good, it seems that Severin did really wish to love Wanda, but it was too late for either of them to regain their innocence.

At the end of the novel, Severin, happily married and secure in his role as a patriarch, explains to his interlocutor, "The treatment was cruel but radical, and the main thing is that I am cured." In ending the lesson, Severin makes this summary judgment of his experience:

> The moral is that woman, as Nature created her and as man up to now has found her attractive, is man's enemy; she can be his slave or his mistress but never his companion. This she can only be when she has the same rights as he and is his equal in education and work. For the time being there is only one alternative: to be the hammer or the anvil. I was fool enough to let a woman make a slave of me, do you understand? Hence the moral of the tale: whoever allows himself to be whipped deserves to be whipped. But as you see, I have taken the blows as well; the rosy mist of supersensuality has lifted, and no one will ever make me believe that the sacred wenches of Benares or Plato's rooster are the images of God. (M 271)

The unequal relationship, as Severin puts it, is afforded by the comedy of the masochistic stage-performance. It is something that, from the masochistic viewpoint of the emasculated man, he can easily accomplish. What the masochistic fantasy offers is the dissolution of the Apollonian mind into Dionysian carnality; the masochistic fantasy is merely a phase that offers a momentary regression into pure sensuality. In the end, by Severin's estimation, masochism is simply a jejune detour on the path to adulthood and procreation. It may purge one of the feminizing impulses that lie hidden, but it is entirely done through the play of signifiers and fantasy. Isolated in his protracted post-adolescent collegiate funk, Severin constructs an abstract libidinal narrative for himself, in order to create a kind of imaginary trauma. Once the cure is delivered, Severin lets himself access a "normal" sexuality by assuming a traditionally prescribed role. What is at issue for Severin in his fantasy is exorcising the ghost of the Oedipus complex, and combating fear with desire.

Proust: Memory, Fantasy, and Nostalgia

Although Proust's *À la recherche du temps perdu* has, over the course of a near-century of criticism, been viewed as a rich source for insights on love, loss, and desire, it has been little treated as a profoundly masochistic text. Aside from an oft-cited scene in *The Guermantes Way*, where the infamous Baron de Charlus is glimpsed in the act of being whipped, masochism is not a concept often linked to the musings of Proust's narrator, Marcel.[5] But through his nostalgia and his fantasies concerning Swann, rife with ambiguity and aestheticization, hallmarks of the masochistic text, Marcel works through his pain over his memories of Gilberte. Throughout the novel, Marcel's relationship with Gilberte (complicated, to say the least) is prefigured by the narrative of Swann's courtship of Odette, which comprises most of "Swann in Love." Marcel's personality would seem to fit with that of a paranoiac; the meaning of the famous maternal kiss would shift depending on the context, and would appear to be completely withheld when Swann happened to drop by in the evening. In this instance, Swann's presence would seem to ignite a potential Oedipal rivalry. In fact, the presence of Swann in the "Combray" portion establishes his character as a vehicle for Marcel's projections regarding his doomed suit of Gilberte, such that Marcel's impressions of Swann's love affair constitute a masochistic fantasy, ambiguous to the point that Swann and Marcel are nearly indistinguishable from one another.[6]

From the very beginning, Swann is made to feel as though Odette is a strange imposition on his desires: "[Odette was] endowed with a kind of beauty which left him indifferent, which aroused in him no desire, which gave him, indeed, a sort of physical repulsion, as one of those women of whom all of us can cite examples, different for each of us, who are the converse of the type which our senses demand" (RT 213). Indeed, Odette seems to be not so much a person but rather a burdensome thing: "[she had] the appearance of being composed of different sections badly fitted together" (RT 215). All the same, Swann feels that pride at Odette's wanting him to visit: "But, after Odette had left him, Swann would think with a smile of her telling how the time would drag until he allowed her to come again" (RT 215). As such, Odette's body becomes a fetish object upon which Swann depends for satisfaction:

> ...the image of Odette de Crécy came to absorb the whole of these day-dreams, if the memory of her could no longer be eliminated from them, then her bodily imperfections would no longer be of the least importance, nor would the conformity of her body, more or less than any other, to the requirements of Swann's taste, since, having become the body of the woman he loved, it must henceforth be the only one capable of causing him joy or anguish. (RT 217)

Odette, as we shall see in the course of the narrative, is the delusion under which Swann shall labor for most of his time in the spotlight.

True to Sacher-Masoch's novel, Swann too plays the part of the flâneur, waiting for a kind of purpose in his life, and perhaps finding it in the impossible prospect of loving Odette. It is also interesting that Marcel, in remembering Swann, should do so after "Combray," where he confines his reminiscences to his own childhood. It is as if this period of Swann's life were Marcel's own adolescence, and in this passage Marcel speaks of Swann's attempts to overcome his juvenile laziness and conscious lack of an identity almost as if they were his own:

> He had so long ceased to direct his life towards an ideal goal, confining himself to the pursuit of ephemeral satisfaction, that he had come to believe, without ever admitting it to himself in so many words, that he would remain in that condition for the rest of his days...in his conversation he took care never to express with any warmth a personal opinion about anything, but instead would supply facts and details which were valid enough in themselves and excused him from showing his real capacities. (RT 229)

Swann's desire for Odette becomes a kind of quest, enough for Marcel to paint it in bluntly mythical terms: "From time to time the shadowy figure of a woman gliding up to Swann, murmuring a few words in his ear, asking him to take her home, would make him start. Anxiously he brushed past all these dim forms, as though among the phantoms of the dead, in the realms of darkness, he had been searching for a lost Eurydice" (RT 252). Following the rules of courtly love, Swann is more than willing to abase himself in front of his potential mistress, as when he chases down Odette's carriage, clutching a bouquet intended for her. The ensuing dialogue is nearly at a screwball-comic pitch, as Swann abruptly loses what little composure he may have had when initially meeting Odette, babbling on in an embarrassing fashion: "No, no, you mustn't speak. You'll get out of breath again. You can easily answer in signs; I shall understand. Really and truly now, you don't mind my doing this?....Tell the truth, now" (RT 254). Odette's response is that of the indulgent parent patting the head of a naïve child: "Still smiling, she shrugged her shoulders ever so slightly, as who should say, 'You're quite mad; you know very well that I like it'" (RT 254). Regardless of its consequences, Swann realizes that he has no choice in the matter about loving Odette, and that such a love has a creative, aesthetic attraction that he cannot deny: "For Swann was once more finding in things, since he had fallen in love, the charm that he had found when, in his adolescence, he had fancied himself an artist; with this difference, that the charm that lay in them now was conferred by Odette alone" (RT 261). Swann is now firmly in Odette's power, even if the nature of their relationship has not been defined, causing him to feel groundless jealousy, the effects of which consume him later in the novel.[7]

Very quickly Swann understands that his obsession punishes him in the same way that it brings him aesthetic joy. Swann's jealousy attached to Odette instantiates itself in discrete moments and images that wound him:

> His jealousy, like an octopus which throws out a first, then a second, and finally a third tentacle, fastened itself firmly to that particular moment, five o'clock in the afternoon, then to another, then to another again. But Swann was incapable of inventing his sufferings. They were only the memory, the perpetuation of a suffering that had come to him from without....And thus his jealousy did even more than the happy, sensual feeling he had originally experienced for Odette had done to alter Swann's character, completely changing, in the eyes of the world, even the outward signs by which that character had been intelligible. (RT 309)

Swann's obsession with Odette is primarily masochistic, in that his affections are governed by a series of discrete, traumatic moments which might, perhaps, add up to love. Proust's method of casting back the mind of the narrator in order to recover these scenes is more than something of an aesthetic gambit—it is also a question of Marcel's remembrance of Swann, recast in his own image. For all of this, the question is not so crucial when dealing with Swann himself, but rather the memories of Marcel, and his parallel pursuit of Gilberte. Marcel's identification with Swann represents a fantastical leap in order to conceive of the birth and origins of Gilberte, and as such, what wounds Marcel also wounds the imaginary Swann. His identification with Swann, viewed through the idealizing gauze of the imagination, is purely mythological.

Other set pieces in the novel further foreground the masochistic qualities of the text in the prolonging of Swann's deliciously tormented courtship. Swann's love for Odette, such as it is, is structured around absence and losses: "And such moments as these, in which she forgot Swann's very existence, were more useful to Odette, did more to bind him to her, than all her coquetry. For in this way Swann was kept in that state of painful agitation which had already been powerful enough to cause his love to blossom, on the night when he had failed to find Odette at the Verdurins' and had hunted for her all evening" (RT 322). Although Odette herself turns out to be elusive, her presence and speech do more to wound him than do her absences; Swann cannot bear to hear from her about her various engagements, as he suspects that everyone she mentions is a secret paramour (RT 323). As it is, Odette ruthlessly manages her time spent with Swann, relegating him to the most marginal of roles by forcing him to stand idly by as she prepares herself for an evening on the town:

> Rare though they became, those moments did not occur in vain. By the process of memory, Swann joined the fragments together, abolished the intervals between them, cast, as in molten gold, the image of an Odette compact of kindness and tranquility, for whom he was later to make sacrifices which the other Odette would never have won from him. But how rare those moments were, and how seldom he now saw her! (RT 342–343)

In light of this treatment, Swann feels that his pursuit of Odette is not in serious jeopardy, but that he is fated to be with her, and that this treatment shall continue without abatement. Both time itself, and the life he once imagined for the both of them, seem impossible for him to fathom, as his is a pain triggered by the merest signal from Odette: "But that inner future, that colourless, free-flowing stream, was suddenly convulsed by a single remark from Odette which, penetrating Swann's defences, immobilised it like a block of ice, congealed its fluidity, froze it altogether..." (RT 386–387). Or, as when Swann ruminates on the possibility that Odette is having an affair with Madame Verdurin, Proust brings out the character of Swann's attachment to Odette as a corrosive one that, without which, he would knowingly take leave of his identity:

> Swann had prepared himself for every possibility. Reality must therefore be something that bears no relation to possibilities, any more than the stab of a knife in one's body bears to the gradual movement of the clouds overhead, since those words, "two or three times," carved as it were a cross upon the living tissues of his heart. Strange indeed that those words, "two or three times," nothing more than words, words uttered in the air, at a distance, could so lacerate a man's heart, as if they had actually pierced it, could make a man ill, like a poison he has drunk....And yet this Odette from whom all this evil sprang was no less dear to him, was, on the contrary, more precious, as if, in proportion as his sufferings increased...He wanted to devote more care to her, as one tends a disease which one has suddenly discovered to be more serious. (RT 395)

The symptoms personify the illness. At times, Swann seems to regard Odette as a mere figment of his own devising that could be willed away, as when he wishes for her a "painless" death, brought about by being run over by a carriage, crossing the busy Parisian streets (RT 386). In looking back on his early infatuation, Swann realizes that his humiliation did not emerge over the course of his acquaintance with Odette but had been there from the beginning: "And Swann could distinguish, standing motionless before that scene of remembered happiness, a wretched figure who filled him with such pity, because he did not at first recognize who it was, that he had to lower his eyes lest anyone should observe that they were filled with tears. It was himself" (RT 377).

The end of "Swann in Love" completes the circuit initiated in "Combray." In remembering Gilberte, Marcel realizes that the moments that give him pain are nevertheless structured by his love for her. Moreover, he sees that he had judged Swann wrongly as a young child, being unable to understand his torment at the time; this understanding has arrived through the self-justifying empathy of his reconstructed memories.[8] He understands that there was nothing of *her* in these discrete instances, and that her love had been nothing but a ruse of his own mind and memory (RT 446–447). The end of "Swann in Love," which looks forward to *Within A Budding Grove*, features Marcel's mediation on the transitoriness of female companionship:

> But, forced for so many years now, by a sort of grafting process, to share in the life of feminine humanity, they called to my mind the figure of the dryad, the fair worldling, swiftly walking, brightly coloured, whom they shelter with their branches as she passes beneath them, obliging her to acknowledge, as they

> themselves acknowledge, the power of the season; they recalled to me the happy days of my unquestioning youth, when I would hasten eagerly to the spots where masterpieces of female elegance would be incarnate for a few moments beneath the unconscious, accommodating boughs. (RT 459)

Perpetually out of Marcel's grasp, women appear in his life and then fade, his obsessional tendencies transforming them into objects of longing, deliverers of curses and blessings. As for Marcel, he is all too willing to submit himself to feminine domination, and in doing so he invites trauma into his life. Later, in the second division of *À la recherche du temps perdu,* Marcel muses on his propensity for viewing women as destinations in his life: "We construct our lives for one person, and when at length it is ready to receive her that person does not come; presently she is dead to us, and we live on, prisoners within the walls which were intended only for her" (RT 682). In Proust's masterwork, the suffering that is undergone in the name of memory is resolved only through interrogating those memories from the start, and understanding the shape of one's imagined destiny through those fateful figures chosen to represent it.

Masochism: Approved (Père)version

Throughout this discussion, I have (perhaps all too blithely) taken masochism as being something of widely understood and accepted phenomenon. The idea of masochism has a very pedestrian definition: the enjoyment of suffering in lieu of behavior normally viewed as being pleasurable. Here, I have considered masochism in the analytic sense as a fetish, rather than a psychological attitude. It is one thing to understand masochism as being a quality attached to one's personality (namely, that a person who enjoys studying differential equations must be masochistic), and quite another to encounter the phenomenon analytically. It can be seen that masochism is entirely an aspect of the rampant signification instigated by the classically male libido, in the analytic, "technical" sense.

Freud's critique of masochism condemns it, like other "perversions," as a barrier to normal sexual development. But the concept that masochistic fantasy embodies—the victory of the body's pleasure over the stern proclamations of the superego—presents a challenge to Lacan's dictum that the unconscious is always structured and accessible like a language. The conception of fantasy as '"symptom" cannot apply to masochism as such, because it represents an entirely different sexual order than that which Freudian analysis supports. As Jacqueline Rose observes, depending upon the kind of emphasis put on the symptom, the visual aspect of fantasy can reach any form of the vision within the subject's unconscious, ranging from simple visual impression to full symbolic constitution.[9] In other words, the imaginary's *interpretation* of the symbolic is the key in the masochistic fantasy, not the position of the symbol in discourse. Because masochism does not respond to the typical libidinal "aim," the ironic and illogical beating fantasy completely divests its figures of their full symbolic weight. Fantasy is present not as a symptom signaling repression, but as an end in itself, opening a realm of unrestricted symbolic play where desire can desire whatever object it chooses.

Freud's young girl, by watching the father flail the children, may perhaps feel guilt at being a voyeur, a "non-sexual" being, as Freud intimates. But one could look at this guilt as a projection of Freud's embarrassment at being found out by the girl, who sees him reifying the sexual body according to an ancient fable. She *sees* the violations he perpetrates on behalf of his own desires, and enjoys them nevertheless, regardless of their relation to her sexual being. The more the libido is abstracted from biological drives, the freer one is to attach spurious desires to any combination of circumstances and images; the exploration of this curious fantasy is such that it reveals the power of fantasy itself, and the energy it extends to the fantasist. A significant part of this fantasy is the floating status of the subject, able to light on various aspects of the scenario without regard to libidinal priorities. Not least of these is its voyeuristic dimension, which participates in the visual vocabulary of paranoia and the fetishization of images; in this case, it is the feeling of power in overseeing and directing the domination and humiliation of the subject, even if it is oneself.

The explanation of the value of masochism can also obtain on the level of psychoanalytic reading itself, as it too engages in the power of overseeing the violation of the body. Lacan's analogous study of this reading relation, "Seminar on the Purloined Letter," shows Freud's formidable structuralist interpreter exploring the nature of reading and violation. The multiple levels of perspective on the meaning of the forever-closed letter are shared by an ever-widening circle of readers, each able to see the errors their predecessors have made. Lacan's distinct advantage over Freud is that he reduces Freud's figures to symbols in everyday discourse and in the psychoanalytic dialectic; Lacan's open-ended style enables a certain latitude in reading his own work as well as Freud's. As there shall always be other readers, there shall be extensions and refinements of psychoanalytic theory; each body of work shall have its detractors and "mistakes," ready to be made objects of voyeuristic satisfaction, as with Lacan's reading of "Dora." In this case, the structural oppositions of Lacan and apparitions of desire that haunt them point to those aporias Lacan's allusive style may not have foreclosed yet, so that new readings may be explored. The masochist scenario, by endowing the subject with the power of fantasy, sidesteps the masculine in order to release the possibilities of psychoanalytic reading.

5

Narcissism: Lacan, The Symptom, and the Joycean Uses of Psychoanalysis

Despite modernism's studied pursuit of radically new forms of literary expression, the reverberations of the Victorian *fin-de-siècle*, whose dominant figure was the Paterian artist, charged with bringing forth the beautiful, were still felt by modernism's first generation. Most notably, Oscar Wilde was identified with this artistic pursuit, and his work and public identity were not so easily forgotten. Although capable of potent moral judgments in his work, the perceived shallowness of Wilde's persona projects what may be termed, for lack of a better word, narcissism. The primitive diagnosis of homosexuality, a residual myth which persists even today, is that such an orientation constitutes a case of arrested sexual development. As Freud remarks in "Libido Theory and Narcissism:"

> Object-choice, the step forward in the development of the libido which is made after the narcissistic stage, can take place according to two different types: either according to the narcissistic type, where the subject's own ego is replaced by another one that is as similar as possible, or according to the attachment type, where people who have become precious through satisfying other vital needs are chosen as objects by the libido as well. A strong libidinal fixation to the narcissistic type of object-choice is to be included in the predisposition to manifest homosexuality. (SE 16: 426–427)

However unsophisticated this analysis may seem at first blush, it nevertheless reflects a deeply rooted anxiety about homosexuality's supposed "perversion" of the heterosexual relation. Wilde also distinguishes himself by being, in some respects, the most anti-social of creatures, the writer working from within his imagination, needing solitude in order to write. In this sense, Wilde is doubly perverse for affecting a flamboyant social persona, and also for donning the laurels of the proto-modernist artist.

One might also consider James Joyce's relationship to Wilde. Even though they are poles apart in terms of literary output, they share the Irish modernist traits of exile, censorship, and charges of vulgarity, literary and otherwise.[1] Fortunately for Joyce's own development as an artist, Wilde predated him by a mere twenty years or so, and Joyce could therefore benefit from his inspirational presence and figurative martyrdom. From the first pages of *Ulysses*, Joyce rather explicitly lays claim to Wilde as an idol for his fictional alter ego, Stephen Dedalus. The opening chapter of the novel, with its homosocial triad of Mulligan, Haines, and Stephen, who engage in flippant Wildean banter, contrasts sharply with the comfortable middle-class respectability of Leopold Bloom, who emerges as the novel's central figure. As the self-obsessed Stephen Dedalus was the focus of Joyce's previous novel, *A Portrait of the Artist as a Young Man*, Bloom's psyche, aided with the technique of interior monologue, is the major staging area for the themes of *Ulysses*.

Despite Bloom's mundane surroundings, the kind of ambition Joyce has for his Everymannish protagonist is intriguing. To be Bloom is not only to bear the weight of an estranged wife and unsettled home, but also to measure up to Joyce's Odyssean and modernist conceits. Joyce made no secret of the symbolic keys to his work, even to the point of laying out a plan of sorts for the novel in the Gilbert-Gorman schema, where the "colors," bodily organs, academic disciplines, and narrative "technics" of each chapter are revealed.[2] The outline itself, aside from being a great help to first readings of *Ulysses*, endorses Joyce's own "unofficial" interpretation of the novel as an encyclopedic commentary on every aspect of intellectual and artistic life, history, the canon, and the like. Even decades after its publication, Joyce's presence still attends the text, offering a ready-made apparatus for interpreting his intimidating work. Bloom himself, however, is far from being the kind of aesthetically astute protagonist Joyce makes of Stephen; he is pressed into service by Joyce to be the central figure in the "narcissistic" chapter of *Ulysses*, "Lotus-Eaters."

But is Bloom up to the task of being Joyce's narcissistic exemplar? Although introspective, Bloom identifies himself sexually with Molly (specifically, her *derrière*), is deferential to others in social interaction, and in general lacks the ability to sustain any narcissistic fantasy. With

Ulysses, I seek to locate an instance in which Bloom, Joyce's most fully realized literary character, attempts to fulfill his creator's desire that he should indulge in the kind of narcissism the modern artistic type himself favors. In doing so, Joyce complicates the sexuality of the artist in his work, and raises implicit problems of constructing the narcissist as conclusively gendered in any fashion. By removing the burden of narcissism in *Ulysses* from Stephen (the likeliest suspect), one gains insight into a reading of Bloom as a specimen of the truly Joycean artist, the one who engages in fabricating allusive, symbolic fantasy, only to have it fail him in the end. The question of gender and sexuality in *Ulysses* is deeper than Joyce originally suggested in his presentation of Bloom, in the novel, as a "new womanly man." In this chapter, I shall examine the interaction between the discourses of psychoanalysis, structuralism, and Joycean rhetoric in order to redefine the sexual landscape of Joycean narcissism, not only in *Ulysses*, but also within Joyce's style. Joyce skirts questions of heterosexuality and covers his evasion up by positing an incomplete heterosexual fantasy for Bloom, while deliberately tweaking the act of psychoanalytic reading along the way.

Unlike its colorful forbears of the late Victorian and Edwardian ages, modernist narcissism exists as introspection without an image to project, foregoing the presence of a governing superego. In Lacan's appraisal of Joyce, "Joyce le symptôme," one finds a way of reading Joyce that allows the text to escape psychoanalysis and avoid the late-Lacanian complex of the real, symbolic, and unconscious. *Ulysses* proper is a text that refuses parentage, denying both father and mother, and "Lotus-Eaters" leaves the question of Bloom's heterosexual masculinity more complicated than it first appears on the surface. I propose a reading of Bloom's narcissism as a rejection of sexuality to the extent that he threatens to break out of the symbolism of *Ulysses* and his roles of father, lover, and parent, most of all in light of the final image of "Lotus-Eaters," Bloom's limp penis floating in the bath. Bloom even fails as a narcissist, gives up on desire, and languidly wishes a return to the womb. In doing so, Bloom sidesteps the Law of the Father, the Oedipus complex, and the entire Freudian conceptual scheme in favor of the pleasure of "meaningless," fragmentary fantasy, which itself never produces an autoerotic payoff. Bloom's "narcissistic" chapter frustrates all conventional psychoanalytic readings of the operations of desire. As a coda to this chapter, I offer a discussion of Joyce's relationship with his daughter Lucia, her analysis with Carl Jung, and *Finnegans Wake*.

Freud: The Ambiguity of Narcissism

Despite its promising title, Freud's essay "On Narcissism: An Introduction" fails to provide a detailed psychoanalytic explanation of narcissism's sexual dynamic. Freud's emphasis lies more on the ego's object choices rather than on an account grounded in self-regarding and self-image, after the narrative of the Greek myth of Narcissus. The problem that Freud faces in "On Narcissism" is twofold: he first tries to answer the question of narcissism's relation to the male ego, and then tries to address the difference between the libidinal ego and the ego's object. Throughout, Freud subtly makes the distinction between simple auto-eroticism and the question of narcissism. That he cannot make this difference satisfyingly clear alerts the modern Freudian to the absence of the id-ego-superego triad, which would make its appearance later in the 1923 watershed text *The Ego and the Id.* In the middle stage of Freud's thought, there is only the ego, and the vague shape (and agency) of the unconscious; what Freud calls "conscience" is an impoverished, nebulous stand-in for what would later become the ultra-rational superego (SE 19: 36–37). Yet Freud continues on the same lines as found in the third chapter of *The Ego and the Id* by claiming that the "ego ideal," the "energetic reaction-formation" against object choice, had already been stated in the earlier essay. This is a disingenuous statement on Freud's part, as the moral consequences of the superego are absent in this particular formulation of the psyche.

"On Narcissism" designates two possibilities of cathection for the ego, either external (focusing on a person or object) or ideal (focusing on oneself). The latter choice poses a serious problem for Freud, as his conception of narcissism in the 1919 essay has no real sexual dynamic; instead it is a manifestation of neurosis, with no sexual investment at all. The subject has a profound sense of narcissism in that he has no need of the external world of objects, preferring introspection in all matters (SE 14: 86). The problem of curing the narcissist is relatively straightforward: the therapist must lead the subject back to interaction with the social world. Although this behavior has little erotic import, it does fall into Freud's biographically grounded developmental scheme. Narcissism, Freud asserts, has its origin in the experience of childhood introspection. As Freud investigates the infantile roots of this pathological tendency, he determines that narcissism has some necessary relation to the Oedipus complex, and the idiosyncrasies of parentage. Parents endure a "second childhood" along with their offspring, and this shows that the split between object and ego has somehow been rectified (SE 14: 91). This is reflected in the relationship of the subject's ego to the "ego ideal," rhetorically converted by Freud into the superego, which bears the stamp of the father. The difference between simple inwardness and narcissism manifests itself in the kind of neurosis to which Freud refers. It remains for Freud, in this essay, to define the difference between simple introspection and full-blown narcissism. For a subject's narcissism to be viable, there had to have occurred some trauma between childhood and adulthood, outside of the sexual development narrative. This vague trauma resulting in narcissism remains a mystery for Freud, although here as in all psychological matters, Freud claims that he tries to exclude everything in his inquiry that is "different from nature" (SE 14: 78–79). The same irreconcilable split, between ego and world as well as ego and object, must nevertheless persist in order to define what Freud calls "neurosis." The specter of this neurosis informs the idea of narcissism to the extent that Freud speaks of it in terms of schizophrenia, alienated from the sexual exchange:

> ...an anchorite of this kind, who 'tries to erase every trace of sexual interest' (but only in the popular sense of the word 'sexual') does not even necessarily display any pathogenic allocation of the libido. He may have diverted his sexual interest away from human beings entirely, and yet may have sublimated it into a heightened interest in the divine, in nature, or in the animal kingdom, without his libido having undergone an introversion on to his phantasies or a return to his ego. (SE 14: 80–81)

The principal problem described here is that of managing sublimation without reverting to eroticism. In other words, the engine of Freudian psychoanalytic development, the Oedipus complex, must be dropped in order to counter the problem of narcissism, which eschews the libido entirely: this results in a complete overturning of the developmental Freudian universe. Narcissism ratifies the possibility that not all psychological conditions are grounded in gender, sexual economy, or the withholding of the mother's affections. The idea that art can persist as a necessary impulse separated from the id threatens the dominance of the sexual drive in Freud. One may wish to see this Freudian avoidance of the issue in another way, however, other than as a failure to connect the Oedipal sexual economy with the life of the subject. This early treatment of narcissism may be understood as a purely symbolic, anti-empirical, figurative take on the sexual development of the creative, "fertile" mind—the artisan, the writer, the sculptor, perhaps even the psychoanalyst—who constructs a linguistic phallus to compensate for the absence of the superego's stern, conformist authority.

One option open to the Freudian artist, then, is to construct a kind of artificial ego without the danger of sexual sublimation. By this logic, the artist then must give birth to a kind of incomplete self, minus the id, and in order to plug the void left by the absence of the id, fill the gap with art. Freud remarks on the egocentric nature of art in describing the artist's response to bodily anguish with a couplet by Wilhelm Busch: "Concentrated is his soul...In his molar's narrow hole" (SE 14: 82). This literary example has an interesting meta-Freudian reading; the "molar's narrow hole" evokes castration, extrapolating from the dream symbology of *The Interpretation of Dreams*. Whether it refers to a simple cavity or tooth extraction, the artist must attempt to fill the hole in the place of the phallus, the source of sexual desire. Freud implies that the artist does not sublimate in order to reify sexual desire, but rather to cover the lack of the phallus by turning his self-image, his ego ideal, into his own psychic phallus to admire.

The question of narcissism's possible resolution, and its place within the reductive Freudian view, has a contradictory set of possible answers. Freud even says that the castration complex does not figure into the question of narcissism, because there is no object to focus on, no "loss," simply a mysterious libidinal energy and ego-focus with no discernible outlet for aggression or libidinal cathection. This "energy" cannot be thought of as filling a gap where there was none before. Instead of having been castrated through the Oedipus complex, the only thing for the narcissist to do is to cathect his own ego, thus confusing the process of sublimation (SE 14: 100). The ego itself is subjected to idealization, an action Freud characterizes in Platonic terms. But the reason that narcissism is unsatisfactory as a sexual orientation is that the ego feels the need to be loved by others, and the presence of others disturbs the simple self-to-self relation narcissism promotes. By pursuing affection, the narcissist's paranoia about being unloved is soothed. However, because there is no sexual exchange, there can be no transfer of erotic energy and the narcissist feels no "conscience" (Freud's own term) telling him what to do, as the narcissicist is impotent and lacks self-esteem (SE 14: 98). The implementation of self-love and the choice, perhaps, to become a narcissist, prevent the stigma of impotence from being branded onto the subject. Impotence is the byword for Freud's narcissistic analysis, as it implies a lack of phallic power without the nostalgia for the phallus that accompanies castration. The cure for narcissism, if one is warranted, is the damaging of the ego by paranoia, the fear that one is not being adored (SE 14: 101). By the same token, Freud realizes that the sexual relation can be taken in exchange for the narcissistic relation.

Freud hints in this essay that the artistic impulse assists the subject in resisting the Oedipus complex. The principal way of healing the breach between them is to consider sublimation apart from sexual economy. The impulse to create art no longer stems from sexual neurosis, but from an interposition against the figure of the father, because the subject recognizes that the wound was first inflicted by the father, and he refuses to see himself through the father's eyes: this is the subject's rejection of the Oedipus complex. Narcissism on this level naturally must be idealized and therefore symbolic. In feeling the injury to the self-image, the nascent narcissist is able to project desire outward, but with the sense that everything must serve his own wants, not those of the father. Yet in the split between mere pleasure and ego-cathection, the Freudian narcissist favors the former and thus has no internal self-image with which to fall in love. Rather than being obsessed with one's appearance, Freud's narcissist has no sexual impetus whatsoever, and is prevented from entering the Oedipal economy of desire.

As an early attempt at diagnosing narcissism, Freud's essay makes headway in only defining the structure of the unconscious, which he more fully develops in his work of the 1920s. Because narcissism is relegated to being merely neurosis, and possibly leading to schizophrenia, this points to Freud's denial to make sense of it sexually. In a way, Freud banishes the question to abstract realms, never to be explained fully inside the Oedipus complex. The parallel I wish to draw here with Joyce necessitates an anti-Oedipal reading of Joyce's symbology, which on the whole in *Ulysses* leads to a definite heterosexual economy, but ends up being subverted by the "artistic" mindset that made its composition possible. Joyce's own allusive imagination lays the groundwork for such an unprincipled reading of his work. Joyce's style, by putting Bloom on the spot, demonstrates that play and momentary satisfaction in the text overrule concerns of plot or narrative. The events and mental impressions presented in the narrative of *Ulysses* are traditionally read as being loaded with import, as if the reader were always on the edge of something mysterious and profound; one is induced to read Joyce in an expected fashion given its status as a "Joycean" text.

Confronted with Stephen Dedalus's introspection and artistic bearing, taking up the issue of narcissism in *Ulysses* might very well begin and end with Stephen. Scenes such as the Martello tower sequence ape Wildean drawing-room burlesque:

> — Look at yourself, he said, you dreadful bard!
> Stephen bent forward and peered at the mirror held out to him, cleft by a crooked crack. Hair on end. As he and others see me. Who chose this face for me? This dogsbody to rid of vermin. It asks me too....
> Laughing again, he brought the mirror away from away Stephen's peering eyes.
> — The rage of Caliban at not seeing his face in a mirror, he said. If Wilde were only alive to see you!
> Drawing back and pointing, Stephen said with bitterness:
> — It is a symbol of Irish art. The cracked lookingglass of a servant.
> Buck Mulligan suddenly linked his arm in Stephen's and walked with him round the tower, his razor and mirror clacking in the pocket where he had thrust them.
> — It's not fair to tease you like that, Kinch, is it? he said kindly. God knows you have more spirit than any of them.
> Parried again. He fears the lancet of my art as I fear that of his. The cold steel pen. (U1: 134–137, 141–153)

The joke concerning the action of the lancet is that Stephen fears being "pricked," and what's more, he suspects Mulligan "fears the lancet of his (he)art," implying that he wishes for their friendship to be something more, yet is mindful of Mulligan's affection for the Englishman Haines. Despite Stephen's trepidation, there is a palpable gay (in all senses) nationalism here typical of that felt by young Irish intellectuals who made inroads on the hegemony of English literary dominance, as Ellmann relates in his life of Joyce (JJ 98). It should be noted that in the above excerpt, reference may be made to Stephen as a writer, but he is an artist in the future tense only. With the line "God knows you have more spirit than any them," Mulligan unwittingly betrays Stephen's relative inexperience; he might have just as easily said "talent" or "vision." The mere *pose* of the artist defines Stephen's identity, and he cannot imagine himself into reality (most significantly, he cannot see himself in the mirror, as he merely "peer[s] at" it) by writing. As a result, his inferiority takes on the character of petulant narcissism. He loses Mulligan's affection to Haines, obsesses over his rejection of the affection of his mother, and denies knowledge of his father. But when Joyce pulls away from Stephen's littoral introspection in "Proteus," an alternative reading of male narcissism takes over with the presentation of Bloom as the central figure of the novel.

Despite the congruencies that may be inferred between Freud's essay "On Narcissism" and the "Lotus-Eaters" chapter of *Ulysses*, Joyce's purported depiction of narcissism fails to fulfill the reader's expectations. It is, rather, the confrontation between the intentional constructs of the artist versus the "natural," sensual self-absorption focusing on the body that sets the boundaries for Joyce's consideration of narcissism. In other words, the symbolic narcissist, which one may believe rules Joyce's artistic world, is void of any desires other than intellectual ones. Joyce muddies this issue in his masculinist discourse with his refusal to depict any of his principal male characters in any erotic situation other than an imaginary sexual embrace. As all male desire is fantasy in *Ulysses*, so there are no narcissists, and therefore, no realized art save the art that is the text of *Ulysses*. As such, masculine desire remains inchoate, vague, and unfulfilled.

Joyce and "Lotus-Eaters"

The fifth chapter of *Ulysses*, known as "Lotus-Eaters," provides the reader with a glimpse of how Joyce expands on the sexual turbulence at the core of the novel. The Gilbert-Gorman schema declares that there is a "narcissistic" technique at work in the text, but it is a somewhat misleading assertion. Rather than the thrill of passion promised by a true sexual relation, present in ideational narcissism (sexual attachment to the image of the self), there is in its stead mere satiety and lethargy. The examples Freud provides in his analysis help give direction to the ways in which we may think of Bloom, and allows explanations for Joyce's subversive, misdirecting symbols. Freud's work on narcissism sows the seeds of destruction for the superego, and lets Bloom (as it does Stephen) circumvent the question of masculinity completely by projecting a fantastic womb, to which Bloom shall return without once passing through the Oedipus complex.

There are several correspondences between Freud's discussion of narcissism and the "Lotus-Eaters" episode in *Ulysses*, in which Bloom buys soap, chit-chats idly with an acquaintance, goes to Mass, and imagines himself taking a bath. They are principally literal (the setting of the bath, the instant gratification of the senses, a diminishment of mental activity) and also interpretational (considering the question of Bloom's impotence, further proof that he cannot sustain a sexual relation). One can see Bloom as a kind of inward, impotent Freudian narcissist, who, although he "sees himself as others see him" (the well-traveled mantra describing his character in *Ulysses*), has no image of himself and therefore no reflexivity concerning his own ego. He can see himself *only* as others see him. In a Lacanian sense, Bloom is an unwitting and therefore perfect example of Oedipal confusion. The Oedipal symbolism of *Ulysses* is too easy: a father in search of a son, a mother who seeks the dead son, a son who hates the father. On a symbolic level, Bloom is condemned to repeat the familial triangle over and over. But in considering Bloom as a narcissist, Bloom is clearly unsexual, much after Freud's original description; this is the primary manner in which one views Bloom in the light of Joyce's fiction. Reading against the plot and symbology of *Ulysses*, one finds instead Bloom as a character alone, not multiple but one, his narcissistic status authorized and validated by Joyce.

The whole of the "Lotus-Eaters" chapter centers on the problem of negotiating sexual fantasy, while keeping Bloom rather impotent, at least in a genital sense. In everything Bloom does, he cannot even find the time to fantasize without being interrupted or postponed. This inability to sustain an estimable sexual fantasy precludes Bloom from being a classic narcissist, as he cannot cathect on a mental image. From his chaste, adulterous correspondence with Martha, to his inability to view an attractive woman across the street, to his anticipation of the hot bath that awaits him, Bloom is unable to overcome his own lethargy and participate in a decent fantasy. As the chapter opens, Bloom looks in the window of the Belfast and Oriental Tea Company; he sweats and fiddles with the card in his hat, and reads the package labels. It appears that as he fidgets, he works off a kind of sexual nervousness in anticipation and the same holds for the scene before the window: Bloom *wastes* the energy that he would spend masturbating (a theme throughout the whole of this chapter) in twitchy contemplation. This launches Bloom into a kind of reverie about the origin of the tea, the immediate object of his desire, which leads into a fantasy about Ceylon's exotic climate:

> The far east. Lovely spot it must be: the garden of the world, big lazy leaves to float about on, cactuses, flowery meads, snaky lianas they call them. Wonder is it

> like that. Those Cinghalese lobbing about in the sun in *dolce far niente*, not doing a hand's turn all day. Sleep six months out of twelve. Too hot to quarrel. Influence of the climate. Lethargy. Flowers of idleness. The air feeds most. Azotes. Hothouse in Botanic gardens. Sensitive plants. Waterlilies. Petals too tired to. Sleeping sickness in the air. (U5: 29–36)

The rest of the chapter expands on this sluggishness, as Bloom must fritter away some time before attending Dingam's funeral; in a sense, this entire episode is simply masturbation in various magnitudes. The excerpt above is notable also for its subtle sexual imagery coupling the sluggishness of the bath with implied yet postponed masturbation: "Those Cinghalese lobbing about in the sun in *dolce far niente*, not doing a hand's turn all day." Sensual satiation is enough without going through the exercise of a sexual fantasy. Bloom appears to repeat this scenario for himself, after a fashion, at the end of the chapter. As he walks to the bath, Bloom muses: "Turkish. Massage. Dirt gets rolled up in the navel. Nicer if a nice girl did it. Also I think I. Yes. Do it in the bath. Curious longing I. Water to water. Combine business with pleasure" (U5: 502–504). Bloom could be thinking about urination, but a reading of this "curious" urge (curious and therefore somehow suspect), combined with a semi-sexual touching fantasy, strengthens the case for masturbation, as does his thinking of Molly applying a homeopathic skin treatment of "oatmeal steeped in butter-milk": semen. The flowery motif continues with Bloom's reading of the message, and carries over into his thoughts about Martha. He remarks to himself that women loved the discreet "romantic" language: "Angry tulips with you darling mayflower punish your cactus if you don't please poor forgetmenot how I long violets..." (U5: 264–265). The phrase "punish your cactus" conflates the image of the phallic plant with his earlier meditation on the "Cinghalese" "cactuses," and the mental picture of the men "floating" in summer languor. The exotic image stands in for a kind of florid, mildly exotic sexuality that is mere fantasy for Bloom, and this theme shall return later in a slightly different form at the chapter's end with the image of the bath.

Other elements in the "Lotus-Eaters" describe insubstantial fantasy where mere "play" must suffice, rather than providing real cathection or correspondence with sexual desire. A compelling instance of literary fantasy in *Ulysses*, in which one of the characters reveals the operations of authorized "desire," is Martha's letter to Bloom, responding to his flirtatious overtures. The missive propagates a kind of fantasy relation that threatens to turn into a real one during the course of the novel, but it is never realized. Bloom is apprehensive about meeting her in person (perhaps after "the rosary" on Sunday, he thinks, and this gives Joyce another flower pun); Bloom even hopes a little that he has scared her off with his latest epistolary demands (U5: 274). He reflects that he will endanger himself when he refuses her sexual attention at this imagined meeting: "Thank you: not having any. Usual love scrimmage. Then running around corners. Bad as a row with Molly. Cigar has a cooling effect" (U5: 270–272). That adultery presents very practical problems for him deepens the picture of Bloom as one paralyzed by the demands of performing heterosexually. The enigmatic mental note "Cigar has a cooling effect" can refer to many things. If Bloom smokes one on his first meeting with Martha, he may turn her off with its noxious fumes; a cigar leads to the quelling of sexual desire through the mastery of a symbolic phallus; a precoital cigar may make him lose his erection, therefore allowing him to get out of his duty-bound sexual encounters with Molly. One could also see it as a slightly anachronistic reference to Freud's famous habit—in this instance, Freud's ever-present phallus pokes out, revealing the "real" intentions of Joyce's characters and their desires.

Suzette Henke notes in her reading of Martha's letter that the rejection implicit in Bloom's dispatch intensifies the aura of masochism surrounding their correspondence.[3] However, the impact of this letter has more to do with her engagement in the rules of this epistolary affair and the language of flower symbolism than "real" sexual desire and sex-play. The real problem in analyzing this letter is in her rejection of Bloom's fantasy in the language of flowers, accompanied there by a "yellow flower with flattened petals." This symbolic blossom plays on Bloom's assumed name, Henry Flower, and therefore his cowardice and his impotent state. This poses, as would be expected, difficulties for Bloom's view of his own sexuality:

> I am awfully angry with you. I do wish I could punish you for that. I called you a naughty boy because I do not like that other world. Please tell me what is the real meaning of that word? Are you not happy in your home you poor little naughty boy? (U5: 243–247)

The phrase "other world" (word) appears inexplicably in the text, referring ostensibly to the world of Bloom, but also possibly their furtively shared world of sadomasochistic vocabulary, the "words" to which they seem to be paying lip service. This fantasy has no real mistress, master or slave: by engaging in this type of banter, both parties believe they are effecting transgression, but their words have empty intentions. This sadomasochistic exchange will be horrifically amplified later in a different fashion in the "Circe" episode. There, the textual play becomes serious and is meant explicitly without recourse to the vagaries of reality. It has often been said that "Circe" appears as an eruption of the "unconscious" of *Ulysses*.[4] This is true only to the extent that fantasies are recombined and mutilated in that chapter in the manner of a dream. The presence of "Circe" suggests that there is some connection between fantasy and the "interior life" of the characters in *Ulysses*, chiefly Bloom. But emphasizing the importance of that chapter, in which both Bloom and Stephen suffer at the hands of women (Bloom with his cuckolding and victimization by Bello, Stephen's haunting by his mother), assumes a kind of sexual interest on the part of both men, an interest unfulfilled by actual sexual contact anywhere in the novel's narrative.

In addition to the insubstantial fantasy relation Bloom seems to have constructed, he also seems incapable of sustaining a voyeuristic fantasy that he initiates after tearing up the letter. The interrupted fantasy that occurs in the street, in which a leather-and-stockings-clad woman waits for a cab, seems made to order for Bloom, and yet he seems powerless to continue it. An old acquaintance, Charlie M'Coy, approaches him to discuss recent developments, including Dingam's funeral and the singing careers of both of their wives. This could not have come at a more inopportune time for Bloom, as he strains to see the woman exit the hotel across the way:

> M'Coy. Get rid of him quickly. Take me out of my way. Hate company when you.
> — Hello, Bloom. Where are you off to?
> — Hello, M'Coy. Nowhere in particular.
> — How's the body?
> — Fine. How are you?
> — Just keeping alive, M'Coy said. (U5: 82–88)

The ensuing scene clues the reader in to the way Joyce's technique of interior monologue can hamper Bloom's thought processes, and prevent him from blocking out the outside noise intruding on his thoughts. He cannot see a complete picture of the woman; she appears as a collection of separate images, each with its own fetishistic value. Once the fantasy is initiated by M'Coy's query about the body, the trolley sails into view in front of the already fragmented body of the anonymous woman adjusting her boot, and she does so seemingly for Bloom's eyes only. Already, there can be no narrative here. On top of this, the figure of M'Coy (apparently secure in his marriage) imposes itself on the narration of this fantasy, disrupting it; the fragment "[h]ate company when you" may point to the anxious thought of another man watching him masturbate, and indicates also that this invitation to voyeurism may be a regular occurrence for him. It is also noteworthy that his idea of the baths contains no other figures save himself, alone in the water. Bloom is not necessarily trumped by the sexualized presence of another man, but without the isolation he needs, he is unable to sustain his interest:

> He moved a little to the side of M'Coy's talking head. Getting up in a minute....
>
> Watch! Watch! Silk flash rich stockings white. Watch!
>
> A heavy tramcar honking its gong slewed between.
>
> Lost it. Curse your noisy pugnose. Feels locked out of it. Paradise and the peri. Always happening like that. The very moment. Girl in Eustace street hallway Monday was it settling her garter. Her friend covering the display of. *Esprit de corps.* Well, what are you gaping at? (U5: 124–125, 130–135)

This instance of concealment, counteracted in the masturbation fantasy of "Nausicaa," is foregrounded here in an uncanny way. The consciousness of fantasy as merely fantasy colors one of Bloom's thoughts here: the fragment "Paradise and the peri" signifies his spectator status, as he desires after that which he cannot have. Bloom also comments here on what he is adding to the text of the novel as a kind of supplement to the narrative. The interpretation of the scene, the picture of Bloom's reaction to it, is also the technique of reading Joyce apart from his presence in the text itself. The supplement that is desire is brought to bear on the picture, which is presented to the desiring viewer and turned into fantasy. But, departing from Derrida, the supplement seeks to create no coherent core of meaning underneath or even with the text. Instead, it wants to create a brilliant flash of momentary fulfillment, available in the instant of the text, meant to be enjoyed as read. The strategic deployment of impoverished male fantasy with Stephen and Bloom in *Ulysses* undermines a symbolic, Freudian reading of this novel; as with the readings of Proust, Sacher-Masoch, and James in previous chapters, the signifiers of desire are unhitched from the "masculine" libido.

One characteristic of the uniquely male fantasy is the image of masturbation as somehow emasculating and wasteful. As Bloom imagines himself into the fantastic narrative, we find his anxiety about Boylan present here, as elsewhere, to demoralizing effect. This occurs near the end of the chapter when he meets Bantam Lyons, who shall later in the day make a killing on Bloom's inadvertent suggestion of "Throwaway" as a winning pick for the Royal Ascot. As Lyons snatches away the rolled-up newspaper, Bloom's textual erection becomes only so much garbage at Lyon's insistence on seeing the racing form, when the paper is thrown back at Bloom, unfurled (U5: 539–540). A major thread of the novel's symbolism hangs on the victory of "Throwaway," the rank outsider who carries the day. It is central to Joyce's Bloomean boosterism: the long unnoticed dark horse who, while he does not have heroic qualities, embodies all that is good and human. On a symbolic level this also equates Bloom with the unsung horse, masturbation, the shameful supplement: all that is anti-masculine, anti-hetero, opposed to a kind of overdetermined symbolic, priapic, dominant masculinity. Also, the feminine metaphors that draw the reader's attention to the passive and gentle gestures in the book (Bloom's kindness to old women, Stephen's affection for his younger sister) are easily reversible into positive virtues. These ironic Bloomean associations with the weak and down-trodden play against the kind of symbolic expectation that one naturally might bring to the truly "Joycean" text, one in which the all-powerful signifier assigns meaning through violation (after Lacan), rather than revealing or unpacking it. Joyce, in his play, continually reverses the expectations allusion brings, and abolishes the phallic mode of signification. Therefore, Joyce's depiction of masculine fantasy appears as a parody of male signification. Bloom is a victim of language rather than a master of it, and the same goes for Stephen, the supposed artist.

The final sequence of "Lotus-Eaters" conveys a varied series of images in order to cap off the chapter and bring together the elements of narcissism brought out at various points in this narrative. The chapter ends with the recurrence of Molly's image at the soap shop, previous to Bloom's trip to the baths. The bath itself, it must be noted, does not occur within the context of the chapter, but rather outside of it, as we are again in the realm of fantasy:

> He foresaw his pale body reclined in it at full, naked, in a womb of warmth, oiled by scented melting soap, softly laved. He saw his trunk and limbs riprippled over and sustained, buoyed lightly upward, lemonyellow: his navel, bud

> of flesh: and saw the dark tangled curls of his bush floating, floating hair of the stream around the limp father of thousands, a languid floating flower. (U5: 567–572)

There are two striking features about this foreseen and therefore slightly postponed pleasure. First, there is matter of the womb-like bath in which Bloom finds himself, and second, the limpness of his imaginary penis. Even in fantasy, potency is impossible in light of his self- and outwardly-imposed narcissism. There is no sexual relation possible with Bloom, and the correspondence affair or the simple ogling of a potential dominatrix cannot energize Bloom or draw him out of his flaccid introspection, especially in the company of other men. In addition, the vision of the womb corroborates Freud's implied infantilism in his account of originary narcissism. In this case, the celebration of the male body, sexual pleasure without climax, and a gentle familiarity with the body itself frustrate the Freudian progressive heterosexual narrative. Perhaps regressive and certainly ambiguous, the image at the end of this chapter serves as Joyce's impression of sensual "narcissism," fairly proclaiming Bloom's variable sexual position in *Ulysses*.[5]

To the extent that "Lotus-Eaters" rejects the Law of the Father, it may be read as a queer text of sorts, and this goes doubly so for the historical situation of the novel with the later thought of Freud. In the symbolic shufflings of Joycean play, the conscious managing of psychoanalytic tropes takes center stage. Considering Joyce's ambivalence toward the Freudian "interpretation" of things, it may be seen as a sort of parody, if only to rob psychoanalysis of its analytic powers, and stack the deck to the point where the sexual imagery itself "means" nothing. In this sense, Joyce's work can be characterized as highly anal, involved with the collection and sometimes random presentation of images without regard to their meaning.[6] By concentrating on the text itself as a fetish object, however fragmentary its pleasures, the production of meaning is overturned in the pleasure of the textual moment.

With Jacques Lacan's later work, one may find an aid to explain Joyce's momentary resistance to the Law of the Father, in order to experience the pleasure of the text. In "Joyce le symptôme I," Lacan comes to an appraisal of Joyce as a nascent Lacanian analyst. Joyce foregoes the role of "artist" in favor of being a game player, symbolic magician, and proliferator of text. Joyce presents his artistic persona naïvely in the manner of Bloom, amateur sensualist, rather than Stephen, the forward-looking and pretentious patriarchal artist, with a deep investment in the Oedipus complex. To *read* allusion in Joyce is to join in with the discourse of the Father, to subjugate the text to interpretation, and therefore to seek sanctification in the church of meaning, which in the bathtime moment Joyce burlesques in a parody of the Eucharist. In "Joyce le symptôme I," a seminar conducted on Bloomsday 1975, Lacan confines himself for the most part to *Finnegans Wake*, although his discussion applies, Lacan himself admonishes, to the textual manipulations of *Ulysses*. Beginning with the seminars of the 1970s, Lacan's work takes a definitive turn for the baffling, with his diagrams, disavowals of feminist psychology, and the stressing of the "symptom" (or *sinthome*) as the cornerstone of analysis. In Lacan's later work, he muscles the notion of the unconscious aside and supplants it with linguistic play. The one constant for Lacan remains the topic of desire, and Lacan combines a discussion of Joyce's style, themes and characters with his own obsessions about literary language, desire, and the unconscious.

Lacan declares in this seminar that a literary work can revise a standard Freudian reading with respect to the questions of the unconscious, and the symbols that reveal its associations. Lacan develops the notion that to deny the "conscious" ego the satisfaction of interpreting the unconscious is to reduce the text to a mere object and medium of pleasure. To take things "seriously" is the worst mistake to make with Joyce. By way of illustration, Lacan describes the conflict between the producer of discourse and the artificer who builds meaning into it because he feels the needle of "conscience." To refuse the name of the Father is to reject the unconscious at the same time. To treat Joyce as the "symptom" rescues him from the position of being objectified by the father, and, therefore, rescues him from being victimized by the symbol that links the unconscious to discourse. The reason that critics adduce meaning to Joyce, Lacan remarks, is because of the presence of Joyce, the author, in the text, such that one takes it in "Ernest"; in this joke, Lacan alludes to both Wilde's play and the first name of Freud's biographer Ernest Jones.[7]

Lacan takes pains to distinguish between "symptom" and "symbol," and claims that both ways of reading Joyce cannot be reconciled. One cannot at the same time read Joyce allusively and "for pleasure":

> Je dis Joyce le symptôme—c'est que, le symptôme, le symbole, il l'abolit, si je puis continuer dans cette veine. Ce n'est pas seulement Joyce le symptôme, c'est Joyce en tant que, si je puis dire, désabonné à l'inconscient. (24)

In the end, one confronts the lack of "meaning" in Joyce which denies a unified psychoanalytic reading, which "cancels its subscription to the unconscious," as it were. This is the textual politics of pleasure. The text is not only all that there is, but the preclusion of reading the symptom makes *jouissance* the easiest thing possible, and is the only true mode of reading in the "spirit" of Joyce. The main advantage is avoiding the question of "expectation"; what occurs in the text appears to foreshadow what comes after it, but not necessarily. If the subject matter of *Ulysses* leads us into a blind alley, it is the dead end of the Oedipal narrative. The trinity of Stephen as the imaginary son, Molly as the imaginary mother, and Bloom as the father leads us to that "natural" structuralist-derived reading of the novel. It is also an imposition on the text to accept Joyce's judgment that "Lotus-Eaters" is "narcissistic," when Bloom never once exhibits a trait classically symbolic of narcissism: looking at oneself in a mirror, feeling vain, or being particularly conceited. In a characteristically Joycean fit of disingenuousness, Bloom defies expectations.

As a question of defying "expectation," an alternate form of narcissism means nothing if we are to call it by its "proper" name, fixed to the chapter by Joyce, with willing assistance from Gilbert. Indeed, there is a kind of collaboration that produces pleasure in "symptoms" for their own sake. Lacan outrageously claims that he prides himself, as did the Joyce who wrote *Finnegans Wake*, on obscurity, and that he revels in unintelligibility, such that the sense of his words is excluded (26). Lacan dispenses with the question of his mastery over making language *mean* by reveling in the childish joy of sticking words together for their own sake. In a sense, the real obsessive relation is not typified by the artist's interest in his own work, but in the disavowal of meaning-creation. Leaving one's speech, one's text, for the reader to enjoy for himself or herself, allows the development of a transferential relation—creating, in essence, a text that has no parentage, but that is purely, innocently (in a sense) pleasurable.

There is a striking internal non sequitur as Bloom snatches his letter, walks out of the post office and thinks "Talk: as if that would mend matters" (U5: 76–77). This can be read as Joyce's sly disavowal of the psychoanalytic relation, given Freud's early description of psychoanalysis as the "talking cure." Certainly, there is a strong sense with Bloom that things need mending. If they do, it is an odd way to introduce narcissism as the wound that needs healing from the outset. Although his impotent fantasy leaves things unfulfilled for Bloom, the reader's experience is infinitely more satisfying. This is also the source for perpetually conflicted readings of Joyce's work—whether to put his writing under the rubric of "realist" fiction or that of metafictional explorations of language, the experiments of which are psychological expositions of sorts in themselves.

Sheldon Brivic remarks in his book *The Veil of Signs* that the *jouissance* of Joyce's linguistic play is markedly feminine, and that Lacan equates feminine mystery with the satisfaction provided by Joyce's text.[8] However, this does not take into account the multivalent forms and genres of discourse depicted in Joyce, much less the subtle shadings relating to depictions of fantasy, anxiety and other psychoanalytic phenomena. Calling Joyce's language and writing feminine with regard to *jouissance* is not enough to explain the masculinity of his men, as their seemingly impotent desires and fantasies have to be critically reconstructed from the bottom up. The conflict between the classically tormented artist and the *bricoleur* amateur novelist, already castrated by language, sets up the parallel crises of masculinity and heterosexuality in *Ulysses.* Lacan draws out this conflict in reading Joyce as an "artist" or sensualist, with both positions sexually suspect. To pose as "masculine" for Freud, one plays the heterosexual Oedipal game to conclusion; to overthrow it, what Joyce and Bloom do is merely contrary and calls their sexual roles forever into question.

Coda: Joyce, Psychoanalysis, Fatherhood, and the *Wake*

Because Joyce's work is so eerily aware of any reading that one may take to it, the problem with reading Joyce with reference to theory is that the results of such readings wind up almost always seeming tautological. Psychoanalytic theory is no exception. Aside from the relative toothlessness of garden-variety psychoanalysis when set to the task of devouring the Joycean text, it may seem to be the height of presumption to hunt for meaning within Joyce's work by looking at his life with reference to his writing. At bottom, Joyce's life itself was not all that eventful. As much as any writer ever did, he spent much of his life in his room, writing away, with the occasional domestic trouble or familial crisis, much of it having to do with lack of money. Nevertheless, it cannot be denied that much of Joyce's identity is there in his work, as he used up all the knowledge he could absorb from his circle of friends, collaborators, and interlocutors. One of the unique qualities of Joyce's work is its encyclopedic imperative to say as much as it can, as beautifully as it can: wisely, most of Joyce's best readers and critics shy away from the attempt to comprehend it all, instead leaving the experience of the sheer totality of Joyce's work as part of the pleasure of reading him. Despite Joyce's famous pronouncement that the artist should stand off to the side of the work, "paring his fingernails," Joyce's writing is impossible to conceive apart from his identity, which he ruthlessly mined to exhaustion over the course of his career.

It has also been well noted that Joyce actively despised and distrusted psychoanalysis. His prejudice stemmed from his distaste for the irrelevance of its concepts (as Joyce once remarked to his Boswell, Frank Budgen, "Why all this fuss and bother about the mystery of the unconscious? What about the mystery of the conscious? What do they know about that?"), and its resemblance to a new religion (going to a psychoanalyst, for him, he once said, would feel like going to confession, and he had had enough of that in his life). But perhaps most of all, Joyce felt, as did his contemporary Lawrence, that the investigation of the psyche, the principal subject of his fiction, was better left to artists and historians.

Yet, Joyce seemed to think that while the sauce was no good for the gander, it was perfectly fine for the goose. Interested in Budgen's dream diary, Joyce, rather than starting his own nocturnal journal, began keeping a record of his wife Nora's dreams, with potted Freudian analysis following each description. Weirdly enough, most of the dreams seem to involve the work he was doing on *Ulysses*, but this was unsurprising given his obsessive impromptu discussions with anyone and everyone, including Nora, about the content of the book during the advanced stages of its composition. Joyce's most extended engagement with any form of psychoanalysis occurred during the last half of the composition of *Finnegans Wake*, when he sought treatment for his daughter Lucia's mental illness. In the early thirties, as the material for the *Wake* was taking shape, Lucia's behavior reached a desperate low, manifesting itself in pyromania, fugues of rage and destructiveness, and other erratic behavior, along with an unhealthy erotic attachment to Samuel Beckett, then Joyce's secretary. The crisis over the composition of *Finnegans Wake* seems to parallel the crisis he felt over his daughter Lucia's deteriorating mental condition; Ellmann depicts Joyce as believing that if he solved the problem of writing the *Wake* (a book that even in its early stages nobody really wanted to read), then he could somehow magically solve the problem of Lucia's sanity, and she would be able to lead a somewhat normal life. Unfortunately, Joyce does not seem to have been willing to take steps to normalize Lucia, as he believed her to be some kind of creative genius, and also clairvoyant. In letters to various benefactors and correspondents, Joyce entertained the idea that Lucia simply had an exaggerated personality. He indulged her behavior in many ways, from encouraging her drawings by anonymously subsidizing her art for limited editions of his work, to buying her a 4,000 franc fur coat, asserting in correspondence that it would do more for her self esteem than would psychoanalysis (JJ 662).

Nevertheless, Joyce eventually decided to seek a form of analytic treatment for Lucia. Once the Joyces moved to Zurich, they placed her in the sanitarium of Burghölzli, which had none other than Carl Jung on the staff. Jung had already published comments about *Ulysses*, and seemed eager to take on the task of curing Lucia. From the beginning, Jung's approach was perhaps too perfect, as it fell into line with Joyce's preliminary unofficial diagnosis. The looser Jungian approach, with its affinity for the questions of identity and personae rather than attention to genital structure and Oedipal conflict, probably made the medicine go down more easily, for both Joyce and Lucia. The Jungian interpretation of this situation, straight from the mouth of Jung himself, is that Joyce's animus manifested itself in Lucia's personality, thus validating what Joyce had suspected all along. Privately, Jung confided to his colleagues and fans that the case of Lucia and Joyce was a paradigmatic case of an artist and his muse. One letter of Jung's reads, in part: "If you know anything of my Anima theory, Joyce and his daughter are a classical example of it. She was definitely his 'femme inspiratrice,' which explains his obstinance to have her certified" (JJ 679). Jung was perhaps reluctant to diagnose Lucia fully, as Jung felt that her psychosis, which was already reflecting badly on Joyce, was a manifestation of Joyce's latent psychosis. Also, Joyce was growing more and more uncomfortable with the closeness of the analyst-analysand relationship, as he was jealous of Jung's access to Lucia.

Here the context for Jungian analysis tests her creativity and (admittedly mental) fecundity against the measure of her father's virility, namely, his proficiency as an artist. The Oedipus situation is seen more or less in reverse. The father wishes to keep Lucia close to him and protect her, rather than fearing that a son would eventually would take his place. Lucia's drawing and scribbling, such as they are, are scrutinized by Joyce in a vain effort to uncover the creative thrust Joyce is sure exists within her. Jung's initial diagnosis of schizophrenia is transformed (in Joyce's estimation) into a validation of Lucia's worth as a masculine artistic extension of Joyce himself. The torture of fevered "genius" is somehow made benign by the countersign of the fecund father, doubly so when the father in question is James Joyce, capable of pouring a divine stream of signification, like chrism, over all the physical, psychical, historical, and familial world. Joyce's perception of Lucia as a kind of sybil (his family called her a Cassandra instead) is not in itself unusual in the world of artists and muses, but Ellmann relays a few choice utterances that, in Joyce's opinion, clinched the case for her clairvoyance: in all ways, they reflect his desire for closure and a return to his origins. Addressing him, Lucia once spoke to Joyce in the voice of a native Irishman, a country wholly alien to her: "I want to reconcile you. It is time for some great person of your country to come forward and hold out a hand to you and to us" (JJ 678). Joyce assumed that, because of his literary success, it was time for him to make some symbolic gesture of return. Lucia's terse telegrammatic declaration to Joyce, "You look like Bray head," sent to him while visiting Ireland, echoes the Wakean synonymity of male figures with real-life landscapes (JJ 684).

In the end, Lucia's treatment could well be considered a failure, as her unbalanced behavior persisted throughout the rest of her life. In the middle of the *Wake's* first section, Joyce presents a protracted psychoanalytic riff that throws ambiguous sexual confusion, religious ecstasy, and analytic hubris into the narrative mix. It is hard to resist seeing an encapsulation of Lucia's narrow brush with analysis in the following famous passage:

> ...plus dinky pinks deliberatively summersaulting off her bisexcycle, at the main entrance of the curate's perpetual soutane suit with her one to see and awoh! who picks her up as gingerly as any balmbearer would to feel whereupon the virgin was most hurt and nicely asking: whyre have you been so grace a mauling and where were you chaste me child? Be who, farther potential? and so wider but we grisly old Sykos who done our unsmiling bit on 'alices, when they were yung and easily freudened, in the penumbra of the procuring room and what oracular compression we have had apply to them! could (did we care to see our feebought silence *in camera*) tell our very moistnostrilled one that *father* in such virgated contexts is not always that undemonstrative relative (often held up to our contumacy) who settles our hashbill for us and what an innocent all-

> abroad's adverb such as Michaelly looks like can be suggestive of under the pudendascope, and, finally, what a neurasthene nympholept, endocrine-pineal typus, of inverted parentage with a prepossessing drauma present in her past and a priapic urge for congress with agnates before cognates fundamentally is feeling for under her lubricitous meiosis when she refers with liking to some feeler she fancie's face. And Mm. We could. Yes what need to say? 'Tis as human a little story as paper could well carry...[9]

The sexual anxiety in this passage erupts in the phrase "neurasthene nympholept...of inverse parentage," who has, to be sure, a "priapic urge for congress with agnates before cognates"—here the idea that Lucia is parenting Joyce emerges, that she is a prime source for the *Wake* itself, the very model of a profusion of tongues and signifiers. Noting that there was a trauma and "drauma" in the past implies the initiation of some psychoanalytic narrative, and also the infliction of phantom analytic wounds; this is particularly true of the feminine subject, for whom the analyst must create problems that are not there. This is a rather self-consciously artistic reinterpretation of psychoanalysis, self-conscious in that it protests against the gross reality of sex, the focus of Freudian analysis, which brings the reproductive body so vividly to the fore. This brutish insistence on the reality of the body, in an analytic sense, is necessarily horrific to Joyce, and as it was in *Finnegans Wake*, so it is throughout *Ulysses*. Despite the famous tagline describing *Ulysses* as an epic of the body, throughout Joyce's work there is a deep antipathy for one body in particular, that of the father. In the passage quoted above, the father termed "undemonstrative relative" is a pun on the singularity of a father, of anyone's father: the father exists in the mere abstract.

In the ninth chapter of *Ulysses*, "Scylla and Charybdis," Stephen gets a chance to air his theory about Shakespeare and autobiography, and his explanation contains this bite-sized exposition that could well serve as a summary of the problem of parentage in Joyce's work:

> —A father, Stephen said, battling against hopelessness, is a necessary evil. He wrote the play in the months that followed his father's death. If you hold that he, a graying man with two marriageable daughters, with thirtyfive years of life, *nel mezzo del cammin di nostra vita*, with fifty of experience, is the beardless undergraduate from Wittenberg then you must hold that his seventyyear old mother is the lustful queen. No. The corpse of John Shakespeare does not walk the night. From hour to hour it rots and rots. He rests, disarmed of fatherhood, having devised that mystical estate upon his son. Boccaccio's Calandrino was the first and last man who felt himself with child. Fatherhood, in the sense of conscious begetting, is unknown to man. It is a mystical estate, an apostolic succession, from only begetter to only begotten. On that mystery and not on

> the madonna which cunning Italian intellect flung to the mob of Europe the church is founded and founded irremovably because founded, like the world, macro and microcosm, upon the void. Upon incertitude, upon unlikelihood. *Amor matris*, subjective and objective genetive, may be the only true thing in life. Paternity may be a legal fiction. Who is the father of any son that any son should love him or he any son? (U9: 828–845)

As if that were not enough, Stephen reiterates the impossibility of being a son and father at the same time, underlining the necessary role-play of the artist as sole progenitor of himself and world, divorced from the body: "The son unborn mars beauty: born he brings pain, divides affection, increases care. He is a new male: his growth is his father's decline, his youth his father's envy, his friend his father's enemy" (U9: 854–857).

It goes without saying that this is quite the formulation for Oedipal conflict. But the problem of real-world parenting and dutiful allegiance to one's father is solved rather neatly in *Ulysses*. Stephen avoids contact with his irresponsible father, as his father steadily drinks away Stephen's library with money got from selling his schoolbooks, erasing all traces of Stephen from his house, and eliminating the evidence through a presumably limp organ. The affective bond formed by Bloom and Stephen at the end of the novel outstrips the reach of possible Oedipal conflict; in an arrangement perhaps forgotten by morning, Bloom chooses to be a father, and Stephen accepts the role of being a son to one with a distinctively un-Irish face. For Joyce, the paternal relation is necessarily a fantastic one. The only conflict arises when the phenomenal issues of sex intrude. It is the prerogative of the Joycean artist to be all roles at all times, ready to drop or adopt them as fits aesthetic intention. Certainly this is true of the *Wake*, the central organizing principle of which is the dream-landscape of Humphrey Chimpden Earwicker, and is perhaps anticipated by Stephen, again in the ninth chapter of *Ulysses*:

> When Rutlandbaconsouthamptonshakespeare or another poet of the same name in the comedy of errors wrote *Hamlet* he was not the father of his own son merely but, being no more a son, he was and felt himself the father of all his race, the father of his own grandfather, the father of his unborn grandson who, by the same token, never was born, for nature, as Mr Magee understands her, abhors perfection. (U9: 865–871)

As nature abhors perfection, the artist clings to the ever-present promise of perfection; Catherine Froula notes that because reading *Finnegans*

Wake has as much to do with myth as it does with reading Joyce, it is necessarily and primarily a narcissistic document.[10]

Yet Joyce's penchant for retiring into his own aesthetic world is not merely about his remaking of the world in the artist's image. The sexual anxiety and profusion of sexual imagery at the core of Joyce's later work benefit from his recoiling at the generative aspects of the feminine and masculine body, and indeed at times reflect infantile desires to return to the womb (as in the "Lotus-Eaters" episode), or to be absorbed into the identity of the father. One may see glimpses of this at the end of *Finnegans Wake*, where the return and reabsorption into the world is expressed in terms of feminine reconciliation with the father:

> O bitter ending! I'll slip away before they're up. They'll never see. Nor know. Nor miss me. And it's old and old it's sad and old it's sad and weary and I go back to you, my cold father, my cold mad father, my cold mad feary father, till the near sight of the mere size of him, the moyles and moyles of it, moananoaning, makes me seasilt saltsick and I rush, my only, into your arms. (627–628)

The sight of the size of the father-country, the phenomenal horror of the display of the father-body, causes trauma to the speaker, which only falling back into sleep can fully cure, so that the *Wake* can begin again. An analytic interpretation of this complex of tropes in Joyce would yield a perverse stagnation at the oral stage, classically a feature of childhood; the desire to consume and the fear or desire of being consumed predominates in the encounter with the father. It is tempting to read this as Joyce's implicit condemnation of psychoanalysis as a playpen for the small-minded, but it speaks to Joyce's insistence about overcoming the Freudian claim to read the life of the mind in terms of autobiography. For the most part, Joyce's disengagement with psychoanalysis reveals a resistance to let the figure of the analyst, and analytic discourse, disrupt the ever-important primacy of the artist, who is in Joyce's view the undemonstrative relative, and, in his mind, uncontested father of all.

6

Conclusion: Psychoanalysis, Modernity, and the Philosophical Tradition

La paternité, à côté de la maternité, n'apporte à l'homme que charges et responsabilité morale, frustration momentanée de sa femme, alors que de son corps heureux à elle jaillit le lait pour le bébé, la nourriture primordiale. L'insécurité de la paternité biologique est tempérée, en general, par la certitude de sa paternité, confirmée devant la société, auprès de l'état civil où l'enfant déclaré. Mais, tout au moins dans l'état actuel de nos moeurs, un coït triumphant immediate avec la jeune femme phallique glorifiée ne lui est pas autorisé; il doit subir le rival et, officiellement, aimer l'intrus.

—Françoise Dolto, from *Sexualité Féminine: Libido, Érotisme, Frigidité* [1]

The Psychoanalytic Dialogue

After what I just put on the board, you may think you know everything. Don't.
(S.XX 78)

In the words of Jacques Lacan: in the beginning of the analytic relation, there was love.

The primary place of Freud's genius in the analytic tradition is a necessary fabrication, if I may take this phrase from Lacan, in order for one to believe in psychoanalysis. In every important sense, psychoanalysis begins with Freud, surely as Freud deals with the biological origins of life and sexual development, and their intimate relation to the psyche; the closeness of sexual life to the sense of the human is inextricable from human desire, and the very question of desire seems inert and false when *eros* (in whatever form) is not there.

The correspondence of Freud yields an edifying glimpse into the heated atmosphere of psychoanalysis's beginnings. Typical of the first flush of a new discipline, the enthusiasms of and relationships between contributors were often as important as their intellectual acumen, and many of the writings attending the birth of psychoanalysis testify to the depth and seriousness of what was essentially a collaborative effort. Freud's correspondence with Wilhelm Fliess is particularly poignant for a number of reasons, not least because the ultimate reason for their relationship's distintegration was a dispute over the proper credit for Fliess's touting of originary bisexuality as instrumental in sexual development. The extraordinary thing about the Freud-Fliess correspondence is the tenor of Freud's sharing of discoveries and ideas with Fliess. One cannot help being struck by the propositional invention that would become a hallmark of Freud's writing later on, and the genuine pleasure he takes in his epistolary relationship with Fliess: "Your kindheartedness is one of the reasons I love you. Initially, it seemed to me that you had broken off contact with me because of my remarks about the symptoms distant from the nose, and I did not deem this improbable. Now you surprise me with a discussion that takes those fantasies seriously!" (CL 131). The spirit in which this is offered—that of unfettered excitation over an exchange of ideas—belies the grueling degree of self-analysis to which Freud subjected himself, and indicates his sanguine enthusiasm at finding someone who shares his interests.

The ubiquity and regularity of postal communication no doubt encouraged this type of casual reflection, and judging by the character of some of Freud's remarks, it seems the smallest of whims could move him to tell anything to Fliess; one of the most bizarre is Freud's proclivity for assessing his life and work habits according to the rhythms of menstruation, and his abstraction of these ideas into some kind of belief that the menstrual cycle dictates the length of one's life. Freud's letter of August 1, 1898, shortly after his father's death, calculates to the day the number of menstrual cycles that Bismarck outlived his father, as they were supposedly born on the same day (the first of April 1815), and Freud, transposing his father's dates from the Jewish calendar, compares it to the numerology involved in the determination of the number of months according to the menstrual cycle: "...the life difference is 23 X 28. You undoubtedly know what that must mean" (CL 322). The bemused tone Freud often uses with Fliess is in evidence even here, and in this revelation Freud reveals that he is concerned with the failure of his new direction in thought, and also, perhaps, disconcertingly, with his own physiology. The gestation of psychoanalysis, as it were, is dramatized in Freud's asides about his imagined schedule of menstruation:

> My self-analysis is in fact the most essential thing I have at present and promises to become of the greatest value to me if it reaches its end. In the middle of it, it suddenly ceased for three days, during which I had the feeling of being tied up inside (which patients complain of so much), and I was really disconsolate until I found that these same three days (twenty-eight days ago) were the bearers of identical somatic phenomena. Actually only two bad days with a remission in between. From this one should draw the conclusion that the female period is not conducive to work. Punctually on the fourth day, it started again. Naturally, the pause also had another determinant—the resistance to something surprisingly new. Since then I have been once again intensely preoccupied [with it], mentally fresh, though afflicted with all sorts of minor disturbances that come from the content of the analysis. (CL 270)

The idea of doing a self-analysis, certainly outlandish now, no doubt struck Freud himself at the time as being an unprecedented enterprise. The letters he writes, particularly to Fliess, are the record of his struggles over his coming to self-knowledge; the attraction in reading these letters to Fliess is that they back up the claim that Freud is doing real work in this act of self-creation. Freud's willingness to assign his work stoppage to the vagaries of the female period (as he puts it) indicates an analogical relationship to gestation, and one could only conclude that Freud would have wholeheartedly welcomed the comparison if questioned about it. In this case, this act of analytic creation is taking place without the assistance and midwifery of the presence of a woman, uncharacteristic of the early days of analysis, when a number of important analytic discoveries emerged due to a woman's presence. Neither Anna O., nor Dora, nor the oneiric image of Irma is available to occasion sudden insights into the nature of analysis; the burden of analysis is Freud's alone, with only Fliess's correspondence for company. Lacking a flesh-and-blood interlocutor, Freud must content himself with sharing his insights via the post.

The ultimate mode of psychoanalytic inquiry, that of the dialogue, is absent here. But in his act of self-analysis, with all the "physical" symptoms and birth-pangs which Freud describes, Freud reveals an important element of the analytic insight. Beyond sexuality itself, the psychic life of the individual is a layer of experience analogous to somatic life. As such, they are intimately related and cannot, in a reversal of the Cartesian insight, be separated in any assessment of mental functioning; yet this insight into the analogical relation between the somatic and the psychic is something that is realized only through the frustrations of unfulfilled desire. Lacan warns that "narcissism [may] explain everything," but narcissism, in offering the image of a human being as whole, inviolable and self-sufficient, is also a false theoretical ideal, as well as being unworkable in practice. The inquiry into and dialogue about sexuality keys into the primary need for contact and nourishment, without which no human being could exist; this is why sexuality is the guiding thread in analytic inquiry, as it cannot cater to the needs of the Cartesian mind, stranded in a vacant world with only robots for company. Psychoanalysis fleshes out the life of the mental palimpsest analogous to the narrative of the biological life of the subject: its attachments, loves, and hatreds. It was Freud's insight to discover that the mental life of the subject could have somatic consequences, and that, conversely, aberrant behavior points to a disturbance in the inner experience of the subject:

> How was the *psychic* enfeeblement acquired? There is not much to be got from masturbation in his youth; it would certainly not have had such a result, nor does it seem to have exceeded the usual amount. His relations with the girl, who excited him very much sensually, seem far better suited to produce a disturbance in the required direction; in fact, the case approaches the conditions in the familiar neuroses of men during [long] engagements. But above all, it cannot be disputed that the fear of infection and the decision to use a condom laid the foundation for what I have described as the factor of *alienation* between the somatic and the psychic. It would be the same as in the case of coitus interruptus. In short, Mr. K. has incurred psychic sexual weakness because he spoiled coitus for himself, and, his physical health and production of sexual stimuli being unimpaired, the situation gave rise to the generation of anxiety. One may add that his readiness to take precautions, instead of finding adequate satisfaction in a secure relationship, points to a sexuality which was from the first of no great *strength.* (CL 93)

The split between the somatic and the psychic, as Freud puts it, is much like what Clérambault describes with *l'automatisme mental*, or Lacan's *moi/je* distinction; the fissure in the subject that allows reflection (and makes psychoanalysis possible) also guarantees distortion of somatic stimuli mapped onto the psychic. By the same token, the psychic life of the individual, kept in check by the intersubjective network, can be considered apart from the somatic, such that it alone rather than its relationship to the body can be analyzed as an object. With this, Freud abandons the exclusivity of physiological concerns in his investigations of the neuroses, freeing up the possibility for the "talking cure" to do its work.

This is not to say that the analytic exchange is more problem-free than a physical examination simply because it is in the domain of the intellectual. It seems that the reflexive analytic exchange is beholden to all the other rules governing sexual symbolism: reciprocation, defined power roles, jealousy, and possessiveness. This appears to be the summary of the problem with Fliess, who rebukes Freud for using his idea that bisexuality is the starting point for sexual development, and failing to acknowledge his contribution properly. Freud's businesslike, crestfallen response indicates that he believed his early intellectual contact with Fliess was conducted without regard to the crass commerce of claiming credit for scientific discoveries:

> The universality of the bisexual disposition is all that is mentioned in treatment, and that I need there. Since the experience I candidly reported in "Everyday Life," I have suspected that one of us might come to regret our formerly unrestrained exchange of ideas and have striven successfully to forget the details of your communications. At that time I evidently reproached myself dimly, as I do today in complete clarity, for my generosity or carelessness with your property. (CL 467)

Freud's rude awakening is to the fact that he has become a notable cultural figure, after his initial successes, such that his ideas are "owned" by him; Fliess's hurt feelings over his rejection, dismissal and belittlement smack of rank jealousy. Freud's regret that his discussions with Fliess can no longer be as they once were is obvious, and as the leading light of a new school of thought, his writings are subject to scrutiny as they are underwritten by him, no matter how much collaborative consideration he might extend to others. Just as with the analytic session, the tenor of the ideas exchanged by Freud and Fliess changes dramatically once they are committed to writing by Freud himself; thus authorized to join the body of psychoanalytic thought, they are appropriated by Freud and form part of his legacy, with Fliess relegated to being just one more name on the list of Freud's collaborators.

The problems of psychoanalytic dialogue and the transmission of psychoanalytic knowledge share in the Derridean anxiety over the primacy of the printed page as opposed to speech. In his perverse championing of the former over the latter, Jacques Derrida emphasizes the guarantee (or preference) of knowledge transmitted via the written word. For Lacan, who originates this problem in French thought, his reliance on the concept of full speech is an enthusiastic, romantic gesture toward the intimacy and uninhibited contact of the analytic relation, and the ultimate tragedy of its ending. Thus the conundrum of the psychoanalytic tradition is found in its inevitably tortured context: the modeling of the intimate analytic encounter is based on that of the erotic relation, and such a relation invites a host of questions over how knowledge is transmitted between men, with all the attendant questions of possession, avarice, admiration, acknowledgment and indebtedness.

Seduced and Abandoned: Beyond Psychoanalysis

> The discourse of the other is not the discourse of the abstract other, of the other in the dyad, of my correspondent, nor even of my slave, it is the discourse of the circuit in which I am integrated. I am one of its links. It is the discourse of my father for instance, in so far as my father made mistakes which I am absolutely condemned to reproduce – that's what we call the *super-ego*. I am condemned to reproduce them because I am obliged to pick up again the discourse he bequeathed to me, not simply because I am his son, but because one can't stop the chain of discourse, and it is precisely my duty to transmit it in its aberrant form to someone else.
>
> (S.II 89)

> Here there is a little parenthesis – when one gives rise to two (*quand un fait deux*), there is never a return. They don't revert to making one again, even if it is a new one. *Aufhebung* is one of philosophy's pretty little dreams.
>
> (S.XX 86)

Lacan's fascination with *Beyond the Pleasure Principle* extends farther than his use of the ideas expressed in it and the adoption of its metapsychological viewpoint. One of Lacan's first psychoanalytic works, titled "Beyond the Reality Principle," expressed the need to ground psychoanalytic reading in a social context, one of the hallmarks of Lacanian thought. By doing so, Lacan provides a justification for the application of the psychoanalytic viewpoint as it applies to intersubjective relations, and by extension, discourse and desire. Lacan realized, even in his early work, that the meaning of analytic speech must be rooted in discourse as a whole: this realization allowed Lacan to invert the concepts of analysis to cover *all* intersubjective relations, such that interactions with society as a whole could be read psychoanalytically. Instead of beginning with the reductive Cartesian focus on the individual mind and working outward, Lacan validates the analytic relation from the outside in.

As for the substance of *Beyond the Pleasure Principle*, it is worth noting that in his opposition of *eros* by *thanatos* (the conservative impulse to return to a previous state), Freud accidentally, perhaps, provides the ultimate excuse for the Lacanian return. If the analytic relation with its transference may properly be considered erotic, then its opposite, that of the comforting return to the womb, might be considered as an abnegation of the self, the annihilating desire to submit oneself to the mortality of history and fate. The death drive, participating as it does in the symbolic, is the province of language, tradition, the superego—in "The Freudian Thing," Freud makes his appearance as an object of tradition precisely for this reason. Transference with the Freudian corpus can only be a kind of necrology, effacing the life-experience of the subject beholden to its power. At the same time, this orientation of the ego toward that which is past, the desire to anchor oneself in rational thought, speaks to a need fundamentally opposed to the character of erotic love. There is, in all phases and applications of Freud's ideas, a dangerous fetishizing of the concept that the sexual, which is always assumed to be available to psychoanalysis, is the sum and substance of all explanations of human behavior. Seeking after this special knowledge points to a fundamental dissonance in psychoanalytic thinking. The act of thinking, itself beholden to tradition and the past, wishes to impose order and signification on that which signifies life; the problem of negotiating the acquisition of such knowledge, perhaps involving the presence of a teacher, raises erotic possibilities, which are always to be thwarted.

Lacan's leading example of transference in Seminar VIII, that of Plato's *Symposium*, illustrates this difficulty in more than one way. The practice of Socratic inquiry, more a habit of mind than a store of knowledge, is designed to lead the inquirer to the vision of the Good, and once that is achieved, the image of the teacher should, one would assume, be cast aside. Yet without Plato's intervention, the figure of Socrates would have no vivid depictions of his life on the printed page, nor would Socrates' disciples have gathered in his prison cell to witness his execution. The desire *for* the teacher, the transferential shape of the discourse of one's own search for knowledge, determines in a definitive way the mental landscape of the pupil. For the Lacan of the 1950s, the crisis to be solved in "The Freudian Thing" is that of the structuralization of the Freudian corpus; the recovery of Freud as the leading presence in analysis trumps any gesture of escaping his influence. Freud's apprehension of sexuality (and desire) is not to be eluded or dismissed.

The Lacanian return, rather than loosening the sedimentation of tradition, may be seen as a defensive gesture warding off the ghost of Freud. The Oedipus complex, such as it is, signifies an erotic wish to remove the father from competition for the mother. The transferential relation to the past cannot be described in Oedipal terms, nor can the relation with Freud be described as such. It is, no doubt, a move that obscures and erases the memory of the living presence of Freud. Dealing with the shades of the past may mimic the erotic relation of transference, but it keeps the demon, as it were, safely at bay. The seduction of analysis is the seduction of the possibility of critique and reflection itself. The anxiety of influence is rooted in the belief that going through the body of the text can reach the "living" father; overcoming it, one's realizes that the father's death is a permanent one, and that, in a sense, he was never there.

Dissolution

> If you believe it, that is, that it has already happened because one writes to the dead, so then, living one, hail, once again you have understood nothing, hail and be well, as we say to each other with that desperate compassion each time that we know that one instant later we are going to die for one another, each on his own behalf, hail!
>
> —Jacques Derrida, from *The Post Card*[2]

> I would really like it if, from time to time, I had a response, even a protest.
>
> I left rather worried the last time, to say the least. It seemed altogether bearable to me, nevertheless, when I reread what I had said – that's my way of saying that it was very good. But I wouldn't be displeased if someone could attest to having understood something. It would be enough for a hand to go up for me to give that hand the floor, so to speak.
>
> I see that no one is putting a hand up, and thus I must go on.
>
> (S.XX 90)

Over the course of his career, Lacan continually struggled to find a method of practicing analysis with a distinctive identity. In taking on the question of feminine sexuality, the *Encore* seminar was Lacan's stab at getting "beyond" the masculine libido. But for all their novelty, his pronouncements, in effect, became opaque monuments to his legend. At the end of his long career, his reputation already fixed, Lacan embarked on his controversial seminar only to have his work fall upon deaf ears. Not only does he openly despair about whether or not he is being understood, but he receives resounding silence at this question, as if those present are happy just to be in the presence of the oracle, rather than engaging him. Lacan's plea indicates that he realizes those in attendance are invalidating the spirit of the analytic relation by accepting what he says without objection. Without an interlocutorial presence, the searching drift and erotic exchange of analysis is lost; no mimicry of the analytic relation characterizes his lectures. From here on out, Lacan looks most like a victim of his own persuasiveness and rhetorical power. Lacan has been saddled with a following, and is potentially susceptible to the same fate, as occurred with Freud's hagiographization at the hands of Ernest Jones, whom Lacan roundly mocks in Seminar XXIII. This was why dissolving his school became necessary. In one of the last meetings of his final seminar sequence, Lacan, noting that he has come on behalf of his "*Cause Freudienne*," makes this self-conscious statement: "You see that I've kept this adjective. It is, to you, Lacanian, if you like. Me, I'm Freudian."[3] Lacan attempted to make the best of his own anxieties of influence, perhaps inevitably to voice them himself at the end of his career, when on the other side of the equation, he betrayed his doubts about the future of his work. The search for continuities with the rest of Lacan's work and intellectual milieu is therefore crucial; in the end, Lacan's oeuvre is a record of his personal search for truth about the analytic relation, and its frustrations.

In *The Post Card*, a book devoted to the question of the nature of transference, psychoanalysis, and the "letter" (both alphabetical and epistolary), Derrida poses in a rather broad way the questions of philosophical knowledge: to whom are analytic insights addressed? In Derrida's version, the situation of analytic knowledge is such that the teacher will always be "behind" the student, pointing out his or her mistakes. In other words, one term in the analyst-analysand relation always has a more privileged view than the other, following Lacan's discussion in "Seminar on the Purloined Letter." However, this is a view that Lacan does not necessarily endorse, as there are no *a priori* privileged views with regard to intersubjectivity. There are also no privileged intellectual relationships, no guarantees given to those who conduct a life of intellectual inquiry that they shall be "read" as they wish to be, no assurances that their ideas shall survive in any manner that reveals the "original" set of conditions in which they were formulated. Regarding the practice of psychoanalysis, a discipline with a definitive and well-documented origin and which had, in its early expressions, hopes of one day becoming a science, the phenomenon of intellectual indebtedness is deeply paradoxical. Where it would seem the practice of analysis would demand a face-to-face encounter with one's influences, none is possible.

The later theoretical moves of Lacan, specifically the reduction of analytic discourse to the operation of the *sinthome*, come into greater focus with all of this in mind. With the abolition of the unconscious, there are no ghosts to erupt from beneath the surface of discourse. By the same token, Lacan attempts in his introduction of the *sinthome* to abate any fear of Freud's uncanny return from the land of the dead. The overcoming of the anxiety of influence is found in the "beyond" of inquiry, the realization that all such bonds are tenuous, self-chosen, and contingent. Lacan's weary exclamation of disgust in *Encore* shows his awareness of this fact, and is a protest against those who willfully ignore it, simply content to receive wisdom from the master.

Notes

Chapter 1
Transference, Pedagogy, and Psychoanalytic Traditions: Freud, Lacan, and Plato's *Symposium*

[1] Israel Rosenfeld, *Freud's Megalomania: A Novel* (New York: W.W. Norton & Company, 2000) 128.

[2] In Rudinesco's biography of Lacan (*Jacques Lacan*, translated by Barbara Bray, Columbia, 1999), she briefly discusses the separation of both Lacan and Françoise Dolto from the International Psychoanalytical Association in 1963. Lacan had long been a disruptive presence in the IPA; no doubt the decision to exclude him was principally political, yet the official reason given was that his training analysis, conducted with Rudolph Lowenstein, had not been properly supervised.

[3] Lacan's discussion of speech in the analytic situation, and the "poetics" of Freud's work, may be found in the second half of the Rome Discourse (E:S 77–106).

[4] Although much of Lacan's language throughout his work echoes Hegel (the French Hegel that Lacan doubtlessly picked up in the seminars of Kojève), Lacan's willingness to explore the "negative" term of the dialectic of psychoanalytic thought recalls the Heidegger of the late 1920s and early 1930s, who called for an investigation into the "unthoughts" of philosophy in such essays as "What is Metaphysics?," "The Essence of Truth," and others.

[5] Lacan rejects the *cogito* in the opening paragraph of "The Mirror Stage" (E:S 3).

[6] Freud's use of the word *unsinnig* implies something that is not merely outlandish, but cannot be interpreted because it is not legible; contrast *sinnlos*, which can mean senseless, in the way that a thing can be contradictory or otherwise false. *Gesammelte Werke,* edited by Anna Freud, et al., 18 vols. (London: Imago Publishing Co., Ltd., 1942) vol. 2: 284.

[7] Although Freud does not deal with overtly comic dreams as a "type," his remark here that dreams can fill a comic role by playing with the raw material of the dreamer's life opens up the possibility that some dreams can fall under the definition of "tendentious" jokes, as Freud describes in *Jokes and Their Relation to the Unconscious* (SE 8: 102–115).

[8] The word is the same in Freud's original German text, taken entirely from the French, the present participle form of "revenir," to return or revisit.

[9] Freud concludes his account of this sequence of dreams with a very interesting and rich discussion of *Julius Caesar*, comparing himself to the figure of Brutus, Caesar's treacherous erstwhile confidant. He ends the account with the admission that he played the role of Brutus in a scene performed as a fourteen-year-old at school, with a visiting nephew of his, about the same age as he, playing the part of Caesar. Freud briefly mentions his troubled childhood relations with this nephew, and curtails the entire discussion all too soon.

[10] For a contrast with the material Freud describes in *Interpretation of Dreams*, this letter to Fliess on the occasion of his father's death, dating from November 1896, offers a glimpse into Freud's view of his relationship with his father. Although this letter does not fit within the context of my discussion about Freud's mentor-dreams, it provides a resonant insight into the dependence of Freud's psyche on the figure of his father.

> Dear Wilhelm,
>
> I find it so difficult to write just now that I have put off for a long time thanking you for the moving words in your letter. By one of those dark pathways behind the official consciousness the old man's death has affected me deeply. I valued him highly, understood him very well, and with his peculiar mixture of deep wisdom and fantastic light-heartedness he had a significant effect on my life. By the time he died, his life had long been over, but in (my) inner self the whole past has been reawakened by this event.
>
> I now feel quite uprooted....
>
> I must tell you about a nice dream I had the night after the funeral. I was in a place where I read a sign:
>
> You are requested
to close the eyes.
>
> I immediately recognized the location as the barbershop I visit every day. On the day of the funeral I was kept waiting and therefore arrived a little late at the house of mourning. At that time the family was displeased with me because I had arranged for the funeral to be quiet and simple, which they later agreed was quite justified. They were also somewhat offended by my lateness. The sentence on the sign has a double meaning: one should do one's duty to the dead (an apology as though I had not done it and were in need of leniency), and the actual duty itself. The dream thus stems from the inclination to self-reproach that regularly sets in among the survivors. (CL 202)

[11] My aim in doing this is not to equate psychoanalysis, particularly of the Lacanian variety, with philosophy, whatever the implications of such a move might be.

[12] Josef Breuer and Sigmund Freud, *Studies in Hysteria* (New York: W.W. Norton & Company, 1985) 30.

[13] Martha Nussbaum's "The Speech of Alcibiades" covers similar territory in its reading, which seeks to dethrone the centrality of the Diotima narrative in the *Symposium*; in Nussbaum's view, Alcibiades reintroduces the concreteness of the lover's flesh to the story of the ascent. The other side of the equation, which she does not emphasize as

strongly, is that beyond Alcibiades' need to claim Socrates' body, Socrates also needs Alcibiades, despite Socrates' outward asceticism.

[14] Unsurprisingly, the *Symposium* has been more often than not translated as a proto-Christian text, with its apparent criticism of "pagan" values and fleeting homosexual love, and notions of a spiritual presence (for lack of a better word) motivated by compassion, intelligence, and the reconciliation of opposites (the flesh in service and support of the body, and so forth). Recent translations are skewed toward various topics in the dialogue, somewhat fittingly, as it is the richest of the Platonic dialogues in all senses: narratively, stylistically, comically, and philosophically. It is renowned for being one of the few dialogues where Socrates does not have the last word throughout, and the only one in which Socrates gets his comeuppance from both a woman and an ex-lover. In addition, it is the most prominent Platonic dialogue that explicitly accounts for how other philosophers receive their motivation to investigate the nature of truth, an often painful process of initiation.

[15] Terms from the Greek text are taken from *Platonis Opera*, edited by John Burnet (New York: Oxford University Press, 1903).

[16] Etymological material drawn from *An Intermediate Greek Lexicon*, edited by Henry George Liddell and Robert Scott (New York: Oxford University Press, 2000).

Chapter 2
Clérambault and Heidegger: Of Our Antecedents

[1] The typical erotomaniacal situation depicted by Clérambault is that of a woman being in love with someone of a higher station, or perhaps cultural significance, like an artist, writer, or actor.

[2] Jean Garrabé, "Préface," in Clérambault, Gaëtan Gatian de, *L'automatisme mental* (Paris: Laboratoires Delagrange, 1992) 21.

[3] Elisabeth Rudinesco, *Lacan & Co.: One Hundred Years of French Psychoanalysis, 1925–1985*, translated by Jeffery Mehlman (Chicago: University of Chicago Press, 1991) 23–35.

[4] Rudinesco, *Lacan & Co.*, 23. Clérambault's understanding of psychopathology rested on organic causes, in much the same way as did the work of Ey and Minkowski. The interpretation of these phenomena, extant only in abstraction, reflects the possibilities of the organism, and the breakdowns to which it is susceptible. However, sympathetic as Clérambault's aims may have been with those of the Évolution Psychiatrique, it must be said that Clérambault's work contains nothing in it influenced directly or indirectly by the formally phenomenological offshoots of Husserlian philosophy.

[5] As such, the facts and environment of the mental process can exaggerate and distort mental functioning in much the same way as alcohol or other drugs alter the functioning of the nervous system (OP 466).

[6] As he advanced his theory of "anidéisme," Clérambault provided a taxonomy of psychological phenomena according to either their positive or negative valence. One group of phenomena comes under the heading "Processus Mixtes," which, according to Clérambault, has both positive and negative valences: among these phenomena is the creative process, which stands in for psychosis but is really something more like

brainstorming, the substitution of one thought for another (in Freudian parlance, a parapraxical slip) (OP 64–65).

[7] At the opening meeting of Seminar III, Lacan mentions Clérambault in passing, with reference to his thesis.

[8] Elisabeth Rudinesco, *Jacques Lacan*, translated by Barbara Bray (New York: Columbia University Press, 1999) 222–231.

[9] At the same time as she faults Lacan for this, Rudinesco remarks that the poststructural triad of Foucault, Derrida, and Lacan habitually bastardized Heidegger's thought in order to make it simply readable (229). Her reading of Lacan asserts that the importance of truth as an "uncovering" in Lacan's thought is derived from Heidegger, and she claims that Lacan eschewed literality in translating Heidegger to bring out the truly important element of the philosopher's work, namely, "the ability to find in the other that which is in oneself" (229).

[10] Throughout most of this chapter, I shall capitalize "the Other" for clarity's sake and ease of reading. In my discussion, "the Other" simply means "a person who is not the 'I' or 'ego'"; in other words, the version of the Other one usually finds in the phenomenological tradition. Although the capitalization of the "O" has assumed different and significant meanings in the poststructuralist milieu, I do not intend anything else by using the capital O other than the meaning I have outlined above; however, in the discussion of Seminar II, the meaning of the capital "O" shall be thoroughly explored.

[11] Martin Heidegger, *The Fundamental Concepts of Metaphysics: Worldhood, Finitude, Solitude*, translated by William McNeil and Nicholas Walker (Bloomington and Indianapolis: Indiana, 1995) 5. All further references to this work shall be noted parenthetically.

[12] This narrative of Clérambault's last days is, unless specificed otherwise, drawn from the account found in Rudinesco's *Jacques Lacan & Co.*, 105–109.

[13] Serge Tisseron, et al., editors, *La passion des étoffes chez un neuro-psychiatre* (Paris: Solin, 1980) 33. All further references to this edition shall be noted parenthetically. Although this work contains Clérambault's writings and photographs, it also contains a variety of criticial writings about his work.

[14] It is mentioned in the *Les etoffes* collection that Clérambault's favorite book during his recovery was Thomas à Kempis's *Imitation of Christ*, a fifteenth-century series of meditations on the living of a saintly life, emphasizing the denigration of the material world in favor of the spiritual one; its influence as a text in the history of Catholicism (regarding daily practice of the faith) has on occasion been estimated to rival scriptural texts.

[15] Rudinesco, *Jacques Lacan & Co.*, 108.

Chapter 3
Paranoia: Schreber, Lacan and *The Sacred Fount*

[1] Mary Boyle, *Schizophrenia: A Scientific Delusion?* (New York: Routledge, 1990) 183. The author proposes a kind of statistical test demonstrating the effects of *belief* on pattern-recognition, which seems to be at the root of most delusional thinking.

[2] Louis A. Sass, *The Paradoxes of Delusion: Wittgenstein, Schreber, and the Schizophrenic Mind* (Ithaca: Cornell University Press, 1994) 125.

[3] Eugen Bleuler, *Dementia Praecox or the Group of Schizophrenias.* (1908), translated by Joseph Ziskin, M.D. (New York: International Universities Press, 1950). Bleuler's acknowledgment of Freud's work at the beginning of this book, for many years the definitive work on schizophrenia, is interesting in that the work itself goes on to mine the metaphorical side of Freud's ideas about the nature of consciousness, in the process disregarding the role of sexual trauma or other popularly perceived forms of "degeneration" in the emergence of psychotic behavior (337–347).

[4] During his stay at Sonnenstein, Schreber was apparently able to consult Kraepelin's textbook on psychiatry (published in 1899) which included Freud's article on hysteria. Zvi Lothane, *In Defense of Schreber: Soul Murder and Psychiatry* (Hillsdale, NJ: The Analytic Press, 1992) 380.

[5] Luce Irigaray, *Le Langage des dements* (The Hague: Mouton, 1973) 257. For Irigaray, the language of the madman speaks "purely." Also see Lawrence Kirmayer and Ellen Corin, "Inside Knowledge: Cultural Constructions of Insight in Psychosis" in *Insight And Psychosis*, edited by Xavier F. Amador and Anthony S. David (New York: Oxford University Press, 1998) 193–220. Kirmayer and Corin see narrative as being impaired by psychosis, while at the same time providing analytic insight into the illness (198–199): necessarily, they believe the psychotic to be a species of *bricoleur*, in the intellectual sense (203).

[6] Louis A. Sass, *Madness and Modernism: Insanity in the Light of Modern Art, Literature, and Thought* (New York: Basic, 1992). This is a Foucauldian reading of Schreber's memoir, mostly considered alongside *Madness and Civilization*.

[7] Leonard Shengold, *Soul Murder* (New Haven, CT: Yale University Press, 1988) 20. Shengold, who takes the title for his book directly from the Schreberian narrative, terms the psychotic break a "deal with the devil," in that it provides the psychotic subject insulation and a measure of comfort.

[8] Daniel Moritz Schreber, *Illustrated Medical In-door Gymnastics or a System of Medico Hygienic Exercises,* translated by Henry Skelton (London: Williams & Norgate, 1864) 37. All further references to this edition shall be noted parenthetically.

[9] No doubt the latter detail surfaces in the early going of the memoir, where Schreber describes the instigation of sexual excitement in the body belonging primarily to the visual appreciation of the female form; it leads one to wonder whether or not Schreber was attempting to rekindle his soul through this ultimately masturbatory gesture.

[10] The different aspects of Schreber's condition, considered apart from the characterization of his illness upon his emergence from the asylum during one of his sane periods, are evident in the following excerpt from the attendant material on the Schreber case, relating to his lawsuit against the Saxony government for his property rights, which were stripped upon his admittance to the Leipzig asylum. The split between Schreber's professional persona and his private one is clear, at the very least, to the court. Pursuant to this point, the respondent clarifies the extent of Schreber's illness:

> Dr. Weber is now convinced that plaintiff's delusional ideas lead a relatively *separate existence* in his mental life and that outside the religious field which they mainly dominate they affect other fields particularly of daily life *hardly* at all; and that hallucinations from which plaintiff continues to suffer, do not now influence his feeling and thinking to *any significant degree*....For a few years

> appellant has eaten daily as a guest at the family table of the Director of the Asylum without causing any annoyance to the others present. On the contrary Dr. Weber, who looks upon his relation to plaintiff as a friendly one, extols the patient's delicate tact and forbearance which prevented him from molesting the company at table with his miraculous ideas. (MNI 430–431)

In the end, it is Schreber's habituated social self that prevents him from making any untoward moves, socially. His delusional side, firmly kept out of view, does not remake the world in which he lives. It is merely an exaggerated interpretation of the everyday phenomena Schreber experiences.

[11] This strategy is found in *Anti-Oedipus*, which derives, nevertheless, a good deal of its strategies from the later Lacan.

[12] The definition of the term "psychosis" is often determined by the definition of "neurosis," and throughout this century, the definitions of both have altered significantly depending on scientific developments of the period and experimental orientations with regard to psychopathology. Often the difference between them is one of degree rather than kind; neuroses are characterized by low-level anxieties hindering normal societal interaction (especially sexual or familial), while psychoses manifest themselves in perceptual distortions and other hallucinations. With the former, irrational fears arise from bodily stimuli, and with the latter, one's senses cannot be trusted, but rationality rules behavior, extrapolating from false sense-data.

[13] This topic will be covered at greater length in the fifth chapter; in his later work, Lacan's emphasis on the symbolic overshadows the other elements of his analytic outlook, such that analytic interpretation subsumes all aspects of experience.

[14] Michel Arrivé, *Langage et psychanalyse, linguistique et inconscient: Freud, Saussure, Pichon, Lacan* (Paris: Presses Universitaires de France, 1994) 236.

[15] Rudinesco, *Jacques Lacan*, 248–250.

[16] See Rebecca West's *Henry James* (London: Nisbet & Co., 1916) for West's oft-cited remark that the narrator expends more intellectual energy than does Kant in the *Critique of Pure Reason* in the pursuit of his pointless narrative. However, other of West's comments are more revealing:

> One takes it as significant that the unnamed host and hostess of the party never appear save to 'give signals.' The tiny, desperate figures this phrase shows the mind's eye, semaphoring to each other across incredibly extended polished vistas to keep their courage under these looming, soaring vaults, may be taken as symbols of the heart and intellect which Mr. James had now forgotten in his elaboration of their social envelope. (108)

[17] See Nicola Bradbury, *Henry James: The Later Novels* (Oxford: Clarendon, 1979). Her claim that James's later novels deny one a sense of a community of individual readers (33) may be taken as a nod to the claustrophobic feel of James's later prose.

[18] Laurel Bollinger, "'Miracles Are Expensive': The Complicated Metaphors of Subjectivity in *The Sacred Fount*," *The Henry James Review* 20.1 (1999) 51–68.

[19] See Adeline R. Tintner, *Henry James and the Lust of the Eyes* (Baton Rouge: Louisiana State University Press, 1993), where *The Sacred Fount* constitutes a form of

commedia dell'arte (149); also see Susan Winnett, "Mise en Crypte: The Man and the Mask," *The Henry James Review* 5.3 (1984) 220–226, where the mask participates in some kind of DeManian undecidability.

[20] As Scott Derrick notes in his book *Monumental Anxieties: Homoerotic Desire and Feminine Influence in 19th-Century U.S. Literature* (New Brunswick: Rutgers University Press, 1997), the brutality indicated by James in the narrative and the expository narration of the novel mirrors the predatory world of the novel itself.

[21] The most significant treatment of this topic is found in Adeline R. Tintner's "A Gay Sacred Fount: The Reader as Detective," *Twentieth Century Literature* 41.2 (1995) 224–40. However, Tinter's interpretation completely ignores the narrator's flirtations with Ford Obert, which would seem to be the most plainly homoerotic writing that James had ever done.

[22] James L Glass, *Delusion: Internal Dimensions of Political Life* (Chicago: University of Chicago Press, 1985) 256. Glass's political description of madness casts schizophrenia as being, in essence, a private language that symbolizes the effective death of the subject to his community.

[23] See Paul Ricoeur's *Freud and Philosophy* (New Haven: Yale University Press, 1970). Ricoeur's definitive treatment of the hermeneutic status of psychoanalysis underscores this last point, that Freud's path of inquiry can best be seen as a kind of search for the truth about human motives, questions, and proper behavior in the same vein as, perhaps, Platonic philosophy—the same bent toward self-examination obtains.

[24] Donna M. Orange, *Emotional Understanding: Studies in Psychoanalytic Epistemology* (New York: Guilford, 1995) 204.

[25] R.D. Laing's Sartrean analysis of schizophrenia in *The Divided Self* (London: Penguin, 1987) powerfully illustrates his patients' fears of being "consumed" by the Other. Although Laing himself does not make the connection, the troped behavior of the mental patient who firmly believes himself to be Napoleon bears out Laing's thoughts on this score. The schizophrenic subject must, to survive, become "bigger" than he actually is, so that he cannot be swallowed up.

Chapter 4
Masochism: Reading Fantasy with Lacan, Sacher-Masoch, and Proust

[1] The concept of the "female imaginary" has been well treated in a great number of texts, most notably in works by Judith Butler, among others. For simplicity's sake, those discussions will be not be treated here.

The concept of the imaginary itself takes on, perhaps, a feminine cast, just as with the Aristotlean duo ὕλη and μορφή; the symbolic, rigid and abstract, imposes forms on the yielding imaginary, and so forth. None of this is, one can assume, lost on Lacan himself.

[2] Kaja Silverman, *Male Subjectivity at the Margins* (New York: Routledge, 1992) 203. All further references to this work shall be noted parenthetically.

[3] Michel Foucault, *The Order of Things*, translated by Alan M. Sheridan (New York: Vintage, 1970) 209.

[4] John K. Noyes, *The Mastery of Submission: Inventions of Masochism* (Ithaca: Cornell University Press, 1997) 96. Noyes's example here is that of Bernini's *The Ecstasy of St. Theresa*, a favorite of Lacan's, and which tellingly adorns the cover of the Seuil edition of Séminaire XX.

[5] A typical example of this is found in Nick Mansfield's *Masochism: The Art of Power* (London: Praeger, 1997) 34–36, in which only the whipping of the Baron is discussed.

[6] Mieke Bal, *The Mottled Screen: Reading Proust Visually*, translated by Anna-Louise Milne (Stanford: Stanford University Press, 1997) 87. It is worth noting here that Bal claims that the "paternal image" provided by Swann is "generationally" ambiguous in relation to Marcel.

[7] Philippe Willemart, *Proust, Poète et Psychanalyste* (Paris: L'Harmattan, 1999) 89.

[8] Ingrid Wasenaar, *Proustian Passions: The Uses of Self-Justification for* À la recherche du temps perdu (Oxford: Oxford University Press, 2000) 79.

[9] Jacqueline Rose, *Sexuality in the Field of Vision* (New York: Verso, 1986) 43.

Chapter 5
Narcissism: Lacan, The Symptom, and the Joycean Uses of Psychoanalysis

[1] Joyce's interest in Wilde was at once intellectual and nationalistic. While living in Trieste, he once considered translating Wilde's "The Soul of Man Under Socialism" into Italian, and approved of a friend's lead production in a season of Irish drama, *The Importance of Being Earnest*. See Richard Ellmann, *James Joyce* (New York: Oxford University Press, 1982).

[2] This chart can be found in, among other places, Richard Ellmann's *Ulysses on the Liffey* (New York: Oxford University Press, 1972).

[3] Suzette A. Henke, *James Joyce and the Politics of Desire* (New York: Routledge, 1990) 108.

[4] This is by now a cliché, and it is best outlined in Hugh Kenner's "Circe" in Clive Hart and David Hayman, *James Joyce's Ulysses: Critical Essays* (Berkeley: University of California Press, 1974) 341–362, where he undertakes a fairly orthodox structuralist reading of this chapter. The analysis is somewhat self-limiting in its consideration of *Ulysses* as a text with multivalent readings, of all things.

[5] In her fascinating study *James Joyce and the Burden of Disease* (Lexington: University of Kentucky Press, 1995), Kathleen Ferris conjectures that perhaps Joyce himself, like Bloom, had suffered from impotence (97–99). Evidence suggests that Joyce attempted, during the time of the composition of *Ulysses*, to induce Nora to "meet" other men, and possibly sleep with them. Ferris also acknowledges that this gambit was more likely part of Joyce's schemes to stage-manage certain aspects of his life and friendships in order to provide more material for the novel; in his *James Joyce and the Making of Ulysses* (London: Grayson & Grayson, 1937), Frank Budgen enumerates some of these peccadilloes in detail.

[6] Calvin Thomas, *Male Matters: Masculinity, Anxiety, and the Male Body on the Line* (Urbana and Chicago: University of Illinois Press, 1996) 160.

[7] Jacques Lacan, "Joyce le symptôme I," in *Joyce avec Lacan*, edited by Jacques Aubert (Paris: Navarin Editeur, 1987) 24. All other references to this text shall be noted parenthetically.

[8] Sheldon Brivic, *The Veil of Signs: Joyce, Lacan, and Perception* (Urbana and Chicago: University of Illinois Press, 1991) 18.

[9] James Joyce, *Finnegans Wake* (New York: Penguin, 1999) 115. All further references to this work shall be noted parenthetically.

[10] Christine Froula, *Modernism's Body: Sex, Culture, and Joyce* (New York: Columbia University Press, 1996) 202–203.

Chapter 6
Conclusion: Psychoanalysis, Modernity and the Philosophical Tradition

[1] Françoise Dolto, *Sexualité Féminine: Libido, Érotisme, Frigidité* (Paris: Scarabée & Compagnie, 1982) 143.

[2] Jacques Derrida, *The Post Card: From Socrates to Freud and Beyond*, translated by Alan Bass (Chicago: University of Chicago Press, 1987) 148.

[3] My translation, from an unpublished transcript of the seminar session of July 12, 1980.

Bibliography

Arrivé, Michel. *Langage et psychanalyse, linguistique et inconscient: Freud, Saussure, Pichon, Lacan.* Paris: Presses Universitaires de France, 1994.

Bal, Mieke. *The Mottled Screen: Reading Proust Visually.* Translated by Anna-Louise Milne. Stanford: Stanford University Press, 1997.

Bleuler, Eugen. *Dementia Praecox or the Group of Schizophrenias* (1908). Translated by Joseph Ziskin, M.D. New York: International Universities Press, 1950.

Bollinger, Laurel. "'Miracles Are Expensive': The Complicated Metaphors of Subjectivity in *The Sacred Fount.*" *The Henry James Review* 20.1 (1999): 51–68.

Boyle, Mary. *Schizophrenia: A Scientific Delusion?* New York: Routledge, 1990.

Bradbury, Nicola. *Henry James: The Later Novels.* Oxford: Clarendon, 1979.

Breuer, Josef and Sigmund Freud. *Studies in Hysteria.* New York: W.W. Norton & Company, 1985.

Brivic, Sheldon. *The Veil of Signs: Joyce, Lacan, and Perception.* Urbana and Chicago: University of Illinois Press, 1991.

Budgen, Frank. *James Joyce and the Making of Ulysses.* London: Grayson & Grayson, 1937.

Clérambault, Gaëtan Gatian de. *Oeuvres Psychiatriques.* 2 vols. Paris: Presses Universitaires de France, 1942.

———. *La passion des étoffes chez un neuro-psychiatre.* Edited by Serge Tisseron, et al. Paris: Solin, 1980.

Deleuze, Gilles. "Coldness and Cruelty." In *Masochism,* translated by Jean McNeil, 7–138. New York: W.W. Norton & Company, 1992.

Derrick, Scott S. *Monumental Anxieties: Homoerotic Desire and Feminine Influence in 19th-Century U.S. Literature.* New Brunswick: Rutgers University Press, 1997.

Derrida, Jacques. *The Post Card: From Socrates to Freud and Beyond.* Translated by Alan Bass. Chicago: University of Chicago Press, 1987.

Dolto, Françoise. *Sexualité Féminine: Libido, Érotisme, Frigidité.* Paris: Scarabée & Compagnie, 1982.

Ellmann, Richard. *James Joyce.* New and revised edition. New York: Oxford University Press, 1982.

———. *Ulysses on the Liffey.* New York: Oxford University Press, 1972.

Ferris, Kathleen. *James Joyce and the Burden of Disease.* Lexington: University of Kentucky Press, 1995.

Foucault, Michel. *The Order of Things*. Translated by Alan M. Sheridan. New York: Vintage, 1970.

Freud, Sigmund. "'A Child Is Being Beaten,' A Contribution to the Study of the Origin of Sexual Perversions." In *The Standard Edition of the Complete Psychological Works of Sigmund Freud*, translated and edited by James Strachey, et al., 24 vols., vol. 17: 179–204. London: The Hogarth Press, 1953.

———. *The Complete Letters of Sigmund Freud to Wilhelm Fliess 1887–1904*. Translated and edited by Jeffrey Moussaieff Masson. Cambridge, Mass.: Belknap, 1985.

———. "The Economic Problem of Masochism." *Standard Edition*, vol. 19: 159–170.

———. *The Ego and the Id*. *Standard Edition*, vol. 19: 12–66.

———. "Femininity." *Standard Edition*, vol. 22: 112–135.

———. *Gesammelte Werke*. Edited by Anna Freud, et al., 18 vols. London: Imago Publishing Co., Ltd., 1942.

———. *The Interpretation of Dreams*. *Standard Edition*, vols. 4 and 5.

———. *Jokes and Their Relation to the Unconscious*. *Standard Edition*, vol. 8: 9–236.

———. "Libido Theory and Narcissism." *Standard Edition*, vol. 16: 412–430.

———. "On Narcissism: An Introduction." *Standard Edition*, vol. 14: 73–102.

———. "Psycho-analytic Notes Upon a Biographical Account of a Case of Paranoia." *Standard Edition*, vol. 12: 220–247.

Froula, Christine. *Modernism's Body: Sex, Culture, and Joyce*. New York: Columbia University Press, 1996.

Garrabé, Jean. "Préface." In Clérambault, Gaëtan Gatian de, *L'automatisme mental*, 9–31. Paris: Laboratoires Delagrange, 1992.

Glass, James L., *Delusion: Internal Dimensions of Political Life*. Chicago: University of Chicago Press, 1985.

Heidegger, Martin. *Being and Time*. Translated by John MacQuarrie and Edward Robinson. New York: Harper, 1962.

———. *The Fundamental Concepts of Metaphysics: Worldhood, Finitude, Solitude*. Translated by William McNeil and Nicholas Walker. Bloomington and Indianapolis: Indiana, 1995.

Henke, Suzette A. *James Joyce and the Politics of Desire*. New York: Routledge, 1990.

Irigaray, Luce. *Le langage des déments*. The Hague: Mouton, 1973.

James, Henry. *The Sacred Fount*. Introduction by Leon Edel. Afterword by R.P. Blackmur. New York: New Directions, 1995.

Joyce, James. *Finnegans Wake*. New York: Penguin, 1999.

———. *Ulysses: The Corrected Text*. Edited by Hans Walter Gabler. New York: Vintage, 1984.

Kenner, Hugh. "Circe." In *James Joyce's Ulysses: Critical Essays*, edited by Clive Hart and David Hayman, 341–362. Berkeley: University of California Press, 1977.

Kirmayer, Lawrence, and Ellen Corin. "Inside Knowledge: Cultural Constructions of Insight in Psychosis." In *Insight and Psychosis*, edited by Xavier F. Amador and Anthony S. David, 193–220. New York: Oxford University Press, 1998.

Lacan, Jacques. *De la psychose paranoïaque dans ses rapports avec la personnalité*. Paris: Éditions de Seuil, 1975.

———. "De nos antécédents." In *Écrits*, 65–72. Paris: Éditions de Seuil, 1966.

———. "The Freudian Thing, or the Meaning of the Return to Freud in Psychoanalysis." In *Écrits: A Selection*, translated by Bruce Fink, in collaboration with Héloïse Fink and Russell Grigg, 107–137. New York: W.W. Norton & Company, 2002.

———. "The Function and Field of Speech and Language in Psychoanalysis." *Écrits: A Selection*: 31–106.

———. "Guiding Remarks for a Congress on Feminine Sexuality." In *Feminine Sexuality: Jacques Lacan and the école freudienne*, edited by Juliet Mitchell and Jacqueline Rose, translated by Jacqueline Rose, 86–98. New York: W.W. Norton & Company, 1985.

———. "Intervention on Transference." *Feminine Sexuality*: 61–73.

———. "Joyce le symptôme I." In *Joyce avec Lacan*, edited by Jacques Aubert, 21–29. Paris: Navarin Editeur, 1987.

———. "The Mirror Stage as Formative of the *I* Function as Revealed in Psychoanalytic Experience." *Écrits: A Selection*: 3–9.

———. *The Seminar of Jacques Lacan: Book II, The Ego in Freud's Theory and in the Technique of Psychoanalysis (1954–1955)*. Translated by Sylvana Tomaselli, with notes by John Forrester. New York: W.W. Norton & Company, 1991.

———. *The Seminar of Jacques Lacan, Book III: The Psychoses (1955–1956)*. Edited by Jacques-Alain Miller. Translated by Russell Grigg. New York: W.W. Norton & Company, 1992.

———. *The Seminar of Jacques Lacan, Book VIII: Transference (1960–1961)*. Unpublished translation by Cormac Gallagher, from an unedited transcript.

———. *The Seminar of Jacques Lacan, Book XX: On Feminine Sexuality, The Limits of Love and Knowledge, Encore (1972–1973)*. Edited by Jacques-Alain Miller. Translated with notes by Bruce Fink. New York: W.W. Norton & Company, 1998.

———. "Seminar of 12 July 1980." Unpublished and unedited transcript.

———. "Seminar of 21 January 1975." *Feminine Sexuality*: 162–171.

———. "The Signification of the Phallus." *Écrits: A Selection*: 271–280.

Laing, R.D. *The Divided Self*. London: Penguin, 1987.

Liddell, Henry George, and Robert Scott, editors. *An Intermediate Greek Lexicon*. New York: Oxford University Press, 2000.

Lothane, Zvi. *In Defense of Schreber: Soul Murder and Psychiatry*. Hillsdale, NJ: The Analytic Press, 1992.

Mansfield, Nick. *Masochism: The Art of Power*. London: Praeger, 1997.

Moron, Pierre, editor. *Clérambault, Maître de Lacan*. Paris: Le Plessis-Robinson, 1993.

Noyes, John K. *The Mastery of Submission: Inventions of Masochism*. Ithaca: Cornell University Press, 1997.

Orange, Donna M. *Emotional Understanding: Studies in Psychoanalytic Epistemology*. New York: Guilford, 1995.

Plato. *Platonis Opera*. Edited by John Burnet. New York: Oxford University Press, 1903.

Plato. *Symposium*. Translated by Alexander Nehamas and Paul Woodruff. Indianapolis: Hackett, 1989.

Proust, Marcel. *Remembrance of Things Past*, Vol. 1, *Swann's Way, Within a Budding Grove*. Translated by C.K. Scott-Moncrieff and Terence Kilmartin. New York: Vintage, 1982.

Ricoeur, Paul. *Freud and Philosophy*. New Haven, CT: Yale University Press, 1970.

Rose, Jacqueline. *Sexuality in the Field of Vision*. New York: Verso, 1986.

Rosenfeld, Israel. *Freud's Megalomania: A Novel.* New York: W.W. Norton & Company, 2001.

Rudinesco, Elisabeth. *Jacques Lacan.* Translated by Barbara Bray. New York: Columbia University Press, 1999.

———. *Lacan & Co.: One Hundred Years of French Psychoanalysis, 1925–1985.* Translated by Jeffery Mehlman. Chicago: University of Chicago Press, 1991.

Sacher-Masoch, Leopold. *Venus in Furs. Masochism*: 141–293.

Sass, Louis A. *Madness and Modernism: Insanity in the Light of Modern Art, Literature, and Thought.* New York: Basic, 1992.

———. *The Paradoxes of Delusion: Wittgenstein, Schreber, and the Schizophrenic Mind.* Ithaca: Cornell University Press, 1994.

Schreber, Daniel Moritz. *Illustrated Medical In-door Gymnastics or a System of Medico Hygienic Exercises.* Translated by Henry Skelton. London: Williams & Norgate, 1864.

Schreber, Daniel Paul. *Memoirs of My Nervous Illness.* Translated and edited by Ida Macalpine and Richard A. Hunter. Introduction by Rosemary Dinnage. New York: New York Review of Books, 2000.

Shengold, Leonard. *Soul Murder.* New Haven, CT: Yale University Press, 1988.

Silverman, Kaja. *Male Subjectivity at the Margins.* New York: Routledge, 1992.

Thomas, Calvin. *Male Matters: Masculinity, Anxiety, and the Male Body on the Line.* Urbana and Chicago: University of Illinois Press, 1996.

Tintner, Adeline R. "A Gay Sacred Fount: The Reader as Detective." *Twentieth Century Literature* 41.2 (1995): 224–40.

Wasenaar, Ingrid. *Proustian Passions: The Uses of Self-Justification for* À la recherche du temps perdu. New York: Oxford University Press, 2000.

West, Rebecca. *Henry James.* London: Nisbet & Co., 1916.

Willemart, Philippe. *Proust, Poète et Psychanalyste.* Paris: L'Harmattan, 1999.

Winnett, Susan, "Mise en Crypte: The Man and the Mask." *The Henry James Review* 5.3 (1984): 220–226.

Index

STUDIES IN LITERARY CRITICISM & THEORY

Hans Rudnick, General Editor

The focus of this series is on studies of all literary genres that elucidate and interpret works of art in the context of criticism and theory. Theory and criticism are held to provide the hermeneutically most rewarding access to specific authors, works, and issues under consideration. Studies of a comparative nature with special reference to issues of literary history, criticism, and postmodern theory are the distinctive features of this monograph series. Emphasis is on subjects that may set trends, generate discussion, expand horizons beyond present perspectives, and/or redefine previously held notions about "major" and "minor" authors and their achievements within or outside the canon. Approaches may center on works, authors, or abstract notions of criticism and/or theory, including issues of a comparative nature concerning world literature.

For additional information about this series or for the submission of manuscripts, please contact:

Peter Lang Publishing
Acquisitions Department
P.O. Box 1246
Bel Air, Maryland 20104-1246

To order other books in this series, please contact our Customer Service Department:

800-770-LANG (within the U.S.)
(212) 647-7706 (outside the U.S.)
(212) 647-7707 FAX

or browse online by series at:

www.peterlangusa.com